Max Müller

Chips from a German Workshop

Vol.1

Max Müller

Chips from a German Workshop
Vol.1

ISBN/EAN: 9783337385163

Printed in Europe, USA, Canada, Australia, Japan

Cover: Foto ©Suzi / pixelio.de

More available books at **www.hansebooks.com**

CHIPS

from

A GERMAN WORKSHOP.

MAX MÜLLER, M. A.,

FELLOW OF ALL SOULS COLLEGE, OXFORD

VOLUME I.

ESSAYS ON THE SCIENCE OF RELIGION

CHARLES SCRIBNER'S SONS,

1891.

[Published by arrangement with the Author.]

PREFACE.

More than twenty years have passed since my revered friend Bunsen called me one day into his library at Carlton House Terrace, and announced to me with beaming eyes that the publication of the Rig-veda was secure. He had spent many days in seeing the Directors of the East India Company, and explaining to them the importance of this work, and the necessity of having it published in England. At last his efforts had been successful, the funds for printing my edition of the text and commentary of the Sacred Hymns of the Brahmans had been granted, and Bunsen was the first to announce to me the happy result of his literary diplomacy. "Now," he said, "you have got a work for life — a large block that will take years to plane and polish. But mind," he added, "let us have from time to time some chips from your workshop."

I have tried to follow the advice of my departed friend, and I have published almost every year a few articles on such subjects as had engaged my attention, while prosecuting at the same time, as far as altered circumstances would allow, my edition of the Rig-veda, and of other Sanskrit works connected with it. These

articles were chiefly published in the "Edinburgh" and
"Quarterly" Reviews, in the "Oxford Essays," and
"Macmillan's" and "Fraser's" Magazines, in the
"Saturday Review," and in the "Times." In writing
them my principal endeavor has been to bring out even
in the most abstruse subjects the points of real interest
that ought to engage the attention of the public at
large, and never to leave a dark nook or corner without attempting to sweep away the cobwebs of false
learning, and let in the light of real knowledge. Here,
too, I owe much to Bunsen's advice; and when last
year I saw in Cornwall the large heaps of copper ore
piled up around the mines, like so many heaps of rubbish, while the poor people were asking for coppers to
buy bread, I frequently thought of Bunsen's words,
"Your work is not finished when you have brought
the ore from the mine: it must be sifted, smelted, re-
fined and coined before it can be of real use, and con-
tribute towards the intellectual food of mankind." I
can hardly hope that in this my endeavor to be clear
and plain, to follow the threads of every thought to the
very ends, and to place the web of every argument
clearly and fully before my readers, I have always been
successful. Several of the subjects treated in these
essays are, no doubt, obscure and difficult: but there
is no subject, I believe, in the whole realm of human
knowledge, that cannot be rendered clear and intelligible, if we ourselves have perfectly mastered it. And
now while the two last volumes of my edition of the

Rig-veda are passing through the press, I thought the
time had come for gathering up a few armfuls of these
chips and splinters, throwing away what seemed worthless, and putting the rest into some kind of shape, in
order to clear my workshop for other work.

The first and second volumes which I am now publishing contain essays on the early thoughts of mankind, whether religious or mythological, and on early
traditions and customs. There is to my mind no subject more absorbing than the tracing the origin and
first growth of human thought ;—not theoretically, or
in accordance with the Hegelian laws of thought, or
the Comtean epochs ; but historically, and like an Indian trapper, spying for every footprint, every layer,
every broken blade that might tell and testify of the
former presence of man in his early wanderings and
searchings after light and truth.

In the languages of mankind, in which everything
new is old and everything old is new, an inexhaustible mine has been discovered for researches of this
kind. Language still bears the impress of the earliest
thoughts of man, obliterated, it may be, buried under
new thoughts, yet here and there still recoverable in
their sharp original outline. The growth of language
is continuous, and by continuing our researches backward from the most modern to the most ancient strata,
the very elements and roots of human speech have
been reached, and with them the elements and roots of
human thought. What lies beyond the beginnings of

language, however interesting it may be to the physiologist, does not yet belong to the history of man, in
the true and original sense of that word. Man means
the thinker, and the first manifestation of thought is
speech.

But more surprising than the continuity in the
growth of language, is the continuity in the growth of
religion. Of religion, too, as of language, it may be
said that in it everything new is old, and everything
old is new, and that there has been no entirely new religion since the beginning of the world. The elements
and roots of religion were there as far back as we can
trace the history of man; and the history of religion,
like the history of language, shows us throughout a
succession of new combinations of the same radical
elements. An intuition of God, a sense of human
weakness and dependence, a belief in a Divine government of the world, a distinction between good and
evil, and a hope of a better life, — these are some of
the radical elements of all religions. Though sometimes hidden, they rise again and again to the surface.
Though frequently distorted, they tend again and
again to their perfect form. Unless they had formed
part of the original dowry of the human soul, religion
itself would have remained an impossibility, and the
tongues of angels would have been to human ears but
as sounding brass or a tinkling cymbal. If we once
understand this clearly, the words of St. Augustine,
which have seemed startling to many of his admir-

ers, become perfectly clear and intelligible, when he says:[1] "What is now called the Christian religion, has existed among the ancients, and was not absent from the beginning of the human race, until Christ came in the flesh: from which time the true religion, which existed already, began to be called Christian." From this point of view the words of Christ too, which startled the Jews, assume their true meaning, when He said to the centurion of Capernaum: "Many shall come from the east and the west, and shall sit down with Abraham, and Isaac, and Jacob, in the kingdom of heaven."

During the last fifty years the accumulation of new and authentic materials for the study of the religions of the world, has been most extraordinary; but such are the difficulties in mastering these materials that I doubt whether the time has yet come for attempting to trace, after the model of the Science of Language, the definite outlines of the Science of Religion. By a succession of the most fortunate circumstances, the canonical books of three of the principal religions of the ancient world have lately been recovered, — the Veda, the Zend-Avesta, and the Tripitaka. But not only have we thus gained access to the most authentic documents from which to study the ancient religion of the Brahmans, the Zoroastrians, and the Buddhists, but by

[1] August. Retr. 1, 13. "Res ipsa, quae nunc religio Christiana nuncupatur, erat apud antiquos, nec defuit ab initio generis humani, quousque Christus veniret in carnem, unde vera religio, quae jam erat, coepit appellari Christiana."

discovering the real origin of Greek, Roman, and likewise of Teutonic, Slavonic, and Celtic mythology, it has become possible to separate the truly religious elements in the sacred traditions of these nations from the mythological crust by which they are surrounded, and thus to gain a clearer insight into the real faith of the ancient Aryan world.

If we turn to the Semitic world, we find that although but few new materials have been discovered from which to study the ancient religions of the Jews, yet a new spirit of inquiry has brought new life into the study of the sacred records of Abraham, Moses, and the Prophets; and the recent researches of Biblical scholars, though starting from the most opposite points, have all helped to bring out the historical interest of the Old Testament, in a manner not dreamt of by former theologians. The same may be said of another Semitic religion, the religion of Mohammed, since the Koran and the literature connected with it were submitted to the searching criticism of real scholars and historians. Some new materials for the study of the Semitic religions have come from the monuments of Babylon and Nineveh. The very images of Bel and Nisroch now stand before our eyes, and the inscriptions on the tablets may hereafter tell us even more of the thoughts of those who bowed their knees before them. The religious worship of the Phenicians and Carthaginians has been illustrated by Movers from the ruins of their ancient temples, and from scattered notices in classical writers; nay, even the religious ideas of the nomads of the Arabian peninsula, previous to the rise of Mohammedanism, have been brought to light by the patient researches of oriental scholars.

There is no lack of idols among the ruined and buried temples of Egypt with which to reconstruct the pantheon of that primeval country; nor need we despair of recovering more and more of the thoughts buried under the hieroglyphics of the inscriptions, or preserved in hieratic and demotic MSS., if we watch the brilliant discoveries that have rewarded the patient researches of the disciples of Champollion.

Besides the Aryan and Semitic families of religion, we have in China three recognized forms of public worship, the religion of Confucius, that of Lao-tse, and that of Fo (Buddha); and here, too, recent publications have shed new light, and have rendered an access to the canonical works of these religions, and an understanding of their various purports, more easy, even to those who have not mastered the intricacies of the Chinese language.

Among the Turanian nations, a few only, such as the Finns and the Mongolians, have preserved some remnants of their ancient worship and mythology, and these too have lately been more carefully collected and explained by d'Ohsson, Castrèn, and others.

In America, the religions of Mexico and Peru had long attracted the attention of theologians; and of late years the impulse imparted to ethnological researches has induced travellers and missionaries to record any traces of religious life that could be discovered among the savage inhabitants of Africa, America, and the Polynesian islands.

It will be seen from these few indications, that there is no lack of materials for the student of religion; but we shall also perceive how difficult it is to master such vast materials. To gain a full knowledge of the Veda, or the Zend-Avesta, or the Tripitaka, of the Old Testament, the Koran, or the sacred books of China, is the work of a whole life. How then is one man to survey the whole field of religious thought, to classify the religions of the world according to definite and permanent criteria, and to describe their characteristic features with a sure and discriminating hand?

Nothing is more difficult to seize than the salient features, the traits that constitute the permanent expression and real character of a religion. Religion seems to be the common property of a large community, and yet it not only varies in numerous sects, as language does in its dialects, but it escapes our firm grasp till we can trace it to its real habitat, the heart of one true believer. We speak glibly of Buddhism and Brahmanism, forgetting that we are generalizing on the most intimate convictions of millions and millions of human souls, divided by half the world and by thousands of years.

It may be said that at all events where a religion possesses canonical books, or a definite number of

articles, the task of the student of religion becomes
easier, and this, no doubt, is true to a certain extent.
But even then we know that the interpretation of
those canonical books varies, so much so that sects ap-
pealing to the same revealed authorities — as, for instance, the founders of the Vedânta and the Sânkhya
systems — accuse each other of error, if not of willful
error or heresy. Articles, too, though drawn up with
a view to define the principal doctrines of a religion,
lose much of their historical value by the treatment
they receive from subsequent schools; and they are
frequently silent on the very points which make religion what it is.

A few instances may serve to show what difficulties
the student of religion has to contend with, before he
can hope firmly to grasp the facts on which his theories are to be based.

Roman Catholic missionaries who had spent their
lives in China, who had every opportunity, while staying at the court of Pekin, of studying in the original
the canonical works of Confucius and their commentaries, who could consult the greatest theologians then
living, and converse with the crowds that thronged the
temples of the capital, differed diametrically in their
opinions as to the most vital points in the state religion
of China. Leconte, Fouquet, Prémare, and Bouvet
thought it undeniable that Confucius, his predecessors
and his disciples, had entertained the noblest ideas on
the constitution of the universe, and had sacrificed

to the true God in the most ancient temple of the
earth. According to Maigrot, Navarette, on the con
trary, and even according to the Jesuit Longobardi,
the adoration of the Chinese was addressed to inan-
imate tablets, meaningless inscriptions, or, in the best
case, to coarse ancestral spirits and beings without
intelligence.[1] If we believe the former, the ancient
deism of China approached the purity of the Christian
religion; if we listen to the latter, the absurd fetich-
ism of the multitude degenerated amongst the educated, into systematic materialism and atheism. In
answer to the peremptory texts quoted by one party,
the other adduced the glosses of accredited interpreters, and the dispute of the missionaries who had
lived in China and knew Chinese had to be settled in
the last instance by a decision of the see of Rome.

There is hardly any religion that has been studied in
its sacred literature, and watched in its external worship with greater care than the modern religion of the
Hindus, and yet it would be extremely hard to give a
faithful and intelligible description of it. Most people who have lived in India would maintain that the
Indian religion, as believed in and practiced at present
by the mass of the people, is idol worship and nothing
else. But let us hear one of the mass of the people,
a Hindu of Benares, who in a lecture delivered before
an English and native audience defends his faith and
the faith of his forefathers against such sweeping accu-

[1] Abel Rémusat, Mélanges, p. 162.

nations. "If by idolatry," he says, "is meant a system of worship which confines our ideas of the Deity to a mere image of clay or stone; which prevents our hearts from being expanded and elevated with lofty notions of the attributes of God; if this is what is meant by idolatry, we disclaim idolatry, we abhor idolatry, and deplore the ignorance or uncharitableness of those that charge us with this groveling system of worship. . . . . But if, firmly believing, as we do, in the omnipresence of God, we behold, by the aid of our imagination, in the form of an image any of His glorious manifestations, ought we to be charged with identifying them with the matter of the image, whilst during those moments of sincere and fervent devotion we do not even think of matter? If at the sight of a portrait of a beloved and venerated friend no longer existing in this world, our heart is filled with sentiments of love and reverence; if we fancy him present in the picture, still looking upon us with his wonted tenderness and affection, and then indulge our feelings of love and gratitude, should we be charged with offering the grossest insult to him — that of fancying him to be no other than a piece of painted paper? . . . . We really lament the ignorance or uncharitableness of those who confound our representative worship with the Phœnician, Grecian, or Roman idolatry as represented by European writers, and then charge us with polytheism in the teeth of thousands of texts in the Puránas, declaring in clear and unmis-

takable terms that there is but one God who manifests
Himself as Brahma, Vishnu, and Rudra (Siva), in
His functions of creation, preservation, and destruc-
tion." [1]

In support of these statements, this eloquent advocate quotes numerous passages from the sacred literature of the Brahmans, and he sums up his view of the
three manifestations of the Deity in the words of their
great poet Kalidâsa, as translated by Mr. Griffith: —

> "In these Three Persons the One God was shown:
> Each First in place, each Last,—not one alone;
> Of Siva, Vishnu, Brahma, each may be
> First, second, third, among the Blessed Three."

If such contradictory views can be held and defended with regard to religious systems still prevalent
amongst us, where we can cross-examine living witnesses, and appeal to chapter and verse in their sacred
writings, what must the difficulty be when we have to
deal with the religions of the past? I do not wish to
disguise these difficulties which are inherent in a comparative study of the religions of the world. I rather
dwell on them strongly, in order to show how much
care and caution is required in so difficult a subject,
and how much indulgence should be shown in judging
of the shortcomings and errors that are unavoidable in

[1] The modern pundit's reply to the missionary who accuses him of
polytheism is: "O, these are only various manifestations of the one God;
the same as, though the sun be one in the heavens, yet he appears in multi-
form refractions upon the lake. The various sects are only different en-
trances to the one city." See W. W. Hunter, Annals of Rural Bengal,
p. 116.

so comprehensive a study. It was supposed at one time that a comparative analysis of the languages of mankind must transcend the powers of man : and yet by the combined and well directed efforts of many scholars, great results have here been obtained, and the principles that must guide the student of the Science of Language are now firmly established. It will be the same with the Science of Religion. By a proper division of labor, the materials that are still wanting will be collected and published and translated, and when that is done, surely man will never rest till he has discovered the purpose that runs through the religions of mankind, and till he has reconstructed the true *Civitas Dei* on foundations as wide as the ends of the world. The Science of Religion may be the last of the sciences which man is destined to elaborate; but when it is elaborated, it will change the aspect of the world, and give a new life to Christianity itself.

The Fathers of the Church, though living in much more dangerous proximity to the ancient religions of the Gentiles, admitted freely that a comparison of Christianity and other religions was useful. "If there is any agreement," Basilius remarked, " between their (the Greeks') doctrines and our own, it may benefit us to know them : if not, then to compare them and to learn how they differ, will help not a little towards confirming that which is the better of the two."[1]

[1] Basilius, *De legendis Graec. libris, c. v.*

But this is not the only advantage of a comparative study of religions. The Science of Religion will for the first time assign to Christianity its right place among the religions of the world; it will shew for the first time fully what was meant by the fullness of time; it will restore to the whole history of the world, in its unconscious progress towards Christianity, its true and sacred character.

Not many years ago great offence was given by an eminent writer who remarked that the time had come when the history of Christianity should be treated in a truly historical spirit,—in the same spirit in which we treat the history of other religions, such as Brahmanism, Buddhism, or Mohammedanism. And yet what can be truer? He must be a man of little faith, who would fear to subject his own religion to the same critical tests to which the historian subjects all other religions. We need not surely crave a tender or merciful treatment for that faith which we hold to be the only true one. We should rather challenge for it the severest tests and trials, as the sailor would for the good ship to which he intrusts his own life, and the lives of those who are most dear to him. In the Science of Religion, we can decline no comparisons, nor claim any immunities for Christianity, as little as the missionary can, when wrestling with the subtle Brahman, or the fanatical Mussulman, or the plain speaking Zulu. And if we send out our missionaries to every part of the world to face every kind of religion, to shrink from no context, to be appalled by no objections, we must not give way at home or within our own hearts to any misgivings, lest a comparative study of the religions of the world could shake the firm foundations on which we must stand or fall.

To the missionary, more particularly, a comparative study of the religions of mankind will be, I believe, of the greatest assistance. Missionaries are apt to look upon all other religions as something totally distinct from their own, as formerly they used to describe the languages of barbarous nations as something more like the twittering of birds than the articulate speech of men. The Science of Language has taught us that there is order and wisdom in all languages, and even the most degraded jargons contain the ruins of former greatness and beauty. The Science of Religion, I hope, will produce a similar change in our views of barbarous forms of faith and worship; and missionaries, instead of looking only for points of difference, will look out more anxiously for any common ground, any spark of the true light that may still be revived, any altar that may be dedicated afresh to the true God.[1]

[1] Jogeth Chandra Gangooly, a native convert, says : " I know from personal experience that the Hindu Scriptures have a great deal of truth. . . . . . If you go to India, and examine the common sayings of the people, you will be surprised to see what a splendid religion the Hindu religion must be. Even the most ignorant women have proverbs that are full of the purest religion. Now I am not going to India to injure Hindu feelings by saying, ' Your Scripture is all nonsense, is good for nothing ; anything outside the Old and New Testament is a humbug.' No, I tell you I will appeal to the Hindu philosophers, and moralists, and poets, at the same time

And from to us at home, a wider view of the religious life of the world may teach many a useful lesson. Immense as is the difference between our own and all other religions of the world — and few can know that difference who have not honestly examined the foundations of their own as well as of other religions — the position which believers and unbelievers occupy with regard to their various forms of faith is very much the same all over the world. The difficulties which trouble us, have troubled the hearts and minds of men as far back as we can trace the beginnings of religious life. The great problems touching the relation of the Finite to the Infinite, of the human mind as the recipient, and of the Divine Spirit as the source of truth, are old problems indeed; and while watching their appearance in different countries, and their treatment under varying circumstances, we shall be able, I believe, to profit ourselves, both by the errors which others committed before us, and by the truth which they discovered. We shall know the rocks that threaten every religion in this changing and shifting world of ours, and having watched many a storm of religious controversy and many a shipwreck in distant seas, we shall face with greater calmness and prudence the troubled waters at home.

If there is one thing which a comparative study of religions places in the clearest light, it is the inevitable

bringing to them my light, and reasoning with them in the spirit of Christ. That will be my work." — "A Brief Account of Joguth Chunder Gangooly, a Brahmin and a Convert to Christianity." Christian Reformer August, 1860.

decay to which every religion is exposed. It may
seem almost like a truism, that no religion can continue to be what it was during the lifetime of its founder and its first apostles. Yet it is but seldom borne
in mind that without constant reformation, i. e. without
a constant return to its fountain-head, every religion,
even the most perfect, nay the most perfect on account of its very perfection, more even than others,
suffers from its contact with the world, as the purest
air suffers from the mere fact of its being breathed.

Whenever we can trace back a religion to its first
beginnings, we find it free from many of the blemishes
that offend us in its later phases. The founders of
the ancient religions of the world, as far as we can
judge, were minds of a high stamp, full of noble aspirations, yearning for truth, devoted to the welfare of
their neighbors, examples of purity and unselfishness.
What they desired to found upon earth was but seldom
realized, and their sayings, if preserved in their original form, offer often a strange contrast to the practice
of those who profess to be their disciples. As soon as a
religion is established, and more particularly when it
has become the religion of a powerful state, the foreign
and worldly elements encroach more and more on the
original foundation, and human interests mar the simplicity and purity of the plan which the founder had
conceived in his own heart, and matured in his com-
munings with his God. Even those who lived with
Buddha misunderstood his words, and at the Great

Council which had to settle the Buddhist canon, Asoka, the Indian Constantine had to remind the assembled priests that "what had been said by Buddha, that alone was well said;" and that certain works ascribed to Buddha, as, for instance, the instructions given to his son, Râhula, were apocryphal, if not heretical.[1] With every century, Buddhism, when it was accepted by nations, differing as widely as Mongols and Hindus, when its sacred writings were translated into languages as wide apart as Samskrit and Chinese, assumed widely different aspects, till at last the Buddhism of the Shamans in the steppes of Tartary is as different from the teaching of the original Samana, as the Christianity of the leader of the Chinese rebels is from the teaching of Christ. If missionaries could show to the Brahmans, the Buddhists, the Zoroastrians, nay, even to the Mohammedans, how much their present faith differs from the faith of their forefathers and founders; if they could place in their hands and read with them in a kindly spirit the original documents on which these various religions profess to be founded, and enable them to distinguish between the doctrines of their own sacred books and the additions of later ages; an important advantage would be gained, and the choice between Christ and other Masters would be rendered far more easy to many a truth seeking soul. But for that purpose it is necessary that we too should see the beam in our own eyes, and learn to distinguish between the

[1] See Burnouf, Lotus de la bonne Loi, Appendice, No. x. § 4.

Christianity of the nineteenth century and the religion
of Christ. If we find that the Christianity of the
nineteenth century does not win as many hearts in
India and China as it ought, let us remember that it
was the Christianity of the first century in all its
dogmatic simplicity, but with its overpowering love of
God and man, that conquered the world and superseded
religions and philosophies, more difficult to conquer
than the religions and philosophical systems of Hindus
and Buddhists. If we can teach something to the
Brahmans in reading with them their sacred hymns,
they too can teach us something when reading with us
the gospel of Christ. Never shall I forget the deep
despondency of a Hindu convert, a real martyr to his
faith, who had pictured to himself from the pages of
the New Testament what a Christian country must
be, and who when he came to Europe found everything so different from what he had imagined in his
lonely meditations at Benares! It was the Bible only
that saved him from returning to his old religion, and
helped him to discern beneath theological futilities,
accumulated during nearly two thousand years, beneath pharisaical hypocrisy, infidelity, and want of
charity, the buried, but still living seed, committed to
the earth by Christ and His Apostles. How can a
missionary in such circumstances meet the surprise
and questions of his pupils, unless he may point to that
seed, and tell them what Christianity was meant to
be; unless he may show that, like all other religions,

Christianity, too, has had its history; that the Christianity of the nineteenth century is not the Christianity of the Middle Ages, that the Christianity of the Middle Ages was not that of the early Councils, that the Christianity of the early Councils was not that of the Apostles, and "that what has been said by Christ, that alone was well said?"

The advantages, however, which missionaries and other defenders of the faith will gain from a comparative study of religions, though important hereafter, are not at present the chief object of these researches. In order to maintain their scientific character, they must be independent of all extraneous considerations: they must aim at truth, trusting that even unpalatable truths, like unpalatable medicine, will reinvigorate the system into which they enter. To those, no doubt, who value the tenets of their religion as the miser values his pearls and precious stones, thinking their value lessened if pearls and stones of the same kind are found in other parts of the world, the Science of Religion will bring many a rude shock: but to the true believer, truth, wherever it appears, is welcome, nor will any doctrine seem the less true or the less precious, because it was seen, not only by Moses or Christ, but likewise by Buddha or Lao-tse. Nor should it be forgotten that while a comparison of ancient religions will certainly show that some of the most vital articles of faith are the common property of the whole of mankind, at least of all who seek the

Lord, if haply they might feel after Him, and find Him, the same comparison alone can possibly teach us what is peculiar to Christianity, and what has secured to it that preëminent position which now it holds in spite of all obloquy. The gain will be greater than the loss, if loss there be, which I, at least, shall never admit.

There is a strong feeling, I know, in the minds of all people against any attempt to treat their own religion as a member of a class, and, in one sense, that feeling is perfectly justified. To each individual, his own religion, if he really believes in it, is something quite inseparable from himself, something unique, that cannot be compared to anything else, or replaced by anything else. Our own religion is, in that respect, something like our own language. In its form it may be like other languages; in its essence and in its relation to ourselves, it stands alone and admits of no peer or rival.

But in the history of the world, our religion, like our own language, is but one out of many; and in order to understand fully the position of Christianity in the history of the world, and its true place among the religions of mankind, we must compare it, not with Judaism only, but with the religious aspirations of the whole world, with all, in fact, that Christianity came either to destroy or to fulfill. From this point of view Christianity forms part, no doubt, of what people call profane history, but by that very fact, profane history

ceases to be profane, and regains throughout that
sacred character of which it had been deprived by a
false distinction. The ancient Fathers of the Church
spoke on these subjects with far greater freedom than
we venture to use in these days. Justin Martyr, in his
"Apology" (A. D. 139), has this memorable passage
("Apol." i. 46) : "One article of our faith then is,
that Christ is the first begotten of God, and we have
already proved Him to be the very Logos (or universal Reason), of which mankind are all partakers; and
therefore those who live according to the Logos are
Christians, notwithstanding they may pass with you for
Atheists; such among the Greeks were Sokrates and
Herakleitos and the like; and such among the Barbarians were Abraham, and Ananias, and Azarias, and
Misael, and Elias, and many others, whose actions, nay
whose very names, I know, would be tedious to relate,
and therefore shall pass them over. So, on the other
side, those who have lived in former times in defiance
of the Logos or Reason, were evil, and enemies to
Christ and murderers of such as lived according to the
Logos; but *they who have made or make the Logos or
Reason the rule of their actions are Christians*, and men
without fear and trembling." [1]

[1] Τὸ Χριστὸν πρωτότοκον τοῦ Θεοῦ εἶναι ἐδιδάχθημεν, καὶ προεμηνύσαμεν λόγον
ὄντα, οὗ πᾶν γένος ἀνθρώπων μετέσχε· καὶ οἱ μετὰ λόγου βιώσαντες Χριστιανοί εἰσι,
κἂν ἄθεοι ἐνομίσθησαν, οἷον ἐν Ἕλλησι μὲν Σωκράτης καὶ Ἡράκλειτος καὶ οἱ ὅμοιοι
αὐτοῖς, ἐν βαρβάροις δὲ Ἀβραὰμ καὶ Ἀνανίας καὶ Ἀζαρίας καὶ Μισαὴλ καὶ Ἠλίας
καὶ ἄλλοι πολλοί, ὧν τὰς πράξεις ἢ τὰ ὀνόματα καταλέγειν μακρὸν εἶναι ἐπιστάμενοι,
τανῦν παραιτούμεθα. Ὥστε καὶ οἱ προγεγενημένοι ἄνευ λόγου βιώσαντες, ἄχρηστοι

" God," says Clement (200 A. D.), " is the cause of all that is good: only of some good gifts He is the primary cause, as of the Old and New Testaments; of others the secondary, as of (Greek) philosophy. But even philosophy may have been given primarily by Him to the Greeks, before the Lord had called the Greeks also. For that philosophy, like a schoolmaster, has guided the Greeks also, as the Law did Israel, towards Christ. Philosophy, therefore, prepares and opens the way to those who are made perfect by Christ." [1]

And again: " It is clear that the same God to whom we owe the Old and New Testaments, gave also to the Greeks their Greek philosophy, by which the Almighty is glorified among the Greeks." [2]

And Clement was by no means the only one who spoke thus freely and fearlessly, though, no doubt, his knowledge of Greek philosophy qualified him better than many of his contemporaries to speak, with authority on such subjects.

[1] Clem. Alex. Strom. Bk. I. cap. v. § 28.

[2] Strom. Bk. VI. cap. v. § 42.

St. Augustine writes: "If the Gentiles also had possibly something divine and true in their doctrines, our Saints did not find fault with it, although for their superstition, idolatry, and pride, and other evil habits, they had to be detested, and, unless they improved, to be punished by divine judgment. For the Apostle Paul, when he said something about God among the Athenians, quoted the testimony of some of the Greeks who had said something of the same kind: and this, if they came to Christ, would be acknowledged in them, and not blamed. St. Cyprian, too, uses such witnesses against the Gentiles. For when he speaks of the Magians, he says that the chief among them, Hostanes, maintains that the true God is invisible, and that true angels sit at His throne; and that Plato agrees with this, and believes in One God, considering the others to be angels or demons; and that Hermes Trismegistus also speaks of One God, and confesses that He is incomprehensible." (Augustinus, "De Baptismo contra Donatistas," lib. VI. cap. xliv.)

Every religion, even the most imperfect and degraded, has something that ought to be sacred to us, for there is in all religions a secret yearning after the true, though unknown God. Whether we see the Papua squatting in dumb meditation before his fetich, or whether we listen to Firdusi exclaiming: "The height and the depth of the whole world have their centre in Thee, O my God! I do not know Thee what Thou art: but I know that Thou art what Thou alone canst

be,"—we ought to feel that the place whereon we
stand is holy ground. There are philosophers, no
doubt, to whom both Christianity and all other religions are exploded errors, things belonging to the past,
and to be replaced by more positive knowledge. To
them the study of the religions of the world could only
have a pathological interest, and their hearts could
never warm at the sparks of truth that light up, like
stars, the dark yet glorious night of the ancient world.
They tell us that the world has passed through the
phases of religious and metaphysical errors, in order to
arrive at the safe haven of positive knowledge of facts.
But if they would but study positive facts, if they
would but read, patiently and thoughtfully, the history
of the world, as it is, not as it might have been: they
would see that, as in geology, so in the history of
human thought, theoretic uniformity does not exist,
and that the past is never altogether lost. The oldest
formations of thought crop out everywhere, and if we
dig but deep enough, we shall find that even the sandy
desert in which we are asked to live, rests everywhere
on the firm foundation of that primeval, yet inde-
structible granite of the human soul — religious faith.

There are other philosophers, again, who would fain
narrow the limits of the Divine government of the
world to the history of the Jewish and of the Christian
nations, who would grudge the very name of religion
to the ancient creeds of the world, and to whom the
name of natural religion has almost become a term of
reproach. To them, too, I should like to say that if

they would but study positive facts, if they would but
read their own Bible, they would find that the greatness of Divine Love cannot be measured by human
standards, and that God has never forsaken a single
human soul that has not first forsaken Him. "He
hath made of one blood all nations of men, for to
dwell on all the face of the earth; and hath determined
the times before appointed, and the bounds of their
habitation: that they should seek the Lord, if haply
they might feel after Him, and find Him, though He
be not far from every one of us." If they would but
dig deep enough, they too would find that what they
contemptuously call natural religion is in reality the
greatest gift that God has bestowed on the children
of man, and that without it, revealed religion itself
would have no firm foundation, no living roots in the
heart of man.

If by the essays here collected I should succeed in
attracting more general attention towards an independent, yet reverent study of the ancient religions of the
world, and in dispelling some of the prejudices with
which so many have regarded the yearnings after truth
embodied in the sacred writings of the Brahmans, the
Zoroastrians, and the Buddhists, in the mythology of
the Greeks and Romans, nay, even in the wild traditions and degraded customs of Polynesian savages, I
shall consider myself amply rewarded for the labor
which they have cost me. That they are not free from
errors, in spite of a careful revision to which they have
been submitted before I published them in this collec

tion, I am fully aware, and I shall be grateful to any one who will point them out, little concerned whether it is done in a seemly or unseemly manner, as long as some new truth is elicited, or some old error effectually exploded. Though I have thought it right in preparing these essays for publication, to alter what I could no longer defend as true, and also, though rarely, to add some new facts that seemed essential for the purpose of establishing what I wished to prove, yet in the main they have been left as they were originally published. I regret that, in consequence, certain statements of facts and opinions are repeated in different articles in almost the same words; but it will easily be seen that this could not have been avoided without either breaking the continuity of an argument, or rewriting large portions of certain essays. If what is contained in these repetitions is true and right, I may appeal to a high authority "that in this country true things and right things require to be repeated a great many times." If otherwise, the very repetition will provoke criticism and insure refutation. I have added to all the articles the dates when they were written, these dates ranging over the last fifteen years; and I must beg my readers to bear these dates in mind when judging both of the form and the matter of these contributions towards a better knowledge of the creeds and prayers, the legends and customs of the ancient world.

M. N'

PARKS END, OXFORD,
October, 1867.

CONTENTS OF FIRST VOLUME.

L

LECTURE ON THE VEDAS,

OR THE

SACRED BOOKS OF THE BRAHMANS,[1]

DELIVERED AT THE

PHILOSOPHICAL INSTITUTION, LEEDS, March, 1865.

I have brought with me one volume of my edition
of the Veda, and I should not wonder if it were the
first copy of the work which has ever reached this
busy town of Leeds.   Nay, I confess I have some
misgivings that I may have undertaken a hopeless
task, and I begin to doubt whether I shall succeed in
explaining to you the interest which I feel for this ancient collection of sacred hymns, — an interest which
has never failed me while devoting to the publication of
this voluminous work the best twenty years of my life.
Many times have I been asked, But what is the Veda?
Why should it be published?   What are we likely to
learn from a book composed nearly four thousand years
ago, and intended from the beginning for an uaculti-
vated race of mere heathens and savages, — a book

---

[1] Some of the points touched upon in this Lecture have been more fully
treated in my *History of Ancient Sanskrit Literature*. As the second
edition of this work has been out of print for several years, I have here
quoted a few passages from it in full.

which the natives of India have never published themselves, although, to the present day, they profess to regard it as the highest authority for their religion,
morals, and philosophy? Are we, the people of England, or of Europe, in the nineteenth century, likely to
gain any new light on religious, moral, or philosophical
questions from the old songs of the Brahmans? And
is it so very certain that the whole book is not a modern
forgery, without any substantial claims to that high
antiquity which is ascribed to it by the Hindus, so that
all the labor bestowed upon it would not only be labor
lost, but throw discredit on our powers of discrimination, and make us a laughing-stock among the shrewd
natives of India? These and similar questions I have
had to answer many times when asked by others, and
some of them when asked by myself, before embarking
on so hazardous an undertaking as the publication of
the Rig-veda and its ancient commentary. And I
believe I am not mistaken in supposing that many of
those who to-night have honored me with their presence
may have entertained similar doubts and misgivings
when invited to listen to a Lecture " On the Vedas, or
the Sacred Books of the Brahmans."

I shall endeavor, therefore, as far as this is possible
within the limits of one Lecture, to answer some of
these questions, and to remove some of these doubts,
by explaining to you, first, what the Veda really is;
and, secondly, what importance it possesses, not only
to the people of India, but to ourselves in Europe, —
and here again, not only to the student of Oriental
languages, but to every student of history, religion, or
philosophy; to every man who has once felt the charm
of tracing that mighty stream of human thought on

which we ourselves are floating onward, back to its
distant mountain-sources; to every one who has a
heart for whatever has once filled the hearts of millions
of human beings with their noblest hopes, and fears,
and aspirations; to every student of mankind in the
fullest sense of that full and weighty word. Whoever
claims that noble title must not forget, whether he ex-
amines the highest achievements of mankind in our
own age, or the miserable failures of former ages, what
man is, and in whose image and after whose likeness
man was made. Whether listening to the shrieks of
the Shaman sorcerers of Tartary, or to the odes of
Pindar, or to the sacred songs of Paul Gerhard :
whether looking at the pagodas of China, or the Par-
thenon of Athens, or the Cathedral of Cologne ; whether
reading the sacred books of the Buddhists, of the Jews,
or of those who worship God in spirit and in truth, we
ought to be able to say, like the Emperor Maximilian,
" Homo sum, humani nihil a me alienum puto;" or,
translating his words somewhat freely, " I am a man ;
nothing pertaining to man I deem foreign to myself."
Yes, we must learn to read in the history of the whole
human race something of our own history ; and as in
looking back on the story of our own life, we all dwell
with a peculiar delight on the earliest chapters of our
childhood, and try to find there the key to many of
the riddles of our later life, it is but natural that the
historian, too, should ponder with most intense interest
over the few relics that have been preserved to him of
the childhood of the human race. These relics are few
indeed, and therefore very precious ; and this I may venture to say, at the outset and without fear of contradiction, that there exists no literary relic that carries us

back to a more primitive, or, if you like, more childlike state in the history of man [1] than the Veda. As the language of the Veda, the Sanskrit, is the most ancient type of the English of the present day (Sanskrit and English are but varieties of one and the same language), so its thoughts and feelings contain in reality the first roots and germs of that intellectual growth which by an unbroken chain connects our own generation with the ancestors of the Aryan race, — with those very people who at the rising and setting of the sun listened with trembling hearts to the songs of the Veda, that told them of bright powers above, and of a life to come after the sun of their own lives had set in the clouds of the evening. Those men were the true ancestors of our race; and the Veda is the oldest book we have in which to study the first beginnings of our language, and of all that is embodied in language. We are by nature Aryan, Indo-European, not Semitic: our spiritual kith and kin are to be found in India, Persia, Greece, Italy, Germany; not in Mesopotamia, Egypt, or Palestine. This is a fact that ought to be clearly perceived, and constantly kept in view, in order to understand the importance which the Veda has for us, after the lapse of more than three thousand years, and after ever so many changes in our language, thought, and religion.

Whatever the intrinsic value of the Veda, if it simply contained the names of kings, the description of battles, the dates of famines, it would still be, by its

---

[1] " In the sciences of law and society, old means not old in chronology, but in structure: that is most archaic which lies nearest to the beginning of human progress considered as a development; and that is most modern which is furthest removed from that beginning." — J. F. McLennan, *Primitive Marriage*, p. 8

ago alone, the most venerable of books. Do we ever find much beyond such matters in Egyptian hieroglyphics, or in Cuneiform inscriptions? In fact, what does the ancient history of the world before Cyrus, before 500 B. C., consist of, but meagre lists of Egyptian, Babylonian, Assyrian dynasties? What do the tablets of Karnak, the palaces of Nineveh, and the cylinders of Babylon tell us about the thoughts of men? All is dead and barren, nowhere a sigh, nowhere a jest, nowhere a glimpse of humanity. There has been but one oasis in that vast desert of ancient Asiatic history, the history of the Jews. Another such oasis is the Veda. Here, too, we come to a stratum of ancient thought, of ancient feelings, hopes, joys, and fears, — of ancient religion. There is perhaps too little of kings and battles in the Veda, and scarcely anything of the chronological framework of history. But poets, surely, are better than kings; hymns and prayers are more worth listening to than the agonies of butchered armies; and guesses at truth more valuable than conquering titles of Egyptian or Babylonian despots. It will be difficult to settle whether the Veda is " the oldest of books," and whether some of the portions of the Old Testament may not be traced back to the same or even an earlier date than the oldest hymns of the Veda. But in the Aryan world, the Veda is certainly the oldest book, and its preservation amounts almost to a marvel.

It is nearly twenty years ago since my attention was first drawn to the Veda, while attending, in the years 1846 and 1847, the Lectures of Eugène Burnouf at the Collège de France. I was then looking out, like most young men at that time of life, for some great

work, and without weighing long the difficu'ties which
had hitherto prevented the publication of the Veda, I
determined to devote all my time to the collection of
the materials necessary for such an undertaking. I had
read the principal works of the later Sanskrit literature,
but had found little there that seemed to be more than
curious. But to publish the Veda, a work that had
never before been published in India or in Europe, that
occupied in the history of Sanskrit literature the same
position which the Old Testament occupies in the history of the Jews, the New Testament in the history of
modern Europe, the Koran in the history of Mohammedanism,—a work which fills a gap in the history of
the human mind, and promises to bring us nearer than
any other work to the first beginnings of Aryan language and Aryan thought,—this seemed to me an undertaking not altogether unworthy a man's life. What
added to the charm of it was that it had once before
been undertaken by Frederick Rosen, a young German
scholar, who died in England before he had finished the
first book, and that after his death no one seemed willing to carry on his work. What I had to do, first of
all, was to copy not only the text, but the commentary
of the Rig-veda, a work which when finished will fill
six of these large volumes. The author, or rather the
compiler of this commentary, Sâyana Âkârya, lived
about 1400 after Christ, that is to say, about as many
centuries after, as the poets of the Veda lived before,
the beginning of our era. Yet through the 3,000
years which separate the original poetry of the Veda
from the latest commentary, there runs an almost continuous stream of tradition, and it is from it, rather than
from his own brain, that Sâyana draws his explanations

of the sacred texts. Numerous MSS., more or less complete, more or less inaccurate, of Sâyana's classical work, existed in the then Royal Library at Paris, in the Library of the East India House, then in Leadenhall Street, and in the Bodleian Library at Oxford. But to copy and collate these MSS. was by no means all. A number of other works were constantly quoted in Sâyana's commentary, and these quotations had all to be verified. It was necessary first to copy these works, and to make indexes to all of them, in order to be able to find any passage that might be referred to in the larger commentary. Many of these works have since been published in Germany and France, but they were not to be procured twenty years ago. The work, of course, proceeded but slowly, and many times I doubted whether I should be able to carry it through. Lastly came the difficulty,—and by no means the smallest,—who was to publish a work that would occupy about six thousand pages in quarto, all in Sanskrit, and of which probably not a hundred copies would ever be sold. Well, I came to England in order to collect more materials at the East India House and at the Bodleian Library, and thanks to the exertions of my generous friend Baron Bunsen, and of the late Professor Wilson, the Board of Directors of the East India Company decided to defray the expenses of a work which, as they stated in their letter, "is in a peculiar manner deserving of the patronage of the East India Company, connected as it is with the early religion, history, and language of the great body of their Indian subjects." It thus became necessary for me to take up my abode in England, which has since become my second home. The first volume was published in 1849, the second in

1853, the third in 1856, the fourth in 1862. The materials for the remaining volumes are ready, so that, if I can but make leisure, there is little doubt that before long the whole work will be complete.

Now, first, as to the name. Veda means originally knowing or knowledge, and this name is given by the Brahmans not to one work, but to the whole body of their most ancient sacred literature. Veda is the same word which appears in the Greek οἶδα, I know, and in the English, wise, wisdom, to wit.[1] The name of Veda is commonly given to four collections of hymns, which are respectively known by the names of " Rig-veda," "Yagur-veda," " Sâma-veda," and " Atharva-veda ; " but for our own purposes, namely for tracing the earliest growth of religious ideas in India, the only important, the only real Veda, is the Rig-veda.

The other so-called Vedas, which deserve the name of Veda no more than the Talmud deserves the name of Bible, contain chiefly extracts from the Rig-veda, together with sacrificial formulas, charms, and incantations, many of them, no doubt, extremely curious, but never likely to interest any one except the Sanskrit scholar by profession.

The Yagur-veda and Sâma-veda may be described as prayer-books, arranged according to the order of

[1] Sanskrit.	Greek.	Gothic.	Anglo-Saxon.	German.
véda,	οἶδα,	vait,	wât,	ich weiss.
véttha,	οἶσθα,	waist,	wâst,	du weisst.
véda,	οἶδε,	vait,	wât,	er weiss.
vidvá,	—	vitu,	—	—
vidáthuḥ,	ἴστον,	vituts,	—	—
vidátuḥ,	ἴστον,	—	—	—
vidmá,	ἴσμεν,	vitum,	witon,	wir wissen.
vidá,	ἴστε,	vituth,	wite,	ihr wisset.
vidáḥ,	ἴσασι,	vitun,	witac.	sie wissen.

certain sacrifices, and intended to be used by certain classes of priests.

Four classes of priests were required in India at the most solemn sacrifices:—

1. The officiating priests, manual labourers, and acolytes; who have chiefly to prepare the sacrificial ground, to dress the altar, slay the victims, and pour out the libations.
2. The choristers, who chant the sacred hymns.
3. The reciters or readers, who repeat certain hymns.
4. The overseers or bishops, who watch and superintend the proceedings of the other priests, and ought to be familiar with all the Vedas.

The formulas and verses to be muttered by the first class are contained in the Yagur-veda-sanhitâ.

The hymns to be sung by the second class are in the Sâma-veda-sanhitâ.

The Atharva-veda is said to be intended for the Brahman or overseer, who is to watch the proceedings of the sacrifice, and to remedy any mistake that may occur.[1]

Fortunately the hymns to be recited by the third class were not arranged in a sacrificial prayer-book, but were preserved in an old collection of hymns, containing all that had been saved of ancient, sacred, and popular poetry, more like the Psalms than like a ritual; a collection made for its own sake, and not for the sake of any sacrificial performances.

I shall, therefore, confine my remarks to the Rig-veda, which in the eyes of the historical student is the Veda *par excellence*. Now Rig-veda means the Veda

of hymns of praise, for *Rich*, which before the initia
soft letter of Veda is changed to *Rig*, is derived from
a root which in Sanskrit means to celebrate.

In the Rig-veda we must distinguish again between
the original collection of the hymns or *Mantras*, called
the "Sanhitâ" or the collection, being entirely metrical
and poetical, and a number of prose works, called
"Brâhmanas" and "Sûtras," written in prose, and giving information on the proper use of the hymns at sacrifices, on their sacred meaning, on their supposed authors, and similar topics. These works, too, go by the
name of "Rig-veda": but though very curious in themselves, they are evidently of a much later period, and
of little help to us in tracing the beginnings of religious life in India. For that purpose we must depend
entirely on the hymns, such as we find them in the Sanhitâ or the collection of the Rig-veda.

Now this collection consists of ten books, and contains altogether 1,028 hymns. As early as about
600 B. C., we find that in the theological schools of
India every verse, every word, every syllable of
the Veda had been carefully counted. The number
of verses as computed in treatises of that date,
varies from 10,402 to 10,622; that of the words is
153,826, that of the syllables 432,000.[1] With these
numbers, and with the description given in these early
treatises of each hymn, of its metre, its deity, its number of verses, our modern MSS. of the Veda corre-
spond as closely as could be expected.

I say our modern MSS., for all our MSS. are modern, and very modern. Few Sanskrit MSS. are more
than four or five hundred years old, the fact being that

[1] *History of Ancient Sanskrit Literature*, second edition, p. 219 seq.

in the damp climate of India no paper will last for
more than a few centuries. How, then, you will naturally ask, can it be proved that the original hymns
were composed between 1200 and 1500 before the
Christian era, if our MSS. only carry us back to
about the same date after the Christian era? It is
not very easy to bridge over this gulf of nearly three
thousand years, but all I can say is that, after carefully
examining every possible objection that can be made
against the date of the Vedic hymns, their claim to
that high antiquity which is ascribed to them has not,
as far as I can judge, been shaken. I shall try to explain on what kind of evidence these claims rest.

You know that we possess no MS. of the Old Testament in Hebrew older than about the tenth century
after the Christian era; yet the Septuagint translation
by itself would be sufficient to prove that the Old
Testament, such as we now read it, existed in MS.
previous, at least, to the third century before our era.
By a similar train of argument, the works to which I
referred before, in which we find every hymn, every
verse, every word and syllable of the Veda accurately
counted by native scholars about five or six hundred
years before Christ, guarantee the existence of the
Veda, such as we now read it, as far back at least as
five or six hundred years before Christ. Now in the
works of that period, the Veda is already considered,
not only as an ancient, but as a sacred book; and, more
than this, its language had ceased to be generally intelligible. The language of India had changed since
the Veda was composed, and learned commentaries
were necessary in order to explain to the people, then
living, the true purport, nay, the proper pronunciation,

of their sacred hymns. But more than this. In certain exegetical compositions, which are generally comprised under the name of "Sûtras," and which are contemporary with, or even anterior to, the treatises on the theological statistics just mentioned, not only are the ancient hymns represented as invested with sacred authority, but that other class of writings, the Brâhmanas, standing half-way between the hymns and the Sûtras, have likewise been raised to the dignity of a revealed literature. Those Brâhmanas, you will remember, are prose treatises, written in illustration of the ancient sacrifices and of the hymns employed at them. Such treatises would only spring up when some kind of explanation began to be wanted both for the ceremonial and for the hymns to be recited at certain sacrifices; and we find, in consequence, that in many cases the authors of the Brâhmanas had already lost the power of understanding the text of the ancient hymns in its natural and grammatical meaning, and that they suggested the most absurd explanations of the various sacrificial acts, most of which, we may charitably suppose, had originally some rational purpose. Thus it becomes evident that the period during which the hymns were composed must have been separated by some centuries, at least, from the period that gave birth to the Brâhmanas, in order to allow time for the hymns growing unintelligible and becoming invested with a sacred character. Secondly, the period during which the Brâhmanas were composed must be separated by some centuries from the authors of the Sûtras, in order to allow time for further changes in the language and more particularly for the growth of a new theology, which ascribed to the Brâhmanas the same excep-

tional and revealed character which the Brâhmanas
themselves ascribed to the hymns. So that we want
previously to 600 b. c., when every syllable of the
Veda was counted, at least two strata of intellectual
and literary growth, of two or three centuries each;
and are thus brought to 1100 or 1200 b. c. as the earliest time when we may suppose the collection of the
Vedic hymns to have been finished. This collection
of hymns again contains, by its own showing, ancient
and modern hymns — the hymns of the sons together
with the hymns of their fathers and earlier ancestors;
so that we cannot well assign a date more recent than
1200 to 1500 before our era, for the original composition of those simple hymns, which up to the present
day are regarded by the Brahmans with the same feelings with which a Mohammedan regards the Koran,
a Jew the Old Testament, a Christian his Gospel.

That the Veda is not quite a modern forgery can be
proved, however, by more tangible evidence. Hiouen-
thsang, a Buddhist pilgrim, who travelled from China
to India in the years 629-645, and who, in his diary
translated from Chinese into French by M. Stanislas
Julien, gives the names of the four Vedas, mentions
some grammatical forms peculiar to the Vedic Sanskrit,
and states that at his time young Brahmans spent all
their time, from the seventh to the thirtieth year of their
age, in learning these sacred texts. At the time when
Hiouen-thsang was travelling in India, Buddhism was
clearly on the decline. But Buddhism was originally
a reaction against Brahmanism, and chiefly against the
exclusive privileges which the Brahmans claimed, and
which from the beginning were represented by them as
based on their revealed writings, the Vedas, and hence

beyond the reach of human attacks. Buddhism, whatever the date of its founder, became the state religion
of India under Asoka, the Constantine of India, in the
middle of the third century B. C. This Asoka was the
third king of a new dynasty founded by Kandragupta,
the well-known contemporary of Alexander and Seleu
cus, about 315 B. C. The preceding dynasty was that
of the Nandas, and it is under this dynasty that the
traditions of the Brahmans place a number of distinguished scholars, whose treatises on the Veda we still
possess, such as Sanaka, Kátyáyana, Ásvaláyana, and
others. Their works, and others written with a similar
object and in the same style, carry us back to about
600 B. C. This period of literature, which is called the
Sûtra period, was preceded, as we saw, by another
class of writings, the Brâhmanas, composed in a very
prolix and tedious style, and containing lengthy lucubrations on the sacrifices and on the duties of the different classes of priests. Each of the three or four
Vedas, or each of the three or four classes of priests,
has its own Brâhmanas and its own Sûtras; and as the
Brâhmanas are presupposed by the Sûtras, while no
Sûtra is ever quoted by the Brâhmanas, it is clear that
the period of the Brâhmana literature must have preceded the period of the Sûtra literature. There are,
however, old and new Brâhmanas; and there are in
the Brâhmanas themselves long lists of teachers who
handed down old Brâhmanas or composed new ones;
so that it seems impossible to accommodate the whole
of that literature in less than two centuries, from about
800 to 600 B. C. Before, however, a single Brâhmana
could have been composed, it was not only necessary
that there should have been one collection of ancient

hymns, like that contained in the ten books of the Rig-
veda, but the three or four classes of priests must have
been established; the officiating priests and the choristers must have had their special prayer-books; nay, these
prayer-books must have undergone certain changes,
because the Brâhmanas presuppose different texts,
called "sâkhâs," of each of these prayer-books, which
are called the "Yajur-veda-sanhitâ," the "Sâma-veda-
sanhitâ," and the "Atharva-veda-sanhitâ." The work
of collecting the prayers for the different classes of
priests, and of adding new hymns and formulas for
purely sacrificial purposes, belonged probably to the
tenth century B. C.; and three generations more would,
at least, be required to account for the various readings
adopted in the prayer-books by different sects, and invested with a kind of sacred authority, long before the
composition of even the earliest among the Brâhmanas.
If, therefore, the years from about 1000 to 800 B. C.
are assigned to this collecting age, the time before 1000
B. C. must be set apart for the free and natural growth
of what was then national and religious, but not yet
sacred and sacrificial poetry. How far back this period
extends it is impossible to tell; it is enough if the
hymns of the Rig-veda can be traced to a period anterior to 1000 B. C.

Much in the chronological arrangement of the three
periods of Vedic literature that are supposed to have
followed the period of the original growth of the
hymns, must of necessity be hypothetical, and has
been put forward rather to invite than to silence criticism. In order to discover truth, we must be truthful
ourselves, and must welcome those who point out our
errors as heartily as those who approve and confirm

our discoveries. What seems, however, to speak
strongly in favor of the historical character of the
three periods of Vedic literature is the uniformity of
style which marks the productions of each. In modern
literature we find, at one and the same time, different
styles of prose and poetry cultivated by one and the
same author. A Goethe writes tragedy, comedy, sat-
ire, lyrical poetry, and scientific prose; but we find
nothing like this in primitive literature. The individual is there much less prominent, and the poet's character disappears in the general character of the layer of
literature to which he belongs. It is the discovery of
such large layers of literature following each other in
regular succession which inspires the critical historian
with confidence in the truly historical character of the
successive literary productions of ancient India. As
in Greece there is an epic age of literature, where we
should look in vain for prose or dramatic poetry; as in
that country we never meet with real elegiac poetry
before the end of the eighth century, nor with iambics
before the same date; as even in more modern times
rhymed heroic poetry appears in England with the
Norman Conquest, and in Germany the Minnesänger
rise and set with the Swabian dynasty, — so, only in a
much more decided manner, we see in the ancient and
spontaneous literature of India, an age of poets fol-
owed by an age of collectors and imitators, that age to
be succeeded by an age of theological prose writers,
and this last by an age of writers of scientific man-
uals. Now wants produced new supplies, and nothing sprang up or was allowed to live, in prose or
poetry, except what was really wanted. If the
works of poets, collectors, imitators, theologians, and

teachers were all mixed up together, — if the Bráhmanas quoted the Sútras, and the hymns alluded to
the Bráhmanas, — an historical restoration of the Vedic
literature of India would be almost an impossibility.
We should suspect artificial influences, and look with
small confidence on the historical character of such a
literary agglomerate. But he who would question the
antiquity of the Veda must explain how the layers of
literature were formed that are super-imposed over the
original stratum of the poetry of the Rishis: he who
would suspect a literary forgery must show how, when,
and for what purpose, the 1,000 hymns of the Rig-
veda could have been forged, and have become the
religious, moral, political, and literary life of the ancient
inhabitants of India.

The idea of revelation, and I mean more particularly
book-revelation, is not a modern idea, nor is it an idea
peculiar to Christianity. Though we look for it in
vain in the literature of Greece and Rome, we find the
literature of India saturated with this idea from beginning to end. In no country, I believe, has the theory
of revelation been so minutely elaborated as in India.
The name for revelation in Sanskrit is "Sruti," which
means hearing; and this title distinguishes the Vedic
hymns, and, at a later time, the Bráhmanas also,
from all other works, which, however sacred and au-
thoritative to the Hindu mind, are admitted to have
been composed by human authors. The Laws of
Manu, for instance, according to the Brahmanic theology, are not revelation; they are not Sruti, but only
Smriti, which means recollection or tradition. If these
laws, or any other work of authority, can be proved on
any point to be at variance with a single passage of the

Veda, their authority is at once overruled. According
to the orthodox views of Indian theologians, not a
single line of the Veda was the work of human authors. The whole Veda is in some way or other the
work of the Deity; and even those who received the
revelation, or, as they express it, those who saw it,
were not supposed to be ordinary mortals, but beings
raised above the level of common humanity, and less
liable, therefore, to error in the reception of revealed
truth. The views entertained of revelation by the orthodox theologians of India are far more minute and
elaborate than those of the most extreme advocates of
verbal inspiration in Europe. The human element,
called "paurusheyatva" in Sanskrit, is driven out of
every corner or hiding-place; and as the Veda is
held to have existed in the mind of the Deity
before the beginning of time, every allusion to
historical events, of which there are not a few, is
explained away with a zeal and ingenuity worthy of
a better cause.

But let me state at once that there is nothing in the
hymns themselves to warrant such extravagant theories. In many a hymn, the author says plainly that
he or his friends made it to please the gods; that he
made it, as a carpenter makes a chariot (Rv. I. 130, 6;
V. 2, 11), or like a beautiful vesture (Rv. V. 29,
15); that he fashioned it in his heart and kept it
in his mind (Rv. I. 171, 2); that he expects, as
his reward, the favor of the god whom he celebrates
(Rv. IV. 6, 21). But though the poets of the Veda
knew nothing of the artificial theories of verbal inspiration, they were not altogether unconscious of
higher influences: nay, they speak of their hymns as

"god-given" ("devattam," Rv. III. 37. 4). One poet says (Rv. VI. 47, 10): "O god (Indra) have mercy, give me my daily bread! Sharpen my mind, like the edge of iron. Whatever I now may utter, longing for thee, do thou accept it; make me possessed of God!" Another utters for the first time the famous hymn, the "Gâyatrî," which now for more than three thousand years has been the daily prayer of every Brahman, and is still repeated every morning by millions of pious worshippers: "Let us meditate on the adorable light of the divine Creator: may he rouse our minds."[1] This consciousness of higher influences, or of divine help in those who uttered for the first time the simple words of prayer, praise, and thanksgiving, is very different, however, from the artificial theories of verbal inspiration which we find in the later theological writings; it is indeed but another expression of that deep-felt dependence on the Deity, of that surrender and denial of all that seems to be self, which was felt more or less by every nation, but by none, I believe, more strongly, more constantly, than by the Indian. "It is He that has made it," — namely, the prayer in which the soul of the poet has thrown off her burden, — is but a variation of, "It is He that has made us," which is the key-note of all religion, whether ancient or modern, whether natural or revealed.

I must say no more to-night of what the Veda is, for I am very anxious to explain to you, as far as it is possible, what I consider to be the real importance of the Veda to the student of history, to the student of religion, to the student of mankind.

[1] "Tat Savitur varenyam bhargo devasya dhîmahi, dhîyo yo naḥ prachodayât." Colebrooke, Miscellaneous Essays, i. 30. Many passages bearing on this subject have been collected by Dr. Muir in the third volume of his Sanskrit Texts, p. 114 seq.

In the study of mankind there can hardly be a subject more deeply interesting than the study of the different forms of religion; and much as I value the Science of Language for the aid which it lends us in unraveling some of the most complicated tissues of the human intellect, I confess that to my mind there is no study more absorbing than that of the Religions of the World,—the study, if I may so call it, of the various languages in which man has spoken to his Maker, and of that language in which his Maker "at sundry times and in divers manners" spake to man.

To my mind the great epochs in the world's history are marked not by the foundation or the destruction of empires, by the migrations of races, or by French revolutions. All this is outward history, made up of events that seem gigantic and overpowering to those only who cannot see beyond and beneath. The real history of man is the history of religion — the wonderful ways by which the different families of the human race advanced towards a truer knowledge and a deeper love of God. This is the foundation that underlies all profane history; it is the light, the soul, and life of history, and without it all history would indeed be profane.

On this subject there are some excellent works in English, such as Mr. Maurice's "Lectures on the Religions of the World," or Mr. Hardwick's "Christ and other Masters;" in German, I need only mention Hegel's "Philosophy of Religion," out of many other learned treatises on the different systems of religion in the East and the West. But in all these works religions are treated very much as languages were treated during the last century. They are rudely classed, either according to the different localities in which they prevailed, just as in Adelung's " Mithridates " you find the languages of the world classified as European, African, American, Asiatic, etc. ; or according to their age, as formerly languages used to be divided into ancient and modern ; or according to their respective dignity, as languages used to be treated as sacred or profane, as classical or illiterate. Now you know that the Science of Language has sanctioned a totally different system of classification ; and that the Comparative Philologist ignores altogether the division of languages according to their locality, or according to their age, or according to their classical or illiterate character. Languages are now classified genealogically, i. e. according to their real relationship; and the most important languages of Asia, Europe, and Africa, — that is to say, of that part of the world on which what we call the history of man has been acted, — have been grouped together into three great divisions, the Aryan or Indo-European Family, the Semitic Family, and the Turanian Class. According to that division you are aware that English, together with all the Teutonic languages of the Continent, Celtic, Slavonic, Greek, Latin with its modern offshoots, such as French and Italian, Persian, and Sanskrit, are so many varieties of one common type of speech : that Sanskrit, the ancient language of the Veda, is no more distinct from the Greek of Homer, or from the Gothic of Ulfilas, or from the Anglo-Saxon of Alfred, than French is from Italian. All these languages together form one family, one whole, in which every member shares certain features in common with all the rest, and is at the same time distinguished from the rest by certain features peculiarly its own. The

same applies to the Semitic family, which comprises, as
its most important members, the Hebrew of the Old
Testament, the Arabic of the Koran, and the ancient
languages on the monuments of Phœnicia and Carthage,
of Babylon and Assyria. These languages, again,
form a compact family, and differ entirely from the
other family, which we called Aryan or Indo-European.
The third group of languages, for we can hardly call it
a family, comprises most of the remaining languages
of Asia, and counts among its principal members the
Tungusic, Mongolic, Turkic, Samoyedic, and Finnic,
together with the languages of Siam, the Malay Islands,
Thibet, and Southern India. Lastly, the Chinese
language stands by itself, as monosyllabic, the only
remnant of the earliest formation of human speech.

Now I believe that the same division which has introduced a new and natural order into the history of
languages, and has enabled us to understand the growth
of human speech in a manner never dreamt of in
former days, will be found applicable to a scientific
study of religions. I shall say nothing to-night of the
Semitic or Turanian or Chinese religions, but confine
my remarks to the religions of the Aryan family.
These religions, though more important in the ancient
history of the world, as the religions of the Greeks and
Romans, of our own Teutonic ancestors and of the
Celtic and Slavonic races, are nevertheless of great importance even at the present day. For although there
are no longer any worshippers of Zeus, or Jupiter, of
Wodan, Esus,[1] or Perkunas,[2] the two religions of

[1] Mommsen, Inscriptiones Helvetica, 4l. Becker, Die inschriftlichen
Überreste der Keltischen Sprache, in Beiträge zur Vergleichenden Sprach-
forschung, vol. iii. p. 341. Lucan, Phars., 1, 445, "Immemesque feris aliarh-
bus Hesus."
[2] Cf. G. Bühler, Über Parjanya, in Benfey's Orient und Occident.

Aryan origin which still survive, Brahmanism and Buddhism, claim together a decided majority among the inhabitants of the globe. Out of the whole population of the world, —

> 31.2 per cent. are Buddhists,
> 13.4 per cent. are Brahmanists,
> ————
> 44.6

which together gives us 44 per cent. for what may be called living Aryan religions. Of the remaining 56 per cent. 15.7 are Mohammedans, 8.7 per cent. non-descript Heathens, 30.7 per cent. Christians, and only 0.3 per cent. Jews.

Now, as a scientific study of the Aryan languages became possible only after the discovery of Sanskrit, a scientific study of the Aryan religion dates really from the discovery of the Veda. The study of Sanskrit brought to light the original documents of three religions, the Sacred Books of the Brahmans, the Sacred Books of the Magians, the followers of Zoroaster, and the Sacred Books of the Buddhists. Fifty years ago, these three collections of sacred writings were all but unknown, their very existence was doubted, and there was not a single scholar who could have translated a line of the Veda, a line of the Zend-Avesta, or a line of the Buddhist Tripitaka. At present large portions of these, the canonical writings of the most ancient and most important religions of the Aryan race, are published and deciphered, and we begin to see a natural progress, and almost a logical necessity, in the growth of these three systems of worship. The oldest,

vol. i, p. 214. In the Old Irish, *erg*, a drop, t as been pointed out as derived from the same root as *paraguay a*.

most primitive, most simple form of Aryan faith finds its expression in the Veda. The Zend-Avesta represents in its language, as well as in its thoughts, a branching off from that more primitive stem; a more or less conscious opposition to the worship of the gods of nature, as adored in the Veda, and a striving after a more spiritual, supreme, moral deity, such as Zoroaster proclaimed under the name of "Ahura mazda," or Ormuzd. Buddhism, lastly, marks a decided schism; a decided antagonism against the established religion of the Brahmans; a denial of the true divinity of the Vedic gods; and a proclamation of new philosophical and social doctrines.

Without the Veda, therefore, neither the reforms of Zoroaster nor the new teaching of Buddha would have been intelligible: we should not know what was behind them, or what forces impelled Zoroaster and Buddha to the founding of new religions; how much they received, how much they destroyed, how much they created. Take but one word in the religious phraseology of those three systems. In the Veda the gods are called Deva. This word in Sanskrit means bright, — brightness or light being one of the most general attributes shared by the various manifestations of the Deity, invoked in the Veda, as Sun, or Sky, or Fire, or Dawn, or Storm. We can see, in fact, how in the minds of the poets of the Veda, deva, from meaning bright, came gradually to mean divine. In the Zend-Avesta the same word "daéva" means evil spirit. Many of the Vedic gods, with Indra at their head, have been degraded to the position of daévas, in order to make room for Ahura mazda, the Wise Spirit, as the supreme deity of the Zoroastrians. In his confession of faith the follower of Zoroaster declares: "I cease to be a worshipper of the daêvas." In Buddhism, again, we find these ancient Devas, Indra and the rest, as merely legendary beings, carried about at shows, as servants of Buddha, as goblins or fabulous heroes; but no longer either worshipped or even feared by those with whom the name of Deva had lost every trace of its original meaning. Thus this one word deva marks the mutual relations of these three religions. But more than this. The same word deva is the Latin *deus*, thus pointing to that common source of language and religion, far beyond the heights of the Vedic Olympus, from which the Romans, as well as the Hindus, draw the names of their deities, and the elements of their language as well as of their religion.

The Veda, by its language and its thoughts, supplies that distant background in the history of all the religions of the Aryan race, which was missed indeed by every careful observer, but which formerly could be supplied by guess-work only. How the Persians came to worship Ormuzd; how the Buddhists came to protest against temples and sacrifices; how Zeus and the Olympian gods came to be what they are in the mind of Homer; or how such beings as Jupiter and Mars came to be worshipped by the Italian peasant, — all these questions, which used to yield material for endless and baseless speculations, can now be answered by a simple reference to the hymns of the Veda. The religion of the Veda is not the source of all the other religions of the Aryan world, nor is Sanskrit the mother of all the Aryan languages. Sanskrit, as compared to Greek and Latin, is an elder sister, not a parent: Sanskrit is the earliest deposit of Aryan speech, as the Veda is the earliest deposit of Aryan faith. But the religion and incipient mythology of the Veda possess the same simplicity and transparency which distinguish the grammar of Sanskrit from Greek, Latin, or German grammar. We can watch in the Veda ideas and their names growing, which in Persia, Greece, and Rome we meet with only as full-grown or as fast decaying. We get one step nearer to that distant source of religious thought and language which has fed the different national streams of Persia, Greece, Rome, and Germany; and we begin to see clearly, what ought never to have been doubted, that there is no religion without God, or, as St. Augustine expressed it, that " there is no false religion which does not contain some elements of truth."

I do not wish by what I have said to raise any exaggerated expectations as to the worth of these ancient hymns of the Veda, and the character of that religion which they indicate rather than fully describe. The historical importance of the Veda can hardly be exaggerated; but its intrinsic merit, and particularly the beauty or elevation of its sentiments, have by many been rated far too high. Large numbers of the Vedic hymns are childish in the extreme: tedious, low, commonplace. The gods are constantly invoked to protect their worshippers, to grant them food, large flocks, large families, and a long life; for all which benefits they are to be rewarded by the praises and sacrifices offered day after day, or at certain seasons of the year. But hidden in this rubbish there are precious stones. Only in order to appreciate them justly, we must try to divest ourselves of the common notions about Poly theism, so repugnant not only to our feelings, but to our understanding. No doubt, if we must employ technical terms, the religion of the Veda is Polytheism, not Monotheism. Deities are invoked by different names, some clear and intelligible, such as "Agni," fire; "Sûrya," the sun; " Ushas," dawn; "Maruts," the storms; "Prithivî," the earth; "Ap," the waters; "Nadî," the rivers: others such as " Varuna," " Mitra," "Indra," which have become proper names, and disclose but dimly their original application to the great aspects of nature, the sky, the sun, the day. But whenever one of these individual gods is invoked, they are not conceived as limited by the powers of others, as superior or inferior in rank. Each god is to the mind of the supplicant as good as all gods. He is felt, at the time, as a real divinity, — as supreme and absolute, — without a suspicion of those limitations which, to our mind, a plurality of gods must entail on every single god. All the rest disappear for a moment from the vision of the poet, and he only who is to fulfil their desires stands in full light before the eyes of the worshippers. In one hymn, ascribed to Manu, the poet says: "Among you, O gods, there is none that is small, none that is young; you are all great indeed." And this is indeed the key-note of the ancient Aryan worship. Yet it would be easy to find in the numerous hymns of the Veda, passages in which almost every important deity is represented as supreme and absolute. Thus in one hymn, Agni (fire) is called "the ruler of the universe," "the lord of men," "the wise king, the father, the brother, the son, the friend of man ; " nay, all the powers and names of the other gods are dis-

tinctly ascribed to Agni.   But though Agni is thus
highly exalted, nothing is said to disparage the divine
character of the other gods. In another hymn another
god, Indra, is said to be greater than all : "The gods,"
it is said, "do not reach thee, Indra, nor men; thou
overcomest all creatures in strength."   Another god,
Soma, is called the king of the world, the king of
heaven and earth, the conqueror of all.   And what more
could human language achieve, in trying to express the
idea of a divine and supreme power, than what another
poet says of another god, Varuna: "Thou art lord of
all, of heaven and earth ; thou art the king of all, of
those who are gods, and of those who are men !"

   This surely is not what is commonly understood by
Polytheism.   Yet it would be equally wrong to call it
Monotheism.   If we must have a name for it, I should
call it Kathenotheism.   The consciousness that all the
deities are but different names of one and the same
godhead, breaks forth indeed here and there in the
Veda.   But it is far from being general.   One poet,
for instance, says (Rv. I. 164, 46) : "They call him
Indra, Mitra, Varuna, Agni; then he is the beautiful-
winged heavenly Garutmat : that which is One the
wise call it in divers manners: they call it Agni,
Yama, Mâtarisvan."   And again (Rv. X. 114, 5):
'Wise poets make the beautiful-winged, though he is
one, manifold by words."

   I shall read you a few Vedic verses, in which the
religious sentiment predominates, and in which we
perceive a yearning after truth, and after the true
God, untrammeled as yet by any names or any traditions [1] (Rv. X. 121):—

   [1] History of Ancient Sanskrit Literature, p. 570.

1. In the beginning there arose the golden Child—He was the one born lord of all that is. He stablished the earth, and this sky;—Who is the God to whom we shall offer our sacrifice?

2. He who gives life, He who gives strength; whose command all the bright gods revere; whose shadow is immortality, whose shadow is death;—Who is the God to whom we shall offer our sacrifice?

3. He who through His power is the one king of the breathing and awakening world—He who governs all, man and beast;—Who is the God to whom we shall offer our sacrifice?

4. He whose greatness these snowy mountains, whose greatness the sea proclaims, with the distant river—He whose these regions are, as it were His two arms;—Who is the God to whom we shall offer our sacrifice?

5. He through whom the sky is bright and the earth firm—He through whom the heaven was stablished,—nay, the highest heaven,—He who measured out the light in the air;—Who is the God to whom we shall offer our sacrifice?

6. He to whom heaven and earth, standing firm by His will, look up, trembling inwardly—He over whom the rising sun shines forth;—Who is the God to whom we shall offer our sacrifice?

7. Wherever the mighty water-clouds went, where they placed the seed and lit the fire, thence arose He who is the sole life of the bright gods;—Who is the God to whom we shall offer our sacrifice?

8. He who by His might looked even over the water-clouds, the clouds which gave strength and lit the sacrifice: He who alone is God above all gods;—

Who is the God to whom we shall offer our sacrifice?

9. May He not destroy us — He the creator of the earth; or He, the righteous, who created the heaven; He also created the bright and mighty waters; — Who is the God to whom we shall offer our sacrifice? [1]

The following may serve as specimens of hymns addressed to individual deities whose names have become the centres of religious thought and legendary traditions; deities, in fact, like Jupiter, Apollo, Mars, or Minerva, no longer mere germs, but fully developed forms of early thought and language: —

HYMN TO INDRA (Rv. I. 53). [2]

1. Keep silence well! [3] we offer praises to the great Indra in the house of the sacrificer. Does he find treasure for those who are like sleepers? Mean praise is not valued among the munificent.

2. Thou art the giver of horses, Indra, thou art the giver of cows, the giver of corn, the strong lord

[1] A last verse is added, which entirely spoils the poetical beauty and the whole character of the hymn. Its later origin seems to have struck even native critics, for the author of the Pada text did not receive it. "O Prajâpati, no other than thou hast embraced all these created things; may what we desired when we called on thee, be granted to us, may we be lords of riches."

[2] I subjoin for some of the hymns here translated, the translation of the late Professor Wilson, in order to show what kind of difference there is between the traditional rendering of the Vedic hymns, as adopted by him, and their interpretation according to the rules of modern scholarship: —

1. We ever offer fitting praise to the mighty Indra, in the dwelling of the worshipper, by which he (the deity) has quickly acquired riches, as (a thief) hastily carries (off the property) of the sleeping. Praise ill expressed is not valued among the munificent.

2. Thou Indra, art the giver of horses, of cattle, of barley, the master

[3] Favete linguis.

of wealth; the old guide of man, disappointing no desires, a friend to friends:—to him we address this song.

3. O powerful Indra, achiever of many works, most brilliant god—all this wealth around here is known to be thine alone: take from it, conqueror, bring it hither! do not stint the desire of the worshipper who longs for thee!

4. On these days thou art gracious, and on these nights,[1] keeping off the enemy from our cows and from our stud. Tearing[2] the fiend night after night with the help of Indra, let us rejoice in food, freed from haters.

5. Let us rejoice, Indra, in treasure and food, in wealth of manifold delight and splendor. Let us rejoice in the blessing of the gods, which gives us the strength of offspring, gives us cows first and horses.

6. These draughts inspired thee, O lord of the brave! these were vigor, these libations, in battles,

and protector of wealth, the firmest in friendship, (the being) of many days; thee disappointest not desires (addressed to thee); thee art a friend to our friends: such an Indra we praise.

3. Wise and resplendent Indra, the achiever of great deeds, the riches that are spread around are known to be thine: having collected them, (thou even thy enemies), bring them to me disappoint not the expectation of the worshipper who trusts in thee.

4. Propitiated by these offerings, by these libations, dispel poverty with cattle and horses: may we, subduing our adversary, and relieved from enemies by Indra, (pleased) by our libations, enjoy together abundant food.

5. Indra, may we become possessed of riches, and of food: and with energies agreeable to many, and shining around, may we prosper through thy divine favor, the source of prowess, of cattle, and of horses.

6. Those who were thy allies (the Maruts), brought thee joy: protects

[1] (R.V. I. 112. 25, "áyahbhir aktúbhih," by day and by night: also Rv. III. 31. 16. M. M., "Todtenbestattung." p. 5.

[2] Professor Benfey reads "damyasāt," but all MSS. that I know without exception, read "darṇyasāt."

when for the sake of the poet, the sacrificer, thou struckest down irresistibly ten thousands of enemies.

7. From battle to battle¹ thou advancest bravely, from town to town thou destroyest all this with might, when thou, Indra, with Nâmi as thy friend, struckest down from afar the deceiver Namuki.

8. Thou hast slain Karñaga and Parñaya with the brightest spear of Atithigva. Without a helper thou didst demolish the hundred cities of Vañgrida, which were besieged by Rigisvan.

9. Thou hast felled down with the chariot-wheel those twenty kings of men, who had attacked the friendless Susravas,² and gloriously the sixty thousand and ninety-nine forts.

10. Thou, Indra, hast succoured Susravas with thy succors, Tûrvayâna with thy protections. Thou hast made Kutsa, Atithigva, and Âyu subject to this mighty youthful king.

of the pious, those libations and oblations that were offered thee on slaying Vritra), yielded thee delight, when thou, unimpeded by foes, didst destroy the ten thousand obstacles opposed to him who praised thee and offered thee libations.

7. Humiliator (of adversaries), thou goest from battle to battle, and destroyest by thy might city after city; with thy foe-prostrating associate (the thunderbolt), thou, Indra, didst slay afar off the deceiver named Namuki.

8. Thou hast slain Karñaga and Parñaya with thy bright glancing spear, in the cause of Atithigva; unaided, thou didst demolish the hundred cities of Vañgrida, when besieged by Rigisvan.

9. Thou, renowned Indra, overthrewest by thy unattached overtaken chariot-wheel, the twenty kings of men, who had come against Susravas, unaided, and their sixty thousand and ninety and nine followers.

10. Thou, Indra, hast preserved Susravas by thy succor, Tûrvayâna by thy assistance: thou hast made Kutsa, Atithigva, and Âyu subject to the mighty though youthful Susravas.

¹ For a different translation, see Roth, In Orientals Manuscript, p. 88.
² See Spiegel, Erân, p. 300, on Khol Khosru = Susravas.

11. We who in future, protected by the gods, wish to be thy most blessed friends, we shall praise thee, blessed by thee with offspring, and enjoying henceforth a longer life.

The next hymn is one of many addressed to Agni as the god of fire, not only the fire as a powerful element, but likewise the fire of the hearth and the altar, the guardian of the house, the minister of the sacrifice, the messenger between gods and men:—

Hymn to Agni (Rv. II. 6).

1. Agni, accept this log which I offer to thee, accept this my service; listen well to these my songs.

2. With this log, O Agni, may we worship thee, thou son of strength, conqueror of horses! and with this hymn, thou high-born!

3. May we thy servants serve thee with songs, O granter of riches, thou who lovest songs and delightest in riches.

4. Thou lord of wealth and giver of wealth, be thou wise and powerful; drive away from us the enemies!

5. He gives us rain from heaven, he gives us inviolable strength, he gives us food a thousand-fold.

6. Youngest of the gods, their messenger, their invoker, most deserving of worship, come, at our praise, to him who worships thee and longs for thy help.

7. For thou, O sage, goest wisely between these two

11. Protected by the gods, we remain, Indra, at the close of the sacrifice, thy most fortunate friends; we praise thee, or enjoying through thee without offspring, and a long and prosperous life.

VOL. I.   3

creations (heaven and earth, gods and men), like a
friendly messenger between two hamlets.

8. Thou art wise, and thou hast been pleased; perform thou, intelligent Agni, the sacrifice without interruption, sit down on this sacred grass!

The following hymn, partly laudatory, partly depre-
catory, is addressed to the Maruts or Rudras, the
Storm-gods: —

HYMN TO THE MARUTS (Rv. I. 89).[1]

1. When you thus from afar cast forward your
measure, like a blast of fire, through whom wisdom is
it, through whose design? To whom do you go, to
whom, ye shakers (of the earth)?

2. May your weapons be firm to attack, strong also
to withstand! May yours be the more glorious
strength, not that of the deceitful mortal!

3. When you overthrow what is firm, O ye men,
and whirl about what is heavy, ye pass through the
trees of the earth, through the clefts of the rocks.

4. No real foe of yours is known in heaven, nor in
earth, ye devourers of enemies! May strength be

1 Professor Wilson translates as follows: —

1. When, Maruts, who make (all things) tremble, you direct your awful
(vigour) downwards from afar, as light (descends from heaven), by whose
worship, by whose praise (are you attracted)? To what (place of sacrifice), to whom, indeed, do you repair?

2. Strong be your weapons for driving away (your) foes, firm in resisting
them; yours be the strength that merits praise, not (the strength) of a treach-
erous mortal.

3. Directing Maruts, when you demolish what is stable, when you scatter
what is ponderous, then you make your way through the forest (trees) of
earth and the flanks of the mountains.

4. Destroyers of foes, no adversary of yours is known above the heavens

yours, together with your race, O Rudras, to defy even now.

5. They make the rocks to tremble, they tear asunder the kings of the forest. Come on, Maruts, like madmen, ye gods, with your whole tribe.

6. You have harnessed the spotted deer to your chariots, a red deer draws as leader. Even the earth listened at your approach, and men were frightened.

7. O Rudras, we quickly desire your help for our race. Come now to us with help, as of yore, thus for the sake of the frightened Kanva.

8. Whatever fiend, roused by you or roused by mortals, attacks us, tear him from us by your power, by your strength, by your aid.

9. For you, worshipful and wise, have wholly protected Kanva. Come to us, Maruts, with your whole help, as quickly as lightnings come after the rain.

10. Bounteous givers, ye possess whole strength, whole power, ye shakers (of the earth). Send, O

our (may) upon earth: may your collective strength be quickly exerted, sons of Rudra, to humble (your enemies).

5. They make the mountains tremble, they drive apart the forest trees. On, divine Maruts, whither you will, with all your progeny, like those intoxicated.

6. You have harnessed the spotted deer to your chariot; the red deer yoked between them (side to) drag the car: the firmament listens for your coming, and men are alarmed.

7. Rudras, we have recourse to your assistance for the sake of our progeny: come quickly to the timid Kanva, as you formerly came, for our protection.

8. Should any adversary, instigated by you, or by man, assail us, withhold from him food and strength and your assistance.

9. Praiseless, who are to be unreservedly worshipped, uphold (the worshipper) Kanva: come to us, Maruts, with undivided protective assistance, as the lightnings (bring) the rain.

10. Bounteous givers, you enjoy unimpaired vigour; shakers (of the

Marats, against the proud enemy of the poets, an enemy, like an arrow.

The following is a simple prayer addressed to the Dawn : —

HYMN TO USHAS (Rv. VII. 77).

1. She shines upon us, like a young wife, rousing every living being to go to his work. When the fire had to be kindled by men, she made the light by striking down darkness.

2. She rose up, spreading far and wide, and moving everywhere. She grew in brightness, wearing her brilliant garment. The mother of the cows, (the mornings) the leader of the days, she shone gold-colored, lovely to behold.

3. She, the fortunate, who brings the eye of the gods, who leads the white and lovely steed (of the sun), the Dawn was seen revealed by her rays, with brilliant treasures, following every one.

4. Thou art a blessing where thou art near, drive far away the unfriendly ; make the pasture wide, give us safety ! Scatter the enemy, bring riches ! Raise up wealth to the worshipper, thou mighty Dawn.

5. Shine for us with thy best rays, thou bright Dawn, thou who lengthenest our life, thou the love of all, who givest us food, who givest us wealth in cows, horses, and chariots.

6. Thou daughter of the sky, thou high-born Dawn, whom the Vasishthas magnify with songs, give us riches high and wide : all ye gods protect us always with your blessings.

I must confine myself to shorter extracts, in order to be able to show to you that all the principal elements of real religion are present in the Veda. I remind you again that the Veda contains a great deal of what is childish and foolish, though very little of what is bad and objectionable. Some of its poets ascribe to the gods sentiments and passions unworthy of the Deity, such as anger, revenge, delight in material sacrifices; they likewise represent human nature on a low level of selfishness and worldliness. Many hymns are utterly unmeaning and insipid, and we must search patiently before we meet, here and there, with sentiments that come from the depth of the soul, and with prayers in which we could join ourselves. Yet there are such passages, and they are the really important passages, as marking the highest points to which the religious life of the ancient poets of India had reached: and it is to these that I shall now call your attention.

First of all, the religion of the Veda knows of no idols. The worship of idols in India is a secondary formation, a later degradation of the more primitive worship of ideal gods.

The gods of the Veda are conceived as immortal: passages in which the birth of certain gods is mentioned have a physical meaning: they refer to the birth of the day, the rising of the sun, the return of the year.

The gods are supposed to dwell in heaven, though several of them, as, for instance, Agni, the god of fire, are represented as living among men, or as approaching the sacrifice, and listening to the praises of their worshippers.

Heaven and earth are believed to have been made

or to have been established by certain gods. Elaborate
theories of creation, which abound in the later works,
the Brâhmaṇas, are not to be found in the hymns.
What we find are such passages as : —

" Agni held the earth, he established the heaven by
truthful words " (Rv. I. 67, 5).

" Varuṇa stemmed asunder the wide firmaments ;
he lifted on high the bright and glorious heaven ; he
stretched out apart the starry sky and the earth " (Rv.
VII. 86, 1).

More frequently, however, the poets confess their
ignorance of the beginning of all things, and one of
them exclaims : —

" Who has seen the first-born ? Where was the life,
the blood, the soul of the world ? Who went to ask
this from any that knew it ? "   (Rv. I. 164, 4.) [1]

Or again (Rv. X. 81, 4) : " What was the forest, what
was the tree out of which they shaped heaven and
earth ?   Wise men, ask this indeed in your mind, on
what he stood when he held the worlds ? "

I now come to a more important subject.   We find
in the Veda, what few would have expected to find
there, the two ideas, so contradictory to the human
understanding, and yet so easily reconciled in every
human heart : God has established the eternal laws of
right and wrong, he punishes sin and rewards virtue,
and yet the same God is willing to forgive ; just, yet
merciful : a judge, and yet a father.   Consider, for
instance, the following lines (Rv. I. 41, 4) : " His path
is easy and without thorns, who does what is right."

And again (Rv. I. 41, 9) : " Let man fear Him who
holds the four (dice), before he throws them down

[1] *History of Ancient Sanskrit Literature*, p. 96, note.

(i. e. God who holds the destinies of men in his hand) ;
let no man delight in evil words!"

And then consider the following hymns, and imagine the feelings which alone could have prompted
them : —

HYMN TO VARUNA (Rv. VII. 89).

1. Let me not yet, O Varuna, enter into the house
of clay; have mercy, almighty, have mercy !

2. If I go along trembling, like a cloud driven by
the wind ; have mercy, almighty, have mercy !

3. Through want of strength, thou strong and bright
god, have I gone wrong; have mercy, almighty, have
mercy !

4. Thirst came upon the worshipper, though he stood
in the midst of the waters; have mercy, almighty,
have mercy !

5. Whenever we men, O Varuna, commit an offense
before the heavenly host, whenever we break the law
through thoughtlessness ; punish us not, O god, for that
offense.

And again (Rv. VII. 86) : —

1. Wise and mighty are the works of him who
stemmed asunder the wide firmaments (heaven and
earth). He lifted on high the bright and glorious
heaven ; he stretched out apart the starry sky and the
earth.

2. Do I say this to my own self? How can I get
unto Varuna? Will he accept my offering without
displeasure? When shall I, with a quiet mind, see
him propitiated?

3. I ask, O Varuna, wishing to know this my sin
I go to ask the wise. The sages all tell me the same
Varuna it is who is angry with thee.

4. Was it an old sin, O Varuna, that thou wishest to destroy thy friend, who always praises thee? Tell me, thou unconquerable lord, and I will quickly turn to thee with praise, freed from sin.

5. Absolve us from the sins of our fathers, and from those which we committed with our own bodies. Release Vasishtha, O king, like a thief who has feasted on stolen oxen; release him like a calf from the rope.

6. It was not our own doing, O Varuna, it was necessity (or temptation), an intoxicating draught, passion, dice, thoughtlessness. The old is there to mislead the young; even sleep brings unrighteousness.

7. Let me without sin give satisfaction to the angry god, like a slave to his bounteous lord. The lord god enlightened the foolish; he, the wisest, leads his worshipper to wealth.

8. O lord Varuna, may this song go well to thy heart! May we prosper in keeping and acquiring! Protect us, O gods, always with your blessings!

The consciousness of sin is a prominent feature in the religion of the Veda, so is likewise the belief that the gods are able to take away from man the heavy burden of his sins. And when we read such passages as " Varuna is merciful even to him who has committed sin" (Rv. VII. 87, 7), we should surely not allow the strange name of Varuna to jar on our ears, but should remember that it is but one of the many names which men invented in their helplessness to express their ideas of the Deity, however partial and imperfect.

The next hymn, which is taken from the Atharva-veda (IV. 16), will show how near the language of the ancient poets of India may approach to the language of the Bible : [1]

1. The great lord of these worlds sees as if he were near. If a man thinks he is walking by stealth, the gods know it all.

2. If a man stands or walks or hides, if he goes to lie down or to get up, what two people sitting together whisper, King Varuna knows it, he is there as the third.

3. This earth, too, belongs to Varuna, the king, and this wide sky with its ends far apart. The two seas (the sky and the ocean) are Varuna's loins ; he is also contained in this small drop of water.

4. He who should flee far beyond the sky, even he would not be rid of Varuna, the king. His spies proceed from heaven towards this world; with thousand eyes they overlook this earth.

5. King Varuna sees all this, what is between heaven and earth, and what is beyond. He has counted the twinklings of the eyes of men. As a player throws the dice, he settles all things.

6. May all thy fatal nooses, which stand spread out seven by seven and threefold, catch the man who tells a lie, may they pass by him who tells the truth.

Another idea which we find in the Veda is that of faith : not only in the sense of trust in the gods, in their power, their protection, their kindness, but in that of belief in their existence. The Latin word

[1] This hymn was first printed and by Professor Roth in a dissertation on the Atharva-veda (Tübingen, 1845), and it has since been translated and annotated by Dr. Muir, in his article on the Vedic Theogony and Cosmogony, p. 81.

sredo, I believe, is the same as the Sanskrit "*sraddhâ*,' and this sraddhâ occurs in the Veda: —

Rv. I. 102, 2. "Sun and moon go on in regular succession, that we may see, Indra, and believe."

Rv. I. 104, 6. "Destroy not our future offspring, O Indra, for we have believed in thy great power."

Rv. I. 55, 5. "When Indra hurls again and again his thunderbolt, then they believe in the brilliant god."[1]

A similar sentiment, namely, that men only believe in the gods when they see their signs and wonders in the sky, is expressed by another poet (Rv. VIII. 21, 14): —

"Thou, Indra, never findest a rich man to be thy friend; wine-swillers despise thee. But when thou thunderest, when thou gatherest (the clouds), then thou art called, like a father."

And with this belief in god, there is also coupled that doubt, that true skepticism, if we may so call it, which is meant to give to faith its real strength. We find passages, even in these early hymns, where the poet asks himself, whether there is really such a god as Indra, — a question immediately succeeded by an answer, as if given to the poet by Indra himself. Thus we read (Rv. VIII. 100, 3): —

"If you wish for strength, offer to Indra a hymn of praise: a true hymn, if Indra truly exist; for some

---

[1] During violent thunder-storms the natives of New Holland are so afraid of Warrugura, the evil spirit, that they seek shelter even in caves haunted by Ingnas, subordinate demons, which at other times they would enter on no account. There, in silent terror, they prostrate themselves with their faces to the ground, waiting until the spirit, having expended his fury, shall retire to Uta (hell) without having discovered their hiding-place. *Transactions of Ethnological Society,* vol. III p. 229. Oldfield, *The Aborigines of Australia.*

one says, Indra does not exist! Who has seen him? Whom shall we praise?"

Then Indra answers through the poet:—

"Here am I, O worshipper, behold me here! in might I surpass all things."

Similar visions occur elsewhere, where the poet, after inviting a god to a sacrifice, or imploring his pardon for his offences, suddenly exclaims that he has seen the god, and that he feels that his prayer is granted. For instance:—

HYMN TO VARUNA (Rv. I. 25).

1. However we break thy laws from day to day, men as we are, O god, Varuna,

2. Do not deliver us unto death, nor to the blow of the furious, nor to the wrath of the spiteful!

3. To propitiate thee O Varuna, we unbend thy mind with songs, as the charioteer a weary steed.

4. Away from me they flee dispirited, intent only on gaining wealth; as birds to their nests.

5. When shall we bring hither the man, who is victory to the warriors; when shall we bring Varuna, the wide-seeing, to be propitiated?

[6. They (Mitra and Varuna) take this in common; gracious, they never fail the faithful giver.]

7. He who knows the place of the birds that fly through the sky, who on the waters knows the ships;—

8. He, the upholder of order, who knows the twelve months with the offspring of each, and knows the month that is engendered afterwards;—

9. He who knows the track of the wind, of the wide, the bright, the mighty; and knows those who reside on high;—

10. He, the upholder of order, Varuna, sits down among his people; he, the wise, sits there to govern.

11. From thence perceiving all wondrous things, he sees what has been and what will be done.

12. May he, the wise Âditya, make our paths straight all our days; may he prolong our lives!

13. Varuna, wearing golden mail, has put on his shining cloak; the spies sat down around him.

14. The god whom the scoffers do not provoke, nor the tormentors of men, nor the plotters of mischief;—

15. He, who gives to men glory, and not half glory, who gives it even to our own selves;—

16. Yearning for him, the far-seeing, my thoughts move onwards, as kine move to their pastures.

17. Let us speak together again, because my honey has been brought: that thou mayest eat what thou likest, like a friend.

18. Did I see the god who is to be seen by all, did I see the chariot above the earth? He must have accepted my prayers.

19. O hear this my calling, Varuna, be gracious now; longing for help, I have called upon thee.

20. Thou, O wise god, art lord of all, of heaven and earth: listen on thy way.

21. That I may live, take from me the upper rope, loose the middle, and remove the lowest!

In conclusion, let me tell you that there is in the Veda no trace of *metempsychosis*, or that transmigration of souls from human to animal bodies, which is generally supposed to be a distinguishing feature of Indian religion. Instead of this, we find what is really the *sine quâ non* of all real religion, a belief in

immortality, and in personal immortality. Without a
belief in personal immortality, religion surely is like an
arch resting on one pillar, like a bridge ending in an
abyss. We cannot wonder at the great difficulties felt
and expressed by Bishop Warburton and other eminent
divines, with regard to the supposed total absence
of the doctrine of immortality or personal immortality
in the Old Testament; and it is equally startling that
the Sadducees who sat in the same council with the
high-priest, openly denied the resurrection.[1] However,
though not expressly asserted anywhere, a belief in
personal immortality is taken for granted in several passages of the Old Testament, and we can hardly think
of Abraham or Moses as without a belief in life and
immortality. But while this difficulty, so keenly felt
with regard to the Jewish religion, ought to make us
careful in the judgments which we form of other religions, and teach us the wisdom of charitable interpretation, it is all the more important to mark that in the
Veda passages occur where immortality of the soul,
personal immortality and personal responsibility after
death, are clearly proclaimed. Thus we read:—

"He who gives alms goes to the highest place in
heaven; he goes to the gods" (Rv. I. 125, 56).

Another poet, after rebuking those who are rich and
do not communicate, says:—

"The kind mortal is greater than the great in
heaven!"

Even the idea, so frequent in the later literature of
the Brahmans, that immortality is secured by a son,
seems implied, unless our translation deceives us, in
one passage of the Veda (VII. 56. 24): "Asmé

[1] Acts xxiii. 30–xxiii. 6.

(Iti) vira/ marutaḥ sushmí astu gánûmâm yáḥ ásura/ vi dharti, apáḥ yéna su·kshitáya tárema, ádha sva·m dkaḥ abhí vaḥ syáma." "O Maruts, may there be to us a strong son, who is a living ruler of men : through whom we may cross the waters on our way to the happy abode; then may we come to your own house!"

One poet prays that he may see again his father and mother after death (Rv. I. 24. 1) ; and the fathers (Pitris) are invoked almost like gods, oblations are offered to them, and they are believed to enjoy, in company with the gods, a life of never-ending felicity (Rv. X. 15, 16).

We find this prayer addressed to Soma (Rv. IX. 113, 7) : —

"Where there is eternal light, in the world where the sun is placed, in that immortal imperishable world place me, O Soma!

" Where king Vaivasvata reigns, where the secret place of heaven is, where these mighty waters are, there make me immortal!

" Where life is free, in the third heaven of heavens, where the worlds are radiant, there make me immortal!

" Where wishes and desires are, where the bowl of the bright Soma is, where there is food and rejoicing, there make me immortal!

" Where there is happiness and delight, where joy and pleasure reside, where the desires of our desire are attained, there make me immortal!" [1]

---

[1] Professor Roth, after quoting several passages from the Veda in which a belief in immortality is expressed, remarks with great truth: " We here find, not without astonishment, beautiful conceptions on immortality expressed in undorned language with childlike conviction. If it were necessary, we might find here the most powerful weapons against the view which

Whether the old Rishis believed likewise in a place of punishment for the wicked, is more doubtful, though vague allusions to it occur in the Rig-veda, and more distinct descriptions are found in the Atharva-veda. In one verse it is said that the dead is rewarded for his good deeds, that he leaves or casts off all evil, and glorified takes his new body (Rv. X. 14, 8).[1] The dogs of Yama, the king of the departed, present some terrible aspects, and Yama is asked to protect the departed from them (Rv. X. 14, 11). Again, a pit (karta) is mentioned into which the lawless are said to be hurled down (Rv. IX. 73, 8), and into which Indra casts those who offer no sacrifices (Rv. I. 121, 13). One poet prays that the Ádityas may preserve him from the destroying wolf, and from falling into the pit (Rv. II. 29, 6). In one passage we read that " those who break the commandments of Varuna and who speak lies are born for that deep place " (Rv. IV. 5, 5).[2]

Surely the discovery of a religion like this, as unexpected as the discovery of the jaw-bone of Abbeville, deserves to arrest our thoughts for a moment, even in the haste and hurry of this busy life. No doubt, for the daily wants of life, the old division of religions into true and false is quite sufficient; as for practical purposes we distinguish only between our own mother-

has lately been revived, and proclaimed as new, that India was the only birthplace of the idea of immortality, and that even the nations of Europe had derived it from that quarter. As if the religious spirit of every gifted race was not able to arrive at it by its own strength." Journal of the German Oriental Society, vol. iv. p. 427. See Dr. Muir's article on " Yama," in the Journal of the Royal Asiatic Society," p. 10.

[1] M. M., " Die Todtenbestattung bei den Brahmanen." Zeitschrift der Deutschen Morgenländischen Gesellschaft, vol. ix. p. xii.

[2] Dr. Muir, article in " Yama." p. 18.

tongue on the one side, and all other foreign languages
on the other. But, from a higher point of view, it would
not be right to ignore the new evidence that has come
to light; and as the study of geology has given us a
truer insight into the stratification of the earth, it is
but natural to expect that a thoughtful study of the
original works of three of the most important religions
of the world, Brahmanism, Magism, and Buddhism,
will modify our views as to the growth or history of
religion, as to the hidden layers of religious thought
beneath the soil on which we stand. Such inquiries
should be undertaken without prejudice and without
fear: the evidence is placed before us; our duty is to
sift it critically, to weigh it honestly, and to wait for the
results.

Three of these results, to which, I believe, a comparative study of religions is sure to lead, I may state
before I conclude this Lecture.

1. We shall learn that religions in their most ancient
form, or in the minds of their authors, are generally
free from many of the blemishes that attach to them in
later times.

2. We shall learn that there is hardly one religion
which does not contain some truth, some important
truth; truth sufficient to enable those who seek the
Lord and feel after Him, to find Him in their hour of
need.

8. We shall learn to appreciate better than ever
what we have in our own religion. No one who has
not examined patiently and honestly the other religions
of the world, can know what Christianity really is, or
can join with such truth and sincerity in the words of
St. Paul: "I am not ashamed of the Gospel of Christ."

II.

CHRIST AND OTHER MASTERS.[1]

In so comprehensive a work as Mr. Hardwick's "Christ and other Masters," the number of facts stated, of topics discussed, of questions raised, is so considerable that in reviewing it we can select only one or two points for special consideration. Mr. Hardwick intends to give in his work, of which the third volume has just been published, a complete panorama of ancient religion. After having discussed in the first volume what he calls the religious tendencies of our age, he enters upon an examination of the difficult problem of the unity of the human race, and proceeds to draw, in a separate chapter, the characteristic features of religion under the Old Testament. Having thus cleared his way, and established some of the principles according to which the religions of the world should be judged, Mr. Hardwick devotes the whole of the second volume to the religions of India. We find there, first of all, a short but very clear account of the religion of the Veda, as far as it is known at present. We then come to a more matter-of-fact repre-

[1] Christ and other Masters. An Historical Inquiry into some of the chief Parallelisms and Contrasts between Christianity and the Religious Systems of the Ancient World, with special reference to prevailing Difficulties and Objections. By Charles Hardwick, M. A., Christian Advocate in the University of Cambridge. Parts I., II., III. Cambridge, 1858.

sentation of Brahmanism, or the religion of the Hindus, as represented in the so-called " Laws of Manu," and in the ancient portions of the two epic poems, the " Râmâyana " and " Mahâbhârata." The next chapter is devoted to the various systems of Indian philosophy, which all partake more or less of a religious character, and form a natural transition to the first subjective system of faith in India, the religion of Buddha. Mr. Hardwick afterwards discusses, in two separate chapters, the apparent and the real correspondences between Hinduism and revealed religion, and throws out some hints how we may best account for the partial glimpses of truth which exist in the Vedas, the canonical books of Buddhism, and the later Purânas. All these questions are handled with such ability, and discussed with so much elegance and eloquence, that the reader becomes hardly aware of the great difficulties of the subject, and carries away, if not quite a complete and correct, at least a very lucid picture of the religious life of ancient India. The third volume, which was published in the beginning of this year, is again extremely interesting, and full of the most varied descriptions. The religions of China are given first, beginning with an account of the national traditions, as collected and fixed by Confucius. Then follows the religious system of Laotse, or the Tao-ism of China, and lastly Buddhism again, only under that modified form which it assumed when introduced from India into China. After this sketch of the religious life of China, the most ancient centre of Eastern civilization, Mr. Hardwick suddenly transports us to the New World, and introduces us to the worship of the wild tribes of America, and to the ruins of the ancient temples in which the civilized races of that continent, especially the Mexicans, once bowed themselves down before their god or gods. Lastly we have to embark on the South Sea, and to visit the various islands which form a chain between the west coast of America and the east coast of Africa, stretching over half of the globe, and inhabited by the descendants of the once united race of the Malayo-Polynesians.

The account which Mr. Hardwick can afford to give of the various systems of religion in so short a compass as he has fixed for himself, must necessarily be very general; and his remarks on the merits and defects peculiar to each, which were more ample in the second volume, have dwindled down to much smaller dimensions in the third. He declares distinctly that he does not write for missionaries. "It is not my leading object," he says, "to conciliate the more thoughtful minds of heathendom in favor of the Christian faith. However laudable that task may be, however fitly it may occupy the highest and the keenest intellect of persons who desire to further the advance of truth and holiness among our heathen fellow-subjects, there are difficulties nearer home which may in fairness be regarded as possessing prior claims on the attention of a Christian Advocate."

We confess that we regret that Mr. Hardwick should have taken this line. If, in writing his criticism on the ancient or modern systems of Pagan religion, he had placed himself face to face with a poor helpless creature, such as the missionaries have to deal with — a man brought up in the faith of his fathers, accustomed to call his god or gods by names sacred to him from his first childhood; a man who had derived much real help and consolation from his belief in these gods; who had abstained from committing crime, because he was afraid of the anger of a Divine Being; who had performed severe penance, because he hoped to appease the anger of the gods; who had given, not only the tenth part of all he valued most, but the half, nay, the whole of his property, as a free offering to his priests, that they might pray for him or absolve him from his sin, — if, in discussing any of the ancient or modern systems of Pagan religion, Mr. Hardwick had tried to address his arguments to such a person, we believe he would himself have felt a more human, real, and hearty interest in his subject. He would more earnestly have endeavored to find out the good elements in every form of religious belief. No sensible missionary could bring himself to tell a man who has done all that he could do, and more than many who have received the true light of the gospel, that he was excluded from all hope of salvation, and by his very birth and color handed over irretrievably to eternal damnation. It is possible to put a charitable interpretation on many doctrines of ancient heathenism, and the practical missionary is constantly obliged to do so. Let us only consider what these doctrines are. They are not theories devised by men who wish to keep out the truth of Christianity, but sacred traditions which millions of human beings are born and brought up to believe in, as we are born and brought up to believe in Christianity. It is the only spiritual food which God in his wisdom has placed within their reach. But if we once begin to think of modern heathenism, and how certain tenets of Laotse resemble the doctrines of Comte or Spinoza, our equanimity, our historical jus-

...ice, our Christian charity, are gone. We become advocates wrangling for victory ; we are no longer tranquil observers, compassionate friends and teachers. Mr. Hardwick sometimes addresses himself to men like Laotse or Buddha, who are now dead and gone more than two thousand years, in a tone of offended orthodoxy, which may or may not be right in modern controversy, but which entirely disregards the fact that it has pleased God to let these men and millions of human beings be born on earth without a chance of ever hearing of the existence of the gospel. We cannot penetrate into the secrets of the Divine wisdom, but we are bound to believe that God has His purpose in all things, and that He will know how to judge those to whom so little has been given. Christianity does not require of us that we should criticize, with our own small wisdom, that Divine policy which has governed the whole world from the very beginning. We pity a man who is born blind — we are not angry with him ; and Mr. Hardwick, in his arguments against the tenets of Buddha or Laotse, seems to us to treat these men too much in the spirit of a policeman who tells a poor blind beggar that he is only shamming blindness. However, if, as a Christian Advocate, Mr. Hardwick found it impossible to entertain, or at least express, any sympathy with the Pagan world, even the cold judgment of the historian would have been better than the excited pleading of a partisan. Surely it is not necessary, in order to prove that our religion is the only true religion, that we should insist on the utter falseness of all other forms of belief. We need not be frightened if we discover traces of truth, traces even of Christian truth, among the sages and lawgivers of other nations.

St. Augustine was not frightened by this discovery, and every thoughtful Christian will feel cheered by the words of that pious philosopher, when he boldly declares, that there is no religion which, among its many errors, does not contain some real and divine truth. It shows a want of faith in God, and in his inscrutable wisdom in the government of the world, if we think we ought to condemn all ancient forms of faith except the religion of the Jews. A true spirit of Christianity will rather lead us to shut our eyes against many things which are revolting to us in the religion of the Chinese, or the wild Americans, or the civilised Hindus, and to try to discover, as well as we can, how even in these degraded forms of worship a spark of light lies hidden somewhere — a spark which may lighten and warm the heart of the Gentiles, " who, by patient continuance in well-doing, seek for glory, and honor, and immortality." There is an under-current of thought in Mr. Hardwick's book which breaks out again and again, and which has certainly prevented him from discovering many a deep lesson which may be learnt in the study of ancient religions. He uses harsh language, because he is thinking, not of the helpless Chinese, or the dreaming Hindu whose tenets he controverts, but of modern philosophers; and he is evidently glad of every opportunity where he can show to the latter that their systems are more *rechauffés* of ancient heathenism. Thus he says, in his introduction to the third volume : —

" I may also be allowed to add, that, in the present chapters, the more thoughtful reader will not fail to recognize the proper tendency of certain current speculations, which are recommended to us on the ground

that they accord entirely with the last discoveries of
science, and embody the deliberate verdicts of the
oracle within us. Notwithstanding all that has been
urged in their behalf, those theories are little more than
a return to long-exploded errors, a resuscitation of extinct volcanoes; or at best, they merely offer to intro-
duce among us an array of civilizing agencies, which,
after trial in other countries, have been all found wanting. The governing class of China, for example, have
long been familiar with the metaphysics of Spinoza.
They have also carried out the social principles of
M. Comte upon the largest possible scale. For ages
they have been what people of the present day are
wishing to become in Europe, with this difference only,
that the heathen legislator who had lost all faith in God
attempted to redress the wrongs and elevate the moral
status of his subjects by the study of political science, or
devising some new scheme of general sociology ; while
the positive philosopher of the present day, who has re-
lapsed into the same positions, is in every case rejecting
a religious system which has proved itself the mightiest
of all civilizers, and the constant champion of the rights
and dignity of men. He offers in the stead of Christianity a specious phase of paganism, by which the nineteenth century after Christ may be assimilated to the
golden age of Mencius and Confucius ; or, in other
words, may consummate its religious freedom, and attain the highest pinnacle of human progress, by revert-
ing to a state of childhood and of moral imbecility."

Few serious-minded persons will like the temper of
this paragraph. The history of ancient religion is too
important, too sacred a subject to be used as a masked
battery against modern infidelity. Nor should a Chris-

tian Advocate ever condescend to defend his cause by
arguments such as a pleader who is somewhat skeptical
as to the merits of his case, may be allowed to use, but
which produce on the mind of the Judge the very opposite effect of that which they are intended to produce.
If we want to understand the religions of antiquity, we
must try, as well as we can, to enter into the religious,
moral, and political atmosphere of the ancient world.
We must do what the historian does. We must become ancients ourselves; otherwise we shall never
understand the motives and meaning of their faith.
Take one instance. There are some nations who
have always regarded death with the utmost horror.
Their whole religion may be said to be a fight against
death, and the chief object of their prayers seems to be
a long life on earth. The Persian clings to life with
intense tenacity, and the same feeling exists among the
Jews. Other nations, on the contrary, regard death in
a different light. Death is to them a passage from one
life to another. No misgiving has ever entered their
minds as to a possible extinction of existence, and at the
first call of the priest — nay, sometimes from a mere
selfish yearning after a better life — they are ready to
put an end to their existence on earth. Feelings of
this kind can hardly be called convictions arrived at by
the individual. They are national peculiarities, and
they exercise an irresistible sway over all who belong
to the same nation. The loyal devotion which the
Slavonic nations feel for their sovereign will make the
most brutalized Russian peasant step into the place
where his comrade has just been struck down, without a thought of his wife, or his mother, or his children,
whom he is never to see again. He does not do this

because, by his own reflection, he has arrived at the conclusion that he is bound to sacrifice himself for his emperor or for his country; he does it because he knows that every one would do the same; and the only feeling of satisfaction in which he would allow himself to indulge is, that he was doing his duty. If, then, we wish to understand the religions of the ancient nations of the world, we must take into account their national character. Nations who value life so little as the Hindus, and some of the American and Malay nations, could not feel the same horror of human sacrifices, for instance, which would be felt by a Jew; and the voluntary death of the widow would inspire her nearest relations with no other feeling but that of compassion and regret at seeing a young bride follow her husband into a distant land. She herself would feel that, in following her husband into death, she was only doing what every other widow would do; she was only doing her duty. In India, where men in the prime of life throw themselves under the car of Jaggernath, to be crushed to death by the idol they believe in; where the plaintiff who cannot get redress starves himself to death at the door of his judge; where the philosopher who thinks he has learnt all which this world can teach him, and who longs for absorption into the Deity, quietly steps into the Ganges, in order to arrive at the other shore of existence, — in such a country, however much we may condemn these practices, we must be on our guard, and not judge the strange religions of such strange creatures according to our own more sober code of morality. Let a man once be impressed with a belief that this life is but a prison, and that he has but to break through its walls in order to breathe the fresh and pure air of a higher life; let him once consider it cowardice to shrink from this act, and a proof of courage and of a firm faith in God to rush back to that eternal source from whence he came; and let these views be countenanced by a whole nation, sanctioned by priests, and hallowed by poets, and however we may blame and loathe the custom of human sacrifices and religious suicides, we shall be bound to confess that to such a man, and to a whole nation of such men, the most cruel rites will have a very different meaning from what they would have to us. They are not mere cruelty and brutality. They contain a religious element, and presuppose a belief in immortality, and an indifference with regard to worldly pleasures, which, if directed in a different channel, might produce martyrs and heroes. Here, at least, there is no danger of modern heresy aping ancient paganism; and we feel at liberty to express our sympathy and compassion, even with the most degraded of our brethren. The Fijians, for instance, commit almost every species of atrocity; but we can still discover, as Wilkes remarked in his "Exploring Expedition," that the source of many of their abhorrent practices is a belief in a future state, guided by no just notions of religious or moral obligations. They immolate themselves; they think it right to destroy their best friends to free them from the miseries of this life; they actually consider it a duty, and perhaps a painful duty, that the son should strangle his parents, if requested to do so. Some of the Fijians, when interrupted by Europeans in the act of strangling their mother, simply replied that she was their mother, and they were her children, and they ought to put her to death. On reaching the grave the mother sat down, when they all, including children, grandchildren, relations, and friends, took an affectionate leave of her. A rope, made of twisted tapa, was then passed twice around her neck by her sons, who took hold of it and strangled her, after which she was put into her grave, with the usual ceremonies. They returned to feast and mourn, after which she was entirely forgotten, as though she had not existed. No doubt these are revolting rites; but the phase of human thought which they disclose is far from being simply revolting. There is in these immolations, even in their most degraded form, a grain of that superhuman faith which we admire in the temptation of Abraham; and we feel that the time will come, nay, that it is coming, when the voice of the Angel of the Lord will reach those distant islands, and give a higher and better purpose to the wild ravings of their religion.

It is among these tribes that the missionary, if he can speak a language which they understand, gains the most rapid influence. But he must first learn himself to understand the nature of these savages, and to translate the wild yells of their devotion into articulate language. There is, perhaps, no race of men so low and degraded as the Papuas. It has frequently been asserted they had no religion at all. And yet these same Papuas, if they want to know whether what they are going to undertake is right or wrong, squat before their karwar, clasp the hands over the forehead, and bow repeatedly, at the same time stating their intentions. If they are seized with any nervous feeling during this process, it is considered as a bad sign, and the project is abandoned for a time; if otherwise, the idol is supposed to approve. Here we have but to translate

what they in their helpless language call "nervous feeling" by our word "conscience," and we shall not only
understand what they really mean, but confess, perhaps, that it would be well for us if in our own hearts
the karwar occupied the same prominent place which it
occupies in the cottage of every Papua.

March 1858.

III.

THE VEDA AND ZEND-AVESTA.

——

THE VEDA.

THE main stream of the Aryan nations has always flowed towards the northwest. No historian can tell us by what impulse these adventurous nomads were driven on through Asia towards the isles and shores of Europe. The first start of this world-wide migration belongs to a period far beyond the reach of documentary history; to times when the soil of Europe had not been trodden by either Celts, Germans, Slavonians, Romans, or Greeks. But whatever it was, the impulse was as irresistible as the spell which, in our own times, sends the Celtic tribes towards the prairies or the regions of gold across the Atlantic. It requires a strong will, or a great amount of inertness, to be able to withstand the impetus of such national, or rather ethnical movements. Few will stay behind when all are going. But to let one's friends depart, and then to set out ourselves, — to take a road which, lead where it may, can never lead us to join those again who speak our language and worship our gods, — is a course which only men of strong individuality and great self-dependence are capable of pursuing. It was the course adopted by the southern branch of the Aryan family, the Brahmanic Aryas of India and the Zoroastrians of Iran.

At the first dawn of traditional history we see those Aryan tribes migrating across the snow of the Himalaya southward towards the "Seven Rivers" (the Indus, the five rivers of the Penjâb, and the Sarasvati), and ever since India has been called their home. That before this time they had been living in more northern regions, within the same precincts with the ancestors of the Greeks, the Italians, Slavonians, Germans, and Celts, is a fact as firmly established as that the Normans of William the Conqueror were the Northmen of Scandinavia. The evidence of language is irrefragable, and it is the only evidence worth listening to with regard to ante-historical periods. It would have been next to impossible to discover any traces of relationship between the swarthy natives of India and their conquerors, whether Alexander or Clive, but for the testimony borne by language. What other evidence could have reached back to times when Greece was not yet peopled by Greeks, nor India by Hindus? Yet these are the times of which we are speaking. What authority would have been strong enough to persuade the Grecian army, that their gods and their hero ancestors were the same as those of king Porus, or to convince the English soldier that the same blood might be running in his veins and in the veins of the dark Bengalese? And yet there is not an English jury nowadays, which, after examining the hoary documents of language, would reject the claim of a common descent and a spiritual relationship between Hindu, Greek, and Teuton. Many words still live in India and in England that have witnessed the first separation of the northern and southern Aryans, and these are witnesses not to be shaken by any cross-examination. The terms for God, for house, for father, mother, son, daughter, for dog and cow, for heart and tears, for axe and tree, identical in all the Indo-European idioms, are like the watchwords of soldiers. We challenge the coming stranger; and whether he answer with the lips of a Greek, a German, or an Indian, we recognise him as one of ourselves. Though the historian may shake his head, though the physiologist may doubt, and the poet scorn the idea, all must yield before the facts furnished by language. There was a time when the ancestors of the Celts, the Germans, the Slavonians, the Greeks and Italians, the Persians and Hindus, were living together beneath the same roof, separate from the ancestors of the Semitic and Turanian races.

It is more difficult to prove that the Hindu was the last to leave this common home, that he saw his brothers all depart towards the setting sun, and that then, turning towards the south and the east, he started alone in search of a new world. But as in his language and in his grammar he has preserved something of what seems peculiar to each of the northern dialects singly, as he agrees with the Greek and the German where the Greek and the German differ from all the rest, and as no other language has carried off so large a share of the common Aryan heirloom, — whether roots, grammar, words, myths, or legends, — it is natural to suppose that, though perhaps the eldest brother, the Hindu was the last to leave the central home of the Aryan family.

The Aryan nations, who pursued a northwesterly direction, stand before us in history as the principal nations of northwestern Asia and Europe. They have been the prominent actors in the great drama of history, and have carried to their fullest growth all the elements of active life with which our nature is endowed. They have perfected society and morals; and we learn from their literature and works of art the elements of science, the laws of art, and the principles of philosophy. In continual struggle with each other and with Semitic and Turanian races, these Aryan nations have become the rulers of history, and it seems to be their mission to link all parts of the world together by the chains of civilization, commerce, and religion. In a word, they represent the Aryan man in his historical character.

But while most of the members of the Aryan family followed this glorious path, the southern tribes were slowly migrating towards the mountains which gird the north of India. After crossing the narrow passes of the Hindukush or the Himálaya, they conquered or drove before them, as it seems without much effort, the aboriginal inhabitants of the trans-Himalayan countries. They took for their guides the principal rivers of Northern India, and were led by them to new homes in their beautiful and fertile valleys. It seems as if the great mountains in the north had afterwards closed for centuries their Cyclopean gates against new immigrations, while, at the same time, the waves of the Indian Ocean kept watch over the southern borders of the peninsula. None of the great conquerors of antiquity — Sesostris, Semiramis, Nebuchadnezzar, or Cyrus — disturbed the peaceful seats of these Aryan settlers. Left to themselves in a world of their own, without a past, and without a future before them, they had nothing but themselves to ponder on. Struggles there must have been in India also. Old dynasties were destroyed, whole families annihilated, and now empires founded. Yet the inward life of the Hindu was not changed by these convulsions. His mind was like the lotus leaf after a shower of rain has passed over it; his character remained the same — passive, meditative, quiet, and thoughtful. A people of this peculiar stamp was never destined to act a prominent part in the history of the world; nay, the exhausting atmosphere of transcendental ideas in which they lived could not but exercise a detrimental influence on the active and moral character of the Indians. Social and political virtues were little cultivated, and the ideas of the useful and the beautiful hardly known to them. With all this, however, they had what the Greek was as little capable of imagining, as they were of realizing the elements of Grecian life. They shut their eyes to this world of outward seeming and activity, to open them full on the world of thought and rest. The ancient Hindus were a nation of philosophers, such as could nowhere have existed except in India, and even there in early times alone. It is with the Hindu mind as if a seed were placed in a hot-house. It will grow rapidly, its colors will be gorgeous, its perfume rich, its fruits precocious and abundant. But never will it be like the oak growing in wind and weather, and striking its roots into real earth, and stretching its branches into real air beneath the stars and the sun of heaven. Both are experiments, — the hot-house flower and the Hindu mind; and as experiments, whether physiological or psychological, both deserve to be studied.

We may divide the whole Aryan family into two branches, the northern and the southern. The northern

nations, Celts, Greeks, Romans, Germans, and Slavonians, have each one act allotted to them on the stage
of history. They have each a national character to
support. Not so the southern tribes. They are absorbed in the struggles of thought, their past is the
problem of creation, their future the problem of existence; and the present, which ought to be the solution
of both, seems never to have attracted their attention,
or called forth their energies. There never was a nation believing so firmly in another world, and so little
concerned about this. Their condition on earth is to
them a problem; their real and eternal life is a simple
fact. Though this is said chiefly with reference to
them before they were brought in contact with foreign
conquerors, traces of this character are still visible in
the Hindus, as described by the companions of Alexander, nay, even in the Hindus of the present day.
The only sphere in which the Indian mind finds itself
at liberty to act, to create, and to worship, is the sphere
of religion and philosophy; and nowhere have religious
and metaphysical ideas struck root so deep in the mind
of a nation as in India. The shape which these ideas
took amongst the different classes of society, and at
different periods of civilization, naturally varies from
coarse superstition to sublime spiritualism. But, taken
as a whole, history supplies no second instance where
the inward life of the soul has so completely absorbed
all the other faculties of a people.

It was natural, therefore, that the literary works of
such a nation, when first discovered in Sanskrit MSS.
by Wilkins, Sir W. Jones, and others, should have attracted the attention of all interested in the history of
the human race. A new page in man's biography was

laid open, and a literature as large as that of Greece or Rome was to be studied. The "Laws of Manu," the two epic poems, the "Râmâyana" and "Mahâbhârata," the six complete systems of philosophy, works on astronomy and medicine, plays, stories, fables, elegies, and lyrical effusions, were read with intense interest, on account of their age not less than their novelty.

Still this interest was confined to a small number of students, and in a few cases only could Indian literature attract the eyes of men who, from the summit of universal history, survey the highest peaks of human excellence. Herder, Schlegel, Humboldt, and Goethe, discovered what was really important in Sanskrit literature. They saw what was genuine and original, in spite of much that seemed artificial. For the artificial, no doubt, has a wide place in Sanskrit literature. Everywhere we find systems, rules and models, castes and schools, but nowhere individuality, no natural growth, and but few signs of strong originality and genius.

There is, however, one period of Sanskrit literature which forms an exception, and which will maintain its place in the history of mankind, when the names of Kâlidâsa and Sakuntalâ will have been long forgotten. It is the most ancient period, the period of the Veda. There is, perhaps, a higher degree of interest attaching to works of higher antiquity; but in the Veda we have more than mere antiquity. We have ancient thought expressed in ancient language. Without insisting on the fact that even chronologically the Veda is the first book of the Aryan nations, we have in it, at all events, a period in the intellectual life of man to which there is no parallel in any other part of the world. | In the hymns of the Veda we see man left to himself to solve the riddle of this world. We see him crawling on like a creature of the earth with all the desires and weaknesses of his animal nature. Food, wealth, and power, a large family and a long life, are the theme of his daily prayers. But he begins to lift up his eyes. He stares at the tent of heaven, and asks who supports it? He opens his ears to the winds, and asks them whence and whither? He is awakened from darkness and slumber by the light of the sun, and Him whom his eyes cannot behold, and who seems to grant him the daily pittance of his existence, he calls "his life, his breath, his brilliant Lord and Protector." He gives names to all the powers of nature, and after he has called the fire "Agni," the sun-light "Indra," the storms "Maruts," and the dawn "Ushas," they all seem to grow naturally into beings like himself, nay, greater than himself. He invokes them, he praises them, he worships them. But still with all these gods around him, beneath him, and above him, the early poet seems ill at rest within himself. There, too, in his own breast, he has discovered a power that wants a name, a power nearer to him than all the gods of nature, a power that is never mute when he prays, never absent when he fears and trembles. It seems to inspire his prayers, and yet to listen to them; it seems to live in him, and yet to support him and all around him. The only name he can find for this mysterious power is "Bráhman;" for bráhman meant originally force, will, wish, and the propulsive power of creation. But this impersonal bráhman, too, as soon as it is named, grows into something strange and divine. It ends by being one of many gods, one of the great triad, worshipped to the present day. And still the thought within him has no real name, that power which is nothing but itself, which supports the gods, the heavens, and every living being, floats before his mind, conceived but not expressed. At last he calls it "Âtman;" for Âtman, originally breath or spirit, comes to mean Self and Self alone; Self whether divine or human; Self whether creating or suffering; Self whether one or all; but always Self, independent and free. "Who has seen the first-born," says the poet, "when he who has no bones (i. e. form) bore him that had bones? Where was the life, the blood, the Self of the world? Who went to ask this from any that knew it?" (Rv. I. 164, 4.) This idea of a divine Self once expressed, everything else must acknowledge its supremacy: "Self is the Lord of all things, Self is the King of all things. As all the spokes of a wheel are contained in the nave and the circumference, all things are contained in this Self; all selves are contained in this Self.[1] Brâhman itself is but Self."[2]

This Âtman also grew; but it grew, as it were, without attributes. The sun is called the Self of all that moves and rests (Rv. I. 115, 1), and still more frequently Self becomes a mere pronoun. But Âtman remained always free from myth and worship, differing in this from the Brâhman (neuter), who has his temples in India even now, and is worshipped as Brâhman (masculine), together with Vishnu and Siva, and other popular gods. The idea of the Âtman or Self, like a pure crystal, was too transparent for poetry, and therefore was handed over to philosophy, which after-

[1] Brihad-âranyaka, IV. 5. 15, ed. Röer, p. 487.
[2] Ibid. p. 478. Khândogya-upanishad, VIII. 3, 3-4.

wards polished, and turned, and watched it as the medium through which all is seen, and in which all is reflected and known. But philosophy is later than the Veda, and it is of the Vaidik period only I have here to speak.[1]

[1] In writing the above, I was thinking rather of the mental process that was necessary for the production of such words as brahman, âtman, and others, than of their idiomatic use in the ancient literature of India. It might be objected, for instance, that brahman, neut. in the sense of creative power or the principal cause of all things, does not occur in the Rig-veda. This is true. But it occurs in that sense in the Atharva-veda, and in several of the Brâhmanas. There we read of "the oldest or greatest Brahman which rules everything that has been or will be." Heaven is said to belong to Brahman alone (Atharva-veda X. 8, 1). In the Brâhmanas, this Brahman is called the first-born, the self-existing, the best of the gods, and heaven and earth are said to have been established by it. Even the gods spirits are identified with it (Satapatha-brâhmana VIII. 4, 5, 9).

In other passages, again, this same Brahman is represented as entering in man (Atharva-veda X. 7, 17), and in this very passage we can watch the transition from the neutral Brahman into Brahman conceived of as a masculine:—

"Ye puruṣe brahma vidus te viduḥ parameshṭhinam,
Yo veda parameshṭhinam, yas ka veda prajâpatim,
Jyeshṭhaṃ ye brâhmaṇaṃ vidus, te skambham anu saṃviduḥ."

"They who know Brahman in man, they know the Highest.
He who knows the Highest, and he who knows Prajâpati (the lord of creatures),
And they who know the oldest Brahmans, they know the Ground."

The word Brâhmana which is here used, is a derivative form of Brahman; but what is most important in these lines is the mixing of neuter and masculine words, of impersonal and personal deities. This process is brought to perfection by changing Brahman, the neuter, even grammatically into Brâhmana, a masculine,—a change which has taken place in the Âranyakas, where we find Brâhmana used as the name of a male deity. It is this Brâhmana, with the accent on the first, not, as has been supposed, brahmán, the priest, that appears again in the later literature as one of the divine triad, Brâhman, Vishnu, Siva.

The word brâhman, as a neuter, is used in the Rig-veda in the sense of prayer also, originally what bursts forth from the soul, and, in one sense, what is revealed. Hence in later times brahman is used collectively for the Veda, the sacred word.

Another word, with the accent on the last syllable, is brahmán, the man

In the Veda, then, we can study a theogony of
which that of Hesiod is but the last chapter. We can
study man's natural growth, and the results to which
it may lead under the most favorable conditions. All
was given him that nature can bestow. We see him
blest with the choicest gifts of the earth, under a glow-
ing and transparent sky, surrounded by all the gran-
deur and all the riches of nature, with a language
"capable of giving soul to the objects of sense, and
body to the abstractions of metaphysics." We have a
right to expect much from him, only we must not expect in his youthful poems the philosophy of the nineteenth century, or the beauties of Pindar, or, with
some again, the truths of Christianity. Few understand children, still fewer understand antiquity. If we
look in the Veda for high poetical diction, for striking
comparisons, for bold combinations, we shall be disappointed. These early poets thought more for themselves than for others. They sought rather, in their
language, to be true to their own thoughts than to
please the imagination of their hearers. With them it
was a great work achieved for the first time, to bind
thoughts and words together, to find expressions or to
form new names. As to similes, we must look to the
words themselves, which, if we compare their radical
and their nominal meaning, will be found full of bold
metaphors. No translation in any modern language
can do them justice. As to beauty, we must discover
it in the absence of all effort, and in the simplicity of
their hearts. Prose was, at that time, unknown, as

who prays, who utters prayers, the priest, and gradually the Brahman by
profession. In this sense it is frequently used in the Rig-veda (I 108, 7 &
but not yet in the sense of Brahman by birth or caste.

well as the distinction between prose and poetry. It was the attempted imitation of those ancient natural strains of thought which in later times gave rise to poetry in our sense of the word, that is to say, to poetry as an art, with its counted syllables, its numerous epithets, its rhyme and rhythm, and all the conventional attributes of " measured thought."

In the Veda itself, however,—even if by Veda we mean the Rig-veda only (the other three, the Sâman, Yagush, and Atharvana, having solely a liturgical interest, and belonging to an entirely different sphere),—in the Rig-veda also, we find much that is artificial, imitated, and therefore modern, if compared with other hymns. It is true that all the 1017 hymns of the Rig-veda were comprised in a collection which existed as such before one of those elaborate theological commentaries known under the name of Brâhmana, was written, that is to say, about 800 B. C. But before the date of their collection these must have existed for centuries. In different songs the names of different kings occur, and we see several generations of royal families pass away before us with different generations of poets. Old songs are mentioned, and new songs. Poets whose compositions we possess are spoken of as the seers of olden times ; their names in other hymns are surrounded by a legendary halo. In some cases, whole books or chapters may be pointed out as more modern and secondary, in thought and language. But on the whole the Rig-veda is a genuine document, even in its most modern portions not later than the time of Lycurgus ; and it exhibits one of the earliest and rudest phases in the history of mankind ; disclosing in its full reality a period of which in Greece we have but traditions and names, such as Orpheus and Linus, and bringing us as near the beginnings in language, thought, and mythology as literary documents can ever bring us in the Aryan world.

Though much time and labor have been spent on the Veda, in England and in Germany, the time has not yet come for translating it as a whole. It is possible and interesting to translate it literally, or in accordance with scholastic commentaries, such as we find in India from Yáska in the fifth century B. C. down to Sáyana in the fourteenth century of the Christian era. This is what Professor Wilson has done in his translation of the first book of the Rig-veda; and by strictly adhering to this principle and excluding conjectural renderings even where they offered themselves most naturally, he has imparted to his work a definite character and a lasting value. The grammar of the Veda, though irregular, and still in a rather floating state, has almost been mastered; the etymology and the meaning of many words, unknown in the later Sanskrit, have been discovered. Many hymns, which are mere prayers for food, for cattle, or for a long life, have been translated, and can leave no doubt as to their real intention. But with the exception of these simple petitions, the whole world of Vedic ideas is so entirely beyond our own intellectual horizon, that instead of translating we can as yet only guess and combine. Here it is no longer a mere question of skillful deciphering. We may collect all the passages where an obscure word occurs, we may compare them and look for a meaning which would be appropriate to all; but the difficulty lies in finding a sense which we can appropriate, and transfer by analogy into our own language and thought. We must be able to translate our feelings and ideas into their language at the same time that we translate their poems and prayers into our language. We must not despair even where their words seem meaningless, and their ideas barren or wild. What seems at first childish may at a happier moment disclose a sublime simplicity, and even in helpless expressions we may recognize aspirations after some high and noble idea. When the scholar has done his work, the poet and philosopher must take it up and finish it. Let the scholar collect, collate, sift, and reject; let him say what is possible or not according to the laws of the Vedic language; let him study the commentaries, the Sûtras, the Brâhmanas, and even later works, in order to exhaust all the sources from which information can be derived. He must not despise the traditions of the Brahmans, even where their misconceptions and the causes of their misconceptions are palpable. To know what a passage cannot mean is frequently the key to its real meaning; and whatever reasons may be pleaded for declining a careful perusal of the traditional interpretations of Yâska or Sâyana, they can all be traced back to an ill-concealed *argumentum paupertatis*. Not a corner in the Brâhmanas, the Sûtras, Yâska, and Sâyana should be left unexplored before we venture to propose a rendering of our own. Sâyana, though the most modern, is on the whole the most sober interpreter. Most of his etymological absurdities must be placed to Yâska's account, and the optional renderings which he allows for metaphysical, theological, or ceremonial purposes, are mostly due to his regard for the Brâhmanas. The Brâhmanas, though nearest in time to the hymns of the Rig-veda, indulge

in the most frivolous and ill-judged interpretations.
When the ancient Rishi exclaims with a troubled heart,
" Who is the greatest of the gods ? Who shall first
be praised by our songs ? " — the author of the Bráhmana sees in the interrogative pronoun " Who " some
divine name, a place is allotted in the sacrificial invocations to a god " Who," and hymns addressed to him
are called " Whoish " hymns.   To make such misunderstandings possible, we must assume a considerable
interval between the composition of the hymns and the
Bráhmanas.   As the authors of the Bráhmanas were
blinded by theology, the authors of the still later Niruk-
tas were deceived by etymological fictions, and both
conspired to mislead by their authority later and more
sensible commentators, such as Sâyana.   Where Sâyana has no authority to mislead him, his commentary
is at all events rational ; but still his scholastic notions
would never allow him to accept the free interpretation which a comparative study of these venerable documents forces upon the unprejudiced scholar. We must
therefore discover ourselves the real meaning of these
ancient poets ; and if we follow them cautiously, we
shall find that with some effort we are still able to
walk in their footsteps. We shall feel that we are
brought face to face and mind to mind with men yet
intelligible to us, after we have freed ourselves from
our modern conceits. We shall not succeed always :
words, verses, nay, whole hymns in the Rig-veda, will
and must remain to us a dead letter. But where we
can inspire those early relics of thought and devotion
with new life, we shall have before us more real antiquity than in all the inscriptions of Egypt or Nineveh ; not only old names and dates, and kingdoms and

battles, but old thoughts, old hopes, old faith, and old
errors, the old Man altogether — old now, but then
young and fresh, and simple and real in his prayers
and in his praises.

The thoughtful bent of the Hindu mind is visible
in the Veda also, but his mystic tendencies are not yet
so fully developed. Of philosophy we find but little,
and what we find is still in its germ. The active side
of life is more prominent, and we meet occasionally
with wars of kings, with rivalries of ministers, with
triumphs and defeats, with war-songs and imprecations. Moral sentiments and worldly wisdom are not
yet absorbed by fantastic intuitions. Still the child
betrays the passions of the man, and there are hymns,
though few in number, in the Veda, so full of thought
and speculation that at this early period no poet in any
other nation could have conceived them. I give but
one specimen, the 129th hymn of the tenth book of
the Rig-veda. It is a hymn which long ago attracted
the attention of that eminent scholar H. T. Colebrooke, and of which, by the kind assistance of a
friend, I am enabled to offer a metrical translation.
In judging it we should bear in mind that it was not
written by a gnostic or by a pantheistic philosopher,
but by a poet who felt all these doubts and problems
as his own, without any wish to convince or to startle,
only uttering what had been weighing on his mind,
just as later poets would sing the doubts and sorrows
of their heart.

"Nor Aught nor Naught existed; yon bright sky
    Was not, nor heaven's broad woof outstretched above.
    What covered all? what sheltered? what concealed?
    Was it the water's fathomless abyss?
    There was not death — yet was there naught immortal,

> There was no confine betwixt day and night;
> The only One breathed breathless by Itself,
> Other than It there nothing since has been.
> Darkness there was, and all at first was veiled
> In gloom profound — an ocean without light —
> The germ that still lay covered in the husk
> Burst forth, one nature, from the fervent heat.
> Then first came love upon it, the new spring
> Of mind — yea, poets in their hearts discerned,
> Pondering, the bond between created things
> And uncreated. Comes this spark from earth
> Piercing and all-pervading, or from heaven?
> Then seeds were sown, and mighty powers arose —
> Nature below, and power and will above —
> Who knows the secret? who proclaimed it here,
> Whence, whence this manifold creation sprang?
> The gods themselves came later into being —
> Who knows from whence this great creation sprang?
> He from whom all this great creation came,
> Whether his will created or was mute,
> The Most High Seer that is in highest heaven,
> He knows it — or perchance even He knows not."

The grammar of the Veda (to turn from the contents to the structure of the work) is important in many respects. The difference between it and the grammar of the epic poems would be sufficient of itself to fix the distance between these two periods of language and literature. Many words have preserved in these early hymns a more primitive form, and therefore agree more closely with cognate words in Greek or Latin. Night, for instance, in the later Sanskrit is niśā, which is a form peculiarly Sanskritic, and agrees in its derivation neither with nox nor with nú. The Vaidik " nas " or " nak," night, is as near to Latin as can be. Thus mouse in the common Sanskrit is " mûshas " or " mûshikâ," both derivative forms if compared with the Latin mus, muris. The Vaidik Sanskrit has preserved the same primitive noun in the plural " mûsh-as " = Lat. mures. There are other words in the

Veda which were lost altogether in the later Sanskrit,
while they were preserved in Greek and Latin. " Dyaus," sky, does not occur as a masculine in the ordinary
Sanskrit ; it occurs in the Veda, and thus bears witness
to the early Aryan worship of Dyaus, the Greek Zeús.
" Ushas," dawn, again in the later Sanskrit is neuter.
In the Veda it is feminine ; and even the secondary
Vaidik form " Ushâsâ " is proved to be of high antiquity
by the nearly corresponding Latin form *Aurora*. Declension and conjugation are richer in forms and more
unsettled in their usage. It is a curious fact, for
instance, that no subjunctive mood existed in the
common Sanskrit. The Greeks and Romans had it,
and even the language of the Avesta showed clear
traces of it. There could be no doubt that the Sanskrit also once possessed this mood, and at last it was
discovered in the hymns of the Rig-veda. Discoveries of this kind may seem trifling, but they are as
delightful to the grammarian as the appearance of a
star, long expected and calculated, is to the astron-
omer. They prove that there is natural order in
language, and that by a careful induction laws can be
established which enable us to guess with great prob-
ability either at the form or meaning of words where
but scanty fragments of the tongue itself have come
down to us.

October, 1853.

By means of laws like that of the Correspondence
of Letters, discovered by Rask and Grimm, it has been
possible to determine the exact form of words in Gothic,
in cases where no trace of them occurred in the literary
documents of the Gothic nation. Single words which
were not to be found in Ulfilas have been recovered by
applying certain laws to their corresponding forms in
Latin or Old High-German, and thus retranslating
them into Gothic. But a much greater conquest
was achieved in Persia. Here comparative philology
has actually had to create and reanimate all the materials of language on which it was afterwards to work.
Little was known of the language of Persia and Media
previous to the "Shahnameh" of Firdusi, composed
about 1000 A. D., and it is due entirely to the inductive method of comparative philology that we have now
before us contemporaneous documents of three periods
of Persian language, deciphered, translated, and explained. We have the language of the Zoroastrians,
the language of the Achaemenians, and the language of
the Sassanians, which represent the history of the Persian tongue in three successive periods — all now rendered intelligible by the aid of comparative philology,
while but fifty years ago their very name and existence
were questioned.

The labors of Anquetil Duperron, who first translated the Zend-Avesta, were those of a bold adventurer — not of a scholar. Rask was the first who, with the materials collected by Duperron and himself, analyzed the language of the Avesta scientifically. He proved, —

1. That Zend was not a corrupted Sanskrit, as supposed by W. Erskine, but that it differed from it as Greek, Latin, or Lithuanian differed from one another and from Sanskrit.

2. That the modern Persian was really derived from Zend as Italian was from Latin ; and

3. That the Avesta, or the works of Zoroaster, must have been reduced to writing at least previously to Alexander's conquest. The opinion that Zend was an artificial language (an opinion held by men of great eminence in oriental philology, beginning with Sir W. Jones) is passed over by Rask as not deserving of refutation.

The first edition of the Zend texts, the critical restitution of the MSS., the outlines of a Zend grammar, with the translation and philological anatomy of considerable portions of the Zoroastrian writings, were the work of the late Eugène Burnouf. He was the real founder of Zend philology. It is clear from his works, and from Bopp's valuable remarks in his " Comparative Grammar," that Zend in its grammar and dictionary is nearer to Sanskrit than any other Indo-European language. Many Zend words can be retranslated into Sanskrit simply by changing the Zend letters into their corresponding forms in Sanskrit. With regard to the Correspondence of Letters in Grimm's sense of the word, Zend ranges with Sanskrit and the classical languages. It differs from Sanskrit principally in its abi-

lants, nasals, and aspirates. The Sanskrit s, for instance, is represented by the Zend h, a change analogous to that of an original s into the Greek aspirate, only that in Greek this change is not general. Thus the geographical name "hapta hendu," which occurs in the Avesta, becomes intelligible if we retranslate the Zend h into the Sanskrit s. For "sapta sindhu," or the Seven Rivers, is the old Vaidik name of India itself, derived from the five rivers of the Penjáb, together with the Indus, and the Sarasvati.

Where Sanskrit differs in words or grammatical peculiarities from the northern members of the Aryan family, it frequently coincides with Zend. The numerals are the same in all these languages up to 100. The name for thousand, however, "sahasra," is peculiar to Sanskrit, and does not occur in any of the Indo-European dialects except in Zend, where it becomes "hazanra." In the same manner the German and Sklavonic languages have a word for thousand peculiar to themselves; as also in Greek and Latin we find many common words which we look for in vain in any of the other Indo-European dialects. These facts are full of historical meaning; and with regard to Zend and Sanskrit, they prove that these two languages continued together long after they were separated from the common Indo-European stock.

Still more striking is the similarity between Persia and India in religion and mythology. Gods unknown to any Indo-European nation are worshipped under the same names in Sanskrit and Zend; and the change of some of the most sacred expressions in Sanskrit into names of evil spirits in Zend, only serves to strengthen the conviction that we have here the usual traces of a

schism which separated a community that had once
been united.

Burnouf, who compared the language and religion
of the Avesta principally with the later classical Sanskrit, inclined at first to the opinion that this schism took
place in Persia, and that the dissenting Brahmans im-
migrated afterwards into India. This is still the prevailing opinion, but it requires to be modified in accordance with new facts elicited from the Veda. Zend,
if compared with classical Sanskrit, exhibits in many
points of grammar, features of a more primitive character than Sanskrit. But it can now be shown, and Burnouf himself admitted it, that when this is the case, the
Vaidik differs on the very same points from the later
Sanskrit, and has preserved the same primitive and
irregular form as the Zend. I still hold, that the name
of Zend was originally a corruption of the Sanskrit
word "khandas" (i. e. metrical language, cf. *chan-
dere*),[1] which is the name given to the language of

[1] The derivation of "khandas," metre, from the same root which yielded
the Latin *scandere*, seems to me still the most plausible. An account of the
various explanations of this word, proposed by Eastern and Western scholars, is to be found in Spiegel's *Grammar of the Parsi language* (preface,
and p. 370), and in his translation of the *Vendidad* (pp. 44 and 343). That
initial *kh* in Sanskrit may represent an original *sk*, has never, so far as I am
aware, been doubted. (Curtius, *Grundzüge*, p. 60.) The fact that the root
"khand," in the sense of stopping or striding, has not been fixed in Sanskrit as a verbal, but only as a nominal base, is no real objection either.
The same thing has happened over and over again, and has been remarked
as the necessary result of the dialectic growth of language by so eminent a
scholar as Theba. (*Zeitschrift der Deutschen Morgenländischen Gesellschaft*
vol. viii. p. 373 seq.) That *scandere* in Latin, in the sense of scanning, is a
late word, does not affect the question at all. What is of real importance is
simply this, that the principal Aryan nations agree in representing metre
as a kind of stepping or striding. Whether this grew from the fact that
ancient poetry was accompanied by dancing or rhythmic choral movements,
is a question which does not concern us here. ("Carmen chorisdenteo tripo-
darunt in verba hoc' *Faun Lance*," etc. Orelli, *Inscript.* No. 2571.) The

the Veda by Pánini and others. When we read in Pánini's grammar that certain forms occur in *khandas*, but not in the classical language, we may almost always translate the word "*khandas*" by "Zend," for nearly all these rules apply equally to the language of the Avesta.

In mythology also, the "*nomina* and *numina*" of the Avesta appear at first sight more primitive than in Manu or the "Mahâbhârata." But if regarded from a Vaidik point of view, this relation shifts at once, and many of the gods of the Zoroastrians come out once more as mere reflections and deflections of the primitive and authentic gods of the Veda. It can now be proved, even by geographical evidence, that the Zoro-

fact remains that the people of India, Greece, and Italy agree in calling the component elements of their verses feet or steps (*vrs?, pes, khandrit pad* or *pâda;* "*padapankti,*" a row of feet, and "*gopâti,*" i. e. *cadente,* are names of Sanskrit metres). It is not too much, therefore, to say that they may have considered metre as a kind of stepping or striding, and that they may accordingly have called it "*mâda.*" If then we find the name for metre in Sanskrit "*khandas,*" i. e. *khandas,* and if we find that words in Latin (from which we collect, as we may gather from *cassado* and *descendo,* meant gradually striding, and that *cassus* in Sanskrit means the same as *scando* in Latin, surely there can be little doubt as to the original intention of the Sanskrit name for metre, namely, "*khandas.*" Hindu grammarians derive khandas either from *khad,* to cover, or from *khad,* to please. Both derivations are possible, as far as mere laws are concerned. But are we to accept the dogmatic interpretation of the theologians of the *khandas,* who tell us that the metres were called "*khandas*" because the gods, when afraid of death, covered themselves with the metres? Or of the Vâjasaneyins, who tell us that the khandas were so called because they pleased Prajâpati? Such artificial interpretations only show that the Brahmans had no traditional feeling as to the etymological meaning of that word, and that we are at liberty to discover, by the ordinary means, its original intention. I shall only mention from among much that has been written on the etymology of khandas, a most happy remark of Professor Kuhn, who traces the Northern *skald,* poet, back to the same root as the Sanskrit khandas, metre. (Kuhn's *Zeitschrift,* vol. iii. p. 430.) Legerlotz, ibid. ii. 278. The transition of *sk* into *kh* is modified by Sanskrit *khandlas* = A.S. *scildor, scealdor,* and German, *schild* = English, *shield.* (Grimm, *Geschichte der Deutschen Sprache,* p. 341.)

astrians had been settled in India before they immi-
grated into Persia. I say the Zoroastrians, for we
have no evidence to bear us out in making the same
assertion of the nations of Persia and Media in general. That the Zoroastrians and their ancestors
started from India during the Vaidik period can be
proved as distinctly as that the inhabitants of Massilia
started from Greece. The geographical traditions in
the first Fargard of the "Vendidad" do not interfere
with this opinion. If ancient and genuine, they
would embody a remembrance preserved by the Zoroastrians, but forgotten by the Vaidik poets — a remembrance of times previous to their first common descent
into the country of the Seven Rivers. If of later
origin, and this is more likely, they may represent a
geographical conception of the Zoroastrians after they
had become acquainted with a larger sphere of countries and nations, subsequent to their emigration from
the land of the Seven Rivers.[1]

These and similar questions of the highest importance for the early history of the Aryan language and
mythology, however, must await their final decision,
until the whole of the Veda and the Avesta shall
have been published. Of this Burnouf was fully
aware, and this was the reason why he postponed the
publication of his researches into the antiquities of
the Iranian nation. The same conviction is shared
by Westergaard and Spiegel, who are each engaged
on an edition of the Avesta, and who, though they
differ on many points, agree in considering the Veda
as the safest key to an understanding of the Avesta.

[1] The purely mythological character of this geographical chapter has
been proved by M. Michel Bréal, Journal Asiatique, 1862.

Professor Roth, of Tübingen, has well expressed the mutual relation of the Veda and Zend-Avesta under the following simile: "The Veda," he writes, "and the Zend-Avesta are two rivers flowing from one fountain-head: the stream of the Veda is the fuller and purer, and has remained truer to its original character; that of the Zend-Avesta has been in various ways polluted, has altered its course, and cannot, with certainty, be traced back to its source."

As to the language of the Achæmenians, presented to us in the Persian text of the cuneiform inscriptions, there was no room for doubt, as soon as it became legible at all, that it was the same tongue as that of the Avesta, only in a second stage of its continuous growth. The process of deciphering these bundles of arrows by means of Zend and Sanskrit has been very much like deciphering an Italian inscription without a knowledge of Italian, simply by means of classical and mediæval Latin. It would have been impossible, even with the quick perception and patient combination of a Grotefend, to read more than the proper names and a few titles on the walls of the Persian palaces, without the aid of Zend and Sanskrit; and it seems almost providential, as Lassen remarked, that these inscriptions, which at any previous period would have been, in the eyes of either classical or oriental scholars, nothing but a quaint conglomerate of nails, wedges, or arrows, should have been rescued from the dust of centuries at the very moment when the discovery and study of Sanskrit and Zend had enabled the scholars of Europe to grapple successfully with their difficulties.

Upon a closer inspection of the language and gram-

mar of these mountain records of the Achæmenian
dynasty, a curious fact came to light which seemed to
disturb the historical relation between the language of
Zoroaster and the language of Darius. At first, historians were satisfied with knowing that the edicts of
Darius could be explained by the language of the
Avesta, and that the difference between the two,
which could be proved to imply a considerable interval
of time, was such as to exclude forever the supposed
historical identity of Darius Hystaspes and Gushtasp,
the mythical pupil of Zoroaster. The language of the
Avesta, though certainly not the language of Zarathustra,[1] displayed a grammar so much more luxuriant,
and forms so much more primitive than the inscriptions, that centuries must have elapsed between the

[1] Spiegel states the results of his last researches into the language of the
different parts of the Avesta in the following words:—

"We are now prepared to attempt an arrangement of the different portions of the Zend-Avesta in the order of their antiquity. First, we place
the second part of the Yasna, as separated in respect to the language of
the Zend-Avesta, yet not composed by Zoroaster himself, since he is named
in the third person; and indeed everything intimates that neither he nor his
disciple Gushtasp is alive. The second place must unquestionably be assigned to the Vendidad. I do not believe that the book was originally
composed as it now stands; it has suffered both restless and later interpola-
tions; still, its present form may be traced to a considerable antiquity.
The antiquity of the work is proved by its contents, which distinctly show
that the ancient literature was not yet completed.

"The case is different with the writings of the last period, among which
I reckon the first part of the Yasna, and the whole of the Tashts. Among
these a theological character is unmistakable, the separate divinities having
their attributes and titles dogmatically fixed.

"Altogether, it is interesting to trace the progress of religion in Parsi
writings. It is a significant fact, that to this added, that is to say, the second
part of the Yasna, nothing is fixed in the doctrine regarding God. In the
writings of the second period, that is in the Vendidad, we trace the advance
to a theological, and, in its way, mild and scientific system. Out of this,
in the last place, there springs the stern and intolerant religion of the Sassanian epoch." From the Rev. J. Murray Mitchell's Translation.

two periods represented by these two strata of language. When, however, the forms of these languages were subjected to a more searching analysis, it became evident that the phonetic system of the cuneiform inscriptions was more primitive and regular than even that of the earlier portions of the Avesta. This difficulty, however, admits of a solution; and, like many difficulties of the kind, it tends to confirm, if rightly explained, the very facts and views which at first it seemed to overthrow. The confusion in the phonetic system of the Zend grammar is no doubt owing to the influence of oral tradition. Oral tradition, particularly if confided to the safeguard of a learned priesthood, is able to preserve, during centuries of growth and change, the sacred accents of a dead language; but it is liable at least to the slow and imperceptible influences of a corrupt pronunciation. Nowhere can we see this more clearly than in the Veda, where grammatical forms that had ceased to be intelligible, were carefully preserved, while the original pronunciation of vowels was lost, and the simple structure of the ancient metres destroyed by the adoption of a more modern pronunciation. The loss of the Digamma in Homer is another case in point. There are no facts to prove that the text of the Avesta, in the shape in which the Parsis of Bombay and Yezd now possess it, was committed to writing previous to the Sassanian dynasty (226 A. D.). After that time it can indeed be traced, and to a great extent be controlled and checked by the Huzvaresh translations made under that dynasty. Additions to it were made, as it seems, even after these Huzvaresh translations; but their number is small, and we have no reason to doubt that the text

of the Avesta, in the days of Arda Virâf, was on the
whole exactly the same as at present. At the time
when these translations were made, it is clear from
their own evidence that the language of Zarathustra
had already suffered, and that the ideas of the Avesta
were no longer fully understood even by the learned.
Before that time we may infer, indeed, that the doctrine of Zoroaster had been committed to writing; for
Alexander is said to have destroyed the books of the
Zoroastrians, — Hermippus of Alexandria is said to
have read them.[1] But whether on the revival of the
Persian religion and literature, that is to say 500 years
after Alexander, the works of Zoroaster were collected
and restored from extant MSS., or from oral tradition,
must remain uncertain, and the disturbed state of the
phonetic system would rather lead us to suppose a
long-continued influence of oral tradition. What the
Zend language might become, if intrusted to the guar-
dianship of memory alone, unassisted by grammatical
study and archæological research, may be seen at the
present day, when some of the Parsis, who are unable
either to read or write, still mutter hymns and prayers
in their temples, which, though to them mere sound,
disclose to the experienced ear of a European scholar
the time-hallowed accents of Zarathustra's speech.

Thus far the history of the Persian language had
been reconstructed by the genius and perseverance of
Grotefend, Burnouf, Lassen, and last, not least, by the
comprehensive labors of Rawlinson, from the ante-historical epoch of Zoroaster down to the age of Darius and
Artaxerxes II. It might have been expected that, after
that time, the contemporaneous historians of Greece

[1] Lectures on the Science of Language, First Series, p. 86.

would have supplied the sequel. Unfortunately the
Greeks cared nothing for any language except their
own ; and little for any other history except as bearing
on themselves. The history of the Persian language
after the Macedonian conquest, and during the Parthian occupation, is indeed but a blank page. The next
glimpse of an authentic contemporaneous document is
the inscription of Ardeshir, the founder of the new national dynasty of the Sassanians. It is written, though,
it may be, with dialectic difference, in what was once
called "Pehlevi," and is now more commonly known
as "Huzvaresh," this being the proper title of the language of the translations of the Avesta. The legends of
Sassanian coins, the bilingual inscriptions of Sassanian
emperors, and the translation of the Avesta by Sassanian
reformers, represent the Persian language in its third
phase. To judge from the specimens given by Anquetil Duperron, it was not to be wondered at that this
dialect, then called "Pehlevi," should have been pronounced an artificial jargon. Even when more genuine specimens of it became known, the language seemed
so overgrown with Semitic and barbarous words, that
it was expelled from the Iranian family. Sir W. Jones
pronounced it to be a dialect of Chaldaic. Spiegel, however, who is now publishing the text of these translations, has established the fact that the language is
truly Aryan, neither Semitic nor barbarous, but Persian in roots and grammar. He accounts for the large
infusion of foreign terms by pointing to the mixed elements in the intellectual and religious life of Persia
during and before that period. There was the Semitic
influence of Babylonia, clearly discernible even in the
characters of the Achæmenian inscriptions ; there was

the slow infiltration of Jewish ideas, customs, and expressions, working sometimes in the palaces of Persian
kings, and always in the bazars of Persian cities, on
high roads and in villages; there was the irresistible
power of the Greek genius, which even under its rude
Macedonian garb emboldened oriental thinkers to a flight
into regions undreamed of in their philosophy; there
were the academies, the libraries, the works of art of
the Seleucidæ; there was Edessa on the Euphrates, a
city where Plato and Aristotle were studied, where
Christian, Jewish, and Buddhist tenets were discussed,
where Ephraem Syrus taught, and Syriac translations
were circulated which have preserved to us the lost
originals of Greek and Christian writers. The title of
the Avesta, under its Semitic form "Apostako," was
known in Syria as well as in Persia, and the true name
of its author, Zarathustra, is not yet changed in Syriac
into the modern Zerdusht. While this intellectual
stream, principally flowing through Semitic channels,
was irrigating and inundating the west of Asia, the
Persian language had been left without literary cultivation. Need we wonder, then, that the men, who at
the rising of a new national dynasty (226) became the
reformers, teachers, and prophets of Persia, should have
formed their language and the whole train of their ideas
on a Semitic model. Motley as their language may appear to a Persian scholar fresh from the Avesta or from
Firdusi, there is hardly a language of modern Europe
which, if closely sifted, would not produce the same impression on a scholar accustomed only to the pure idiom
of Homer, Cicero, Ulfilas, or Cædmon. Moreover, the
soul of the Sassanian language — I mean its grammar
— is Persian, and nothing but Persian; and though

meagre when compared with the grammar of the Avesta, it is richer in forms than the later Parsi, the Deri, or the language of Firdusi. The supposition (once maintained) that Pehlevi was the dialect of the western provinces of Persia is no longer necessary. As well might we imagine (it is Spiegel's apposite remark) that a Turkish work, because it is full of Arabic words, could only have been written on the frontiers of Arabia. We may safely consider the Huzvaresh of the translations of the Avesta as the language of the Sassanian court and hierarchy. Works also like the Bundehesh and Minokhired belong by language and thought to the same period of mystic incubation, when India and Egypt, Babylonia and Greece, were sitting together and gossiping like crazy old women, chattering with toothless gums and silly brains about the dreams and joys of their youth, yet unable to recall one single thought or feeling with that vigor which once gave it life and truth. It was a period of religious and metaphysical delirium, when everything became everything; when Mâyâ and Sophia, Mitra and Christ, Viraf and Isaiah, Budas, Zarvan, and Kronos were mixed up in one jumbled system of insane speculation, from which at last the East was delivered by the positive doctrines of Mohammed, the West by the pure Christianity of the Teutonic nations.

In order to judge fairly of the merits of the Huzvaresh as a language, it must be remembered that we know it only from those speculative works, and from translations made by men whose very language had become technical and artificial in the schools. The idiom spoken by the nation was probably much less infected by this Semitic fashion. Even the translators sometimes give the Semitic terms only as a paraphrase or more distinct expression side by side with the Persian. And, if Spiegel's opinion be right that Parsi, and not Huzvaresh, was the language of the later Sassanian empire, it furnishes a clear proof that Persian had recovered itself, had thrown off the Semitic ingredients, and again become a pure and national speech. This dialect (the Parsi) also exists in translations only; and we owe our knowledge of it to Spiegel, the author of the first Parsi grammar.

This third period in the history of the Persian language, comprehending the Huzvaresh and Parsi, ends with the downfall of the Sassanians. The Arab conquest quenched the last sparks of Persian nationality; and the fire-altars of the Zoroastrians were never to be lighted again, except in the oasis of Yezd and on the soil of that country which the Zoroastrians had quitted as the disinherited sons of Manu. Still the change did not take place at once. Mohl, in his magnificent edition of the "Shahnameh," has treated this period admirably, and it is from him that I derive the following facts. For a time, Persian religion, customs, traditions, and songs survived in the hands of the Persian nobility and landed gentry (the Dihkans) who lived among the people, particularly in the eastern provinces, remote from the capital and the seats of foreign dominion, Baghdad, Kufah, and Mosul. Where should Firdusi have collected the national strains of ancient epic poetry which he revived in the "Shahnameh" (1000 A. D.), if the Persian peasant and the Persian knight had not preserved the memory of their old heathen heroes, even under the vigilant oppression of Mohammedan zealots? True, the first collection of epic traditions was made under the Sassanians. But this work, commenced under Nushirvan, and finished under Yezdegird, the last of the Sassanians, was destroyed by Omar's command. Firdusi himself tells us how this first collection was made by the Dihkan Danishver. "There was a Pehlevan," he says, "of the family of the Dihkans, brave and powerful, wise and illustrious, who loved to study the ancient times, and to collect the stories of past ages. He summoned from all the provinces old men who possessed portions of (i. e. who knew) an ancient work in which many stories were written. He asked them about the origin of kings and illustrious heroes, and how they governed the world which they left to us in this wretched state. These old men recited before him, one after the other, the traditions of the kings and the changes in the empire. The Dihkan listened, and composed a book worthy of his fame. This is the monument he left to mankind, and great and small have celebrated his name."

The collector of this first epic poem, under Yezdegird, is called a Dihkan by Firdusi. Dihkan, according to the Persian dictionaries, means (1) farmer, (2) historian; and the reason commonly assigned for this double meaning is, that the Persian farmers happened to be well read in history. Quatremère, however, has proved that the Dihkans were the landed nobility of Persia; that they kept up a certain independence, even under the sway of the Mohammedan Khalifs, and exercised in the country a sort of jurisdiction in spite of the commissioners sent from Baghdad, the seat of the government. Thus Danishver even is called a Dihkan, although he lived previous to the Arab conquest. With

him, the title was only intended to show that it was in
the country and among the peasants that he picked up
the traditions and songs about Jemshid, Feridun, and
Rustem. Of his work, however, we know nothing.
It was destroyed by Omar; and, though it survived in
an Arabic translation, even this was lost in later times.
The work, therefore, had to be recommenced when in
the eastern provinces of Persia a national, though no
longer a Zoroastrian, feeling began to revive. The
governors of these provinces became independent as
soon as the power of the Khalifs, after its rapid rise,
began to show signs of weakness. Though the Mohammedan religion had taken root, even among the
national party, yet Arabic was no longer countenanced
by the governors of the eastern provinces. Persian
was spoken again at their courts, Persian poets were
encouraged, and ancient national traditions, stripped
of their religious garb, began to be collected anew.
It is said that Jacob, the son of Leis (870), the first
prince of Persian blood who declared himself independent of the Khalifs, procured fragments of Danishver's epic, and had it rearranged and continued.
Then followed the dynasty of the Samanians, who
claimed descent from the Sassanian kings. They, as
well as the later dynasty of the Gaznevides, pursued
the same popular policy. They were strong because
they rested on the support of a national Persian spirit.
The national epic poet of the Samanians was Dakiki, by
birth a Zoroastrian. Firdusi possessed fragments of his
work, and has given a specimen of it in the story of
Gushtasp. The final accomplishment, however, of an
idea, first cherished by Nushirvan, was reserved for
Mahmud the Great, the second king of the Gaznevide

dynasty. By his command collections of all books were made all over the empire. Men who knew ancient poems were summoned to the court. One of them was Aser Berzin, who had spent his whole life in collecting popular accounts of the ancient kings of Persia. Another was Serv Azad, from Merv, who claimed descent from Seriman, and knew all the tales concerning Sam, Zal, and Rustom, which had been preserved in his family. It was from these materials that Firdusi composed his great epic, the "Shahnameh." He himself declares, in many passages of his poem, that he always followed tradition. "Traditions," he says, "have been given by me; nothing of what is worth knowing has been forgotten. All that I shall say, others have said before me: they plucked before me the fruits in the garden of knowledge." He speaks in detail of his predecessors: he even indicates the sources from which he derives different episodes, and it is his constant endeavor to convince his readers that what he relates are not poetical inventions of his own. Thus only can we account for the fact, first pointed out by Burnouf, that many of the heroes in the "Shahnameh" still exhibit the traits, sadly distorted, it is true, but still unmistakable, of Vaidik deities, which had passed through the Zoroastrian schism, the Achæmenian reign, the Macedonian occupation, the Parthian wars, the Sassanian revival, and the Mohammedan conquest, and of which the Dihkans could still sing and tell, when Firdusi's poem impressed the last stamp on the language of Zarathustra. Bopp had discovered already, in his edition of Nalus (1832), that the Zend Vivanhvat was the same as the Sanskrit Vivasvat; and Burnouf, in his "Observations sur la Grammaire Comparée de M.

Bopp," had identified a second personage, the Zend
Keresâspa with the Sanskrit Krisâsva. But the similarity between the Zend Keresâspa and the Garshasp of
the "Shahnameh" opened a new and wide prospect to
Burnouf, and afterwards led him on to the most striking and valuable results. Some of these were published
in his last work on Zend, "Etudes sur la Langue et les
Textes Zends." This is a collection of articles published originally in the "Journal Asiatique," between
1840 and 1846; and it is particularly the fourth essay,
"Le Dieu Homa," which has opened an entirely new
mine for researches into the ancient state of religion
and tradition common to the Aryans before their
schism. Burnouf showed that three of the most famous names in the "Shahnameh," Jemshid, Feridun, and Garshasp, can be traced back to three
heroes mentioned in the Zend-Avesta as the represen-
tatives of the three earliest generations of mankind,
Yima Kshaêta, Thraêtaona, and Keresâspa, and that
the prototypes of these Zoroastrian heroes could be
found again in the Yama-Trita, and Krisâsva of the
Veda. He went even beyond this. He showed that,
as in Sanskrit, the father of Yama is Vivasvat, the
father of Yima in the Avesta is Vivanhvat. He showed
that as Thraêtaona in Persia is the son of Âthwya, the
patronymic of Trita in the Veda is "Âptya." He explained the transition of Thraêtaona into Feridun by
pointing to the Pehlevi form of the name, as given by
Neriosengh, "Fredun." This change of an aspirated
dental into an aspirated labial, which by many is considered a flaw in this argument, is of frequent occurrence.
We have only to think of θήρ and θύρα, of dhûma and
fumus, of modern Greek φίλος and φίλη,—nay, Me-

nonius's "first complaint" would suffice to explain it.
Burnouf again identified Zohák, the King of Persia,
slain by Feridun, whom even Firdusi still knows by
the name of "Ash dahák," with the Azhi dahâka, the
biting serpent, as he translates it, destroyed by Thraêtaona in the Avesta; and with regard to the changes
which these names, and the ideas originally expressed
by them, had to undergo on the intellectual stage of
the Aryan nation, he says: "Il est sans contredit fort
curieux de voir une des divinités Indiennes les plus
vénérées, donner son nom au premier souverain de la
dynastie arlopersanne; c'est un des faits qui attestent
le plus évidemment l'intime union des deux branches de
la grande famille qui s'est étendue, bien de siècles
avant notre ère, depuis le Gange jusqu'à l'Euphrate."

The great achievements of Burnouf in this field of
research have been so often ignored, and what by right
belongs to him has been so confidently ascribed to
others, that a faithful representation of the real state of
the case, as here given, will not appear superfluous.
There is no intention, while giving his due to Burnouf,
to detract from the merits of other scholars. Some
more minute coincidences, particularly in the story of
Feridun, have subsequently been added by Roth, Benfey, and Weber. The first, particularly, has devoted
two most interesting articles to the identification of
Yama-Yima-Jemshid and Trita-Thraêtaona-Feridun.
Trita, who has generally been fixed upon as the Vaidik
original of Feridun, because Traitana, whose name cor-
responds more accurately, occurs but once in the Rig-
veda, is represented in India as one of the many divine
powers ruling the firmament, destroying darkness, and
sending rain, or, as the poets of the Veda are fond of

expressing it, rescuing the cows and slaying the demons that had carried them off. These cows always move along the sky, some dark, some bright-colored. They low over their pasture; they are gathered by the winds; and milked by the bright rays of the sun, they drop from their heavy udders a fertilizing milk upon the parched and thirsty earth. But sometimes, the poet says, they are carried off by robbers and kept in dark caves near the uttermost ends of the sky. Then the earth is without rain; the pious worshipper offers up his prayer to Indra, and Indra rises to conquer the cows for him. He sends his dog to find the scent of the cattle, and after she has heard their lowing, she returns, and the battle commences. Indra hurls his thunderbolt; the Maruts ride at his side; the Rudras roar; till at last the rock is cleft asunder, the demon destroyed, and the cows brought back to their pasture. This is one of the oldest myths or sayings current among the Aryan nations. It appears again in the mythology of Italy, in Greece, in Germany. In the Avesta, the battle is fought between Thraêtaona and Axhi dahâka, the destroying serpent. Traitana takes the place of Indra in this battle in one song of the Veda; more frequently it is Trita, but other gods also share in the same honor. The demon, again, who fights against the gods is likewise called " Ahi," or the serpent, in the Veda. But the characteristic change that has taken place between the Veda and Avesta is that the battle is no longer a conflict of gods and demons for cows, nor of light and darkness for the dawn. It is the battle of a pious man against the power of evil. " Le Zoroastrisme," as Burnouf says, " en se détachant plus franchement de Dieu et de la nature, a

certainement tenu plus de compte de l'homme que n'a
fait le Brahmanisme, et on peut dire qu'il a regagné
en profondeur ce qu'il perdait en étendue. Il ne m'ap-
partient pas d'indiquer ici ce qu'un système qui tend à
développer les instincts les plus nobles de notre nature,
et qui impose à l'homme, comme le plus important de
ses devoirs, celui de lutter constamment contre le prin-
cipe du mal, a pu exercer d'influence sur les destinées
des peuples de l'Asie, chez lesquels il a été adopté à
diverses époques. On peut cependant déjà dire que le
caractère religieux et martial tout à la fois, qui paraît
avec des traits si héroïques dans la plupart des Jeshts,
n'a pas dû être sans action sur la mâle discipline sous
laquelle ont grandi les commencements de la monarchie
de Cyrus."

A thousand years after Cyrus (for Zohák is mentioned by Moses of Khorene in the fifth century) we
find all this forgotten once more, and the vague ru-
mors about Thraétaona and Azhi dahâka are gathered
at last, and arranged and interpreted into something
intelligible to later ages. Zohák is a three-headed
tyrant on the throne of Persia — three-headed, because
the Vaidik Ahî was three-headed, only that one of
Zohák's heads has now become human. Zohák has
killed Jemshíd of the Peshdadian dynasty: Feridun
now conquers Zohák on the banks of the Tigris. He
then strikes him down with his cow-headed mace, and
is on the point of killing him, when, as Firdusi says, a
supernatural voice whispered in his ear, — [1]

"Slay him not now, his time is not yet come,
His punishment must be prolonged awhile;
And as he cannot now survive the wound,
Bind him with heavy chains; convey him straight

[1] Cf. Atkinson's Shahnamah, p. 46.

> Upon the mountain, there within a cave,
> Deep, dark, and horrible, with arms to soothe
> His sufferings, let the murderer lingering die.
> The work of heaven performing, Feridun
> First purified the world from sin and crime.
> Yet Feridun was not an angel, nor
> Composed of musk and ambergris. By justice
> And generosity he gained his fame.
> Do thou but exercise these princely virtues,
> And thou wilt be renowned as Feridun."

As a last stage in the myth of the Vaidik Trnitana
we may mention versions like those given by Sir John
Malcolm and others, who see in Zohâk the representative of an Assyrian invasion lasting during the thousand
years of Zohâk's reign, and who change Feridun into
Arbaces the Mede, the conqueror of Sardanapalus. We
may then look at the whole with the new light which
Burnouf's genius has shed over it, and watch the retro-
grade changes of Arbaces into Feridun, of Feridun into
Phredûn, of Phredûn into Thraêtaona, of Thraêtaona
into Trnitana, — each a separate phase in the dissolv-
ing view of mythology.

As to the language of Persia, its biography is at an
end with the " Shahnameh." What follows exhibits
hardly any signs of either growth or decay. The
language becomes more and more encumbered with
foreign words; but the grammar seems to have arrived
at its lowest ebb, and withstands further change. From
this state of grammatical numbness, languages recover
by a secondary formation, which grows up slowly and
imperceptibly at first in the speech of the people; till
at last the reviving spirit rises upwards, and sweeps
away, like the waters in spring, the frozen surface of
an effete government, priesthood, literature, and grammar.

October, 1853.

IV.

THE AITAREYA-BRÂHMANA.[1]

THE Sanskrit text, with an English translation of the Aitareya-brâhmana, just published at Bombay by Dr. Martin Haug, the Superintendent of Sanskrit Studies in the Poona College, constitutes one of the most important additions lately made to our knowledge of the ancient literature of India. The work is published by the Director of Public Instruction, in behalf of Government, and furnishes a new instance of the liberal and judicious spirit in which Mr. Howard bestows his patronage on works of real and permanent utility. The Aitareya-brâhmana, containing the earliest speculations of the Brahmans on the meaning of their sacrificial prayers, and the purport of their ancient religious rites, is a work which could be properly edited nowhere but in India. It is only a small work of about two hundred pages, but it presupposes so thorough a familiarity with all the externals of the religion of the Brahmans, the various offices of their priests, the times and seasons of their sacred rites, the form of their innumerable sacrificial utensils, and the preparation of their offerings, that no amount of San-

[1] The Aitareya-brâhmanam of the Rig-veda, edited and translated by Martin Haug, Ph. D., Superintendent of Sanskrit Studies in the Poona College. Bombay, 1863. London: Trübner & Co.

skrit scholarship, such as can be gained in England,
would have been sufficient to unravel the intricate
speculations concerning the matters which form the
bulk of the Aitareya-bráhmana. The difficulty was,
not to translate the text word for word, but to gain
a clear, accurate, and living conception of the subjects
there treated. The work was composed by persons,
and for persons, who, in a general way, knew the performance of the Vedic sacrifices as well as we know
the performance of our own sacred rites. If we placed
the English Prayer-book in the hands of a stranger
who had never assisted at an English service, we
should find that, in spite of the simplicity and plain-
ness of its language, it failed to convey to the unini-
tiated a clear idea of what he ought and what he
ought not to do in church. The ancient Indian ceremonial, however, is one of the most artificial and
complicated forms of worship that can well be imagined; and though its details are, no doubt, most
minutely described in the Bráhmanas and the Sútras,
yet, without having seen the actual site on which the
sacrifices are offered, the altars constructed for the
occasion, the instruments employed by different priests,
— the *tout-ensemble*, in fact, of the sacred rites, — the
reader seems to deal with words, but with words only,
and is unable to reproduce in his imagination the acts
and facts which were intended to be conveyed by
them. Various attempts were made to induce some
of the more learned Brahmans to edit and translate
some of their own rituals, and thus enable European
scholars to gain an idea of the actual performance of
their ancient sacrifices, and to enter more easily into
the spirit of the speculations on the mysterious mean

ing of these rituals, which are embodied in the so-
called "Brâhmanas," or " the sayings of the Brahmans." But although, thanks to the enlightened exertions of Dr. Ballantyne and his associates in the
Sanskrit College of Benares, Brahmans might have
been found knowing English quite sufficiently for the
purpose of a rough and ready translation from Sanskrit into English, such was their prejudice against
divulging the secrets of their craft that none could be
persuaded to undertake the ungrateful task. Dr. Haug
tells us of another difficulty, which we had hardly
suspected, — the great scarcity of Brahmans familiar
with the ancient Vedic ritual : —

"Seeing the great difficulties, nay, impossibility of
attaining to anything like a real understanding of the
sacrificial art from all the numerous books I had
collected, I made the greatest efforts to obtain oral
information from some of those few Brahmans who
are known by the name of 'Srotriyas' or 'Srnatis,'
and who alone are the possessors of the sacrificial
mysteries as they descended from the remotest times.
The task was no easy one, and no European scholar
in this country before me ever succeeded in it. This
is not to be wondered at ; for the proper knowledge
of the ritual is everywhere in India now rapidly dying
out, and in many parts, chiefly in those under British
rule, it has already died out."

Dr. Haug succeeded, however, at last in procuring
the assistance of a real Doctor of Divinity, who had
not only performed the minor Vedic sacrifices, such
as the full and new moon offerings but had officiated
at some of the great Soma sacrifices, now very rarely
to be seen in any part of India. He was induced, we

are sorry to say by very mercenary consi lerations, to
perform the principal ceremonies in a secluded part
of Dr. Haug's premises. This lasted five days, and
the same assistance was afterwards rendered by the
same worthy and some of his brethren whenever Dr.
Haug was in any doubt as to the proper meaning of
the ceremonial treatises which give the outlines of the
Vedic sacrifices. Dr. Haug was actually allowed to
taste that sacred beverage, the Soma, which gives
health, wisdom, inspiration, nay immortality, to those
who receive it from the hands of a twice-born priest.
Yet, after describing its preparation, all that Dr. Haug
has to say of it is :—

" The sap of the plant now used at Poona appears
whitish, has a very stringent taste, is bitter, but not
sour ; it is a very nasty drink, and has some intoxicating effect. I tasted it several times, but it was
impossible for me to drink more than some tea-spoon-
fuls."

After having gone through all these ordeals, Dr.
Haug may well say that his explanations of sacrificial
terms, as given in the notes, can be relied upon as
certain ; that they proceed from what he himself witnessed, and what he was able to learn from men who
had inherited the knowledge from the most ancient
times. He speaks with some severity of those scholars
in Europe who have attempted to explain the technical
terms of the Vedic sacrifices without the assistance of
native priests, and without even availing themselves
carefully of the information they might have gained
from native commentaries.

In the preface to his edition of the Aitareya-brâhmana, Dr. Haug has thrown out some new ideas on

the chronology of Vedic literature which deserve
careful consideration. Beginning with the hymns of
the Rig-veda, he admits, indeed, that there are in
that collection ancient and modern hymns, but he
doubts whether it will be possible to draw a sharp
line between what has been called the "Khandas"
period, representing the free growth of sacred poetry,
and the "Manua" period, during which the ancient
hymns were supposed to have been collected and new
ones added, chiefly intended for sacrificial purposes.
Dr. Haug maintains that some hymns of a decidedly
sacrificial character should be ascribed to the earliest
period of Vedic poetry. He takes, for instance, the
hymn describing the horse sacrifice, and he concludes
from the fact that seven priests only are mentioned in
it by name, and that none of them belongs to the class
of the Udgátars (singers) and Brahmans (superintendents), that this hymn was written before the establishment of these two classes of priests. As these
priests are mentioned in other Vedic hymns, he concludes that the hymn describing the horse sacrifice is
of a very early date. Dr. Haug strengthens his case
by a reference to the Zoroastrian ceremonial, in which,
as he says, the chanters and superintendents are entirely unknown, whereas the other two classes, the
Hotars (reciters) and Adhvaryus (assistants) are
mentioned by the same names as "Zaotar" and
"Rathwiskaro." The establishment of the two new
classes of priests would, therefore, seem to have taken
place in India after the Zoroastrians had separated
from the Brahmans; and Dr. Haug would ascribe the
Vedic hymns in which no more than two classes of
priests are mentioned to a period preceding, others in

which the other two classes of priests are mentioned to
a period succeeding, that ancient schism. We must
confess, though doing full justice to Dr. Haug's argument, that he seems to us to stretch what is merely
negative evidence beyond its proper limits. Surely
a poet, though acquainted with all the details of a sacrifice and the titles of all the priests employed in it,
might speak of it in a more general manner than the
author of a manual, and it would be most dangerous
to conclude that whatever was passed over by him in
silence did not exist at the time when he wrote. Secondly, if there were more ancient titles of priests, the
poet would most likely use them in preference to others
that had been but lately introduced. Thirdly, even
the ancient priestly titles had originally a more general
meaning before they were restricted to their technical
significance, just as in Europe *bishop* meant originally
an overseer, *priest* an elder, *deacon* a minister. In
several hymns, some of these titles — for instance, that
of "hotar," invoker — are clearly used as appellatives,
and not as titles. Lastly, one of the priests mentioned
in the hymn on the horse sacrifice, the Agnimindha,
is admitted by Dr. Haug himself to be the same as
the Agnidhra; and if we take this name, like all the
others, in its technical sense, we have to recognize in
him one of the four Brahman priests.[1] We should
thus lose the ground on which Dr. Haug's argument

---

[1] By an accident two lines containing the names of the sixteen priests in
my *History of Ancient Sanskrit Literature* (p. 469) have been misplaced.
Agnidhra and Potri ought to range with the Brahmans, Prațiharți and
Subrahmanya with the Udgâtri. See Âsval. Sûtra IV 1 (p. 336, ed.
 ... India); and M. M., "Todtenbestattung," p. xl-i. It might be said
however, that the Agnimindha was meant as one of the Hotrikamins, or
one of the Seven Priests, the Sapta Hotris. See Haug, *Aitareya-Brahmana*,
vol. I. p. 58.

is chiefly based, and should have to admit the existence
of Brahman priests as early at least as the time in
which the hymn on the horse sacrifice was composed.
But, even admitting that allusions to a more or less
complete ceremonial [1] could be pointed out in certain
hymns, this might help us no doubt in subdividing
and arranging the poetry of the second or Mantra
period, but it would leave the question, whether allusions to ceremonial technicalities are to be considered
as characteristics of later or earlier hymns, entirely
unaffected.   Dr. Haug, who holds that, in the development of the human race, sacrifice comes earlier
than religious poetry, formulas earlier than prayers,
Leviticus earlier than the Psalms, applies this view
to the chronological arrangement of Vedic literature;
and he is, therefore, naturally inclined to look upon
hymns composed for sacrificial purposes, more particularly upon the invocations and formulas of the Yagur-
veda, and upon the Nivids preserved in the Brâhmanas
and Sûtras, as relics of greater antiquity than the free
poetical effusions of the Rishis, which defy ceremonial
rules, ignore the orthodox rank of priests and deities,
and occasionally allude to subjects more appropriate
for profane than for sacred poetry : —

"The first sacrifices," he writes, "were no doubt
simple offerings performed without much ceremonial.
A few appropriate solemn words, indicating the giver,
the nature of the offering, the deity to which, as well
as the purpose for which it was offered, were sufficient.
All this would be embodied in the sacrificial formulas

<hr/>

[1] Many such allusions were collected in my *History of Ancient Sanskrit
Literature*, p. 450 seq.; some of them have lately been independently discovered by others.

known in later times principally by the name of 'Yagush,' whilst the older one appears to have been 'Yâ-
gyâ.' The invocation of the deity by different names,
and its invitation to enjoy the meal prepared, may be
equally old. It was justly regarded as a kind of Yagush, and called 'Nigada' or 'Nivid.'"

In comparing these sacrificial formulas with the bulk
of the Rig-veda hymns, Dr. Haug comes to the conclusion that the former are more ancient. He shows
that certain of these formulas and Nivids were known
to the poets of the hymns, as they undoubtedly were;
but this would only prove that these poets were acquainted with these as well as with other portions of
the ceremonial. It would only confirm the view advocated by others, that certain hymns were clearly
written for ceremonial purposes, though the ceremonial
presupposed by these hymns may in many cases prove
more simple and primitive than the ceremonial laid
down in the Brâhmanas and Sûtras. But if Dr.
Haug tells us that the Rishis tried their poetical tal-
ent first in the composition of Yâgyâs, or verses to be
recited while an offering was thrown into the fire,
and that the Yâgyâs were afterwards extended into
little songs, we must ask, is this fact or theory? And
if we are told that " there can be hardly any doubt
that the hymns which we possess are purely sacrificial,
and made only for sacrificial purposes, and that those
which express more general ideas, or philosophical
thoughts, or confessions of sins, are comparatively
late," we can only repeat our former question. Dr.
Haug, when proceeding to give his proofs that the
purely sacrificial poetry is more ancient than either
profane songs or hymns of a more general religious

character, only produces such collateral evidence as may be found in the literary history of the Jews and the Chinese — evidence which is curious, but not convincing. Among the Aryan nations, it has hitherto been considered, as a general rule, that poetry precedes prose. Now the Yâgyâs and Nivids are prose, and though Dr. Haug calls it rhythmical prose, yet, as compared with the hymns, they are prose; and though such an argument by itself could by no means be considered as sufficient to upset any solid evidence to the contrary, yet it is stronger than the argument derived from the literature of nations who are neither of them Aryan in language or thought.

But though we have tried to show the insufficiency of the arguments advanced by Dr. Haug in support of his theory, we are by no means prepared to deny the great antiquity of some of the sacrificial formulas and invocations, and more particularly of the Nivids to which he for the first time has called attention. There probably existed very ancient Nivids or invocations, but are the Nivids which we possess the identical Nivids alluded to in the hymns? If so, why have they no accents; why do they not form part of the Sanhitâ; why were they not preserved, discussed, and analyzed with the same religious care as the metrical hymns? The Nivids which we now possess may, as Dr. Haug supposes, have inspired the Rishis with the burden of their hymns; but they may equally well have been put together by later compilers from the very hymns of the Rishis. There is many a hymn in the Sanhitâ of the Rig-veda which may be called a "Nivid," *i. e.* an invitation addressed to the gods to come to the sacrifice, and an enumeration

of the principal names of each deity. Those who believe, on more general grounds, that all religion began
with sacrifice and sacrificial formulas, will naturally look
on such hymns and on the Nivids as relics of a more
primitive age; while others who look upon prayer,
praise, and thanksgiving, and the unfettered expression
of devotion and wonderment as the first germs of a religious worship, will treat the same Nivids as productions of a later age. We doubt whether this problem
can be argued on general grounds. Admitting that
the Jews began with sacrifice and ended with psalms,
it would by no means follow that the Aryan nations
did the same, nor would the chronological arrangement
of the ancient literature of China help us much in
forming an opinion of the growth of the Indian mind.
We must take each nation by itself, and try to find out
what they themselves hold as to the relative antiquity
of their literary documents. On general grounds the
problem whether sacrifice or prayer comes first, may
be argued *ad infinitum* just like the problem whether
the hen comes first or the egg. In the special case of
the sacred literature of the Brahmans, we must be
guided by their own tradition, which invariably places
the poetical hymns of the Rig-veda before the ceremonial hymns and formulas of the Yagur-veda and Sâma-
veda. The strongest argument that has yet been
brought forward against this view is, that the formulas
of the Yagur-veda and the sacrificial texts of the
Sâma-veda contain occasionally more archaic forms of
language than the hymns of the Rig-veda. It was
supposed, therefore, that, although the hymns of the
Rig-veda might have been composed at an earlier time,
the sacrificial hymns and formulas were the first to be

collected and to be preserved in the schools by means
of a strict mnemonic discipline. The hymns of the
Rig-veda, some of which have no reference whatever
to the Vedic ceremonial, being collected at a later
time, might have been stripped, while being handed
down by oral tradition, of those grammatical forms
which in the course of time had become obsolete, but
which, if once recognized and sanctioned in theological
seminaries, would have been preserved there with the
most religious care.

According to Dr. Haug, the period during which
the Vedic hymns were composed extends from 1400
to 2000 b. c. The oldest hymns, however, and the
sacrificial formulas he would place between 2000 and
2400 b. c. This period, corresponding to what has
been called the " K'handas" and " Mantra " periods,
would be succeeded by the Brâhmana period, and Dr.
Haug would place the bulk of the Brâhmanas, all
written in prose, between 1400 and 1200 b. c. He
does not attribute much weight to the distinction
made by the Brahmans themselves between revealed
and profane literature, and would place the Sûtras almost contemporaneous with the Brâhmanas. The only
fixed point from which he starts in his chronological
arrangement is the date implied by the position of
the solstitial points mentioned in a little treatise, the
" Gyotisha," a date which has been accurately fixed
by the Rev. R. Main at 1186 b. c.[1] Dr. Haug fully
admits that such an observation was an absolute necessity for the Brahmans in regulating their calendar —

" The proper time," he writes, " of commencing and
ending their sacrifices, principally the so-called ' Sattras'

[1] See preface to the fourth volume of my edition of the Rig-veda.

or sacrificial sessions, could not be known without
an accurate knowledge of the time of the sun's
northern and southern progress. The knowledge of
the calendar forms such an essential part of the
ritual, that many important conditions of the latter
cannot be carried out without the former. The sacrifices are allowed to commence only at certain lucky
constellations, and in certain months. So, for instance,
as a rule, no great sacrifice can commence during the
sun's southern progress; for this is regarded up to the
present day as an unlucky period by the Brahmans,
in which even to die is believed to be a misfortune.
The great sacrifices generally take place in spring, in
the months of Kaitra and Vaiśākha (April and May).
The Sattras, which lasted for one year, were, as one
may learn from a careful perusal of the fourth book of
the Aitareya-brâhmana, nothing but an imitation of
the sun's yearly course. They were divided into two
distinct parts, each consisting of six months of thirty
days each; in the midst of both was the Vishuvat,
i.e. 'equator or central day,' cutting the whole Sat-
tra into two halves. The ceremonies were in both
halves exactly the same, but they were in the latter
half performed in an inverted order."

This argument of Dr. Haug's seems correct as far as
the date of the establishment of the ceremonial is concerned, and it is curious that several scholars who have
lately written on the origin of the Vedic calendar, and
the possibility of its foreign origin, should not have perceived the intimate relation between that calendar and
the whole ceremonial system of the Brahmans. Dr.
Haug is, no doubt, perfectly right when he claims the
invention of the Nakshatras, or the Lunar Zodiac of the

Bráhmana, if we may so call it, for India; he may be right, also, when he assigns the twelfth century as the earliest date for the origin of that simple astronomical system on which the calendar of the Vedic festivals is founded. He calls the theories of others, who have lately tried to claim the first discovery of the Nakshatras for China, Babylon, or some other Asiatic country, absurd, and takes no notice of the sanguine expectations of certain scholars, who imagine they will soon have discovered the very names of the Indian Nakshatras in Babylonian inscriptions. But does it follow that, because the ceremonial presupposes an observation of the solstitial points in about the twelfth century, therefore the theological works in which that ceremonial is explained, commented upon, and furnished with all kinds of mysterious meanings, were composed at that early date? We see no stringency whatever in this argument of Dr. Haug's, and we think it will be necessary to look for other anchors by which to fix the drifting wrecks of Vedic literature.

Dr. Haug's two volumes, containing the text of the Aitareya-bráhmana, translation, and notes, would probably never have been published, if they had not received the patronage of the Bombay Government. However interesting the Bráhmanas may be to students of Indian literature, they are of small interest to the general reader. The greater portion of them is simply twaddle, and what is worse, theological twaddle. No person who is not acquainted beforehand with the place which the Bráhmanas fill in the history of the Indian mind, could read more than ten pages without being disgusted. To the historian, however, and to the philosopher, they are of infinite importance: to the for-

mier as a real link between the ancient and modern literature of India; to the latter as a most important phase
in the growth of the human mind, in its passage from
health to disease. Such books, which no circulating
library would touch, are just the books which Govern-
ments, if possible, or Universities and learned societies,
should patronize; and if we congratulate Dr. Haug on
having secured the enlightened patronage of the Bombay Government, we may congratulate Mr. Howard
and the Bombay Government on having, in this instance, secured the services of a *bona fide* scholar like
Dr. Haug.[1]

March, 1864.

[1] A few paragraphs in this review, in which allusion was made to certain
charges of what might be called "literary rattening," brought by Dr. Haug
against some Sanskrit scholars, and more particularly against the editor of
the *Indische Studien* at Berlin, have here been omitted, as no longer of any
interest. They may be seen, however, in the ninth volume of that period-
ical, where my review has been reprinted, though, as usual, very incorrectly.
It was not I who first brought these accusations, nor should I have felt justified in alluding to them, if the evidence placed before me had not convinced me that there was some foundation for them. I am willing to admit
that the language of Dr. Haug and others may have been too severe, but
few will think that a very loud and boisterous denial to the best was an answer
that the criticisms were quite undeserved. If, by alluding to these matters
and frankly expressing my disapproval of them, I have given unnecessary
pain, I sincerely regret it. So much for the past. As to the future, care, I
trust, will be taken, — for the sake of the good fame of German scholarship,
which, though living in England, I have quite as much at heart as if living
in Germany, — not to give even the faintest countenance to similar sus-
picions. If my remarks should help in producing that result, I shall be
glad to bow my head in silence under the vials of wrath that have been
poured upon it.

V.

ON THE

STUDY OF THE ZEND-AVESTA IN INDIA.[1]

— • —

SANSKRIT scholars resident in India enjoy considerable advantages over those who devote themselves to
the study of the ancient literature of the Brahmans in
this country, or in France and Germany. Although
Sanskrit is no longer spoken by the great mass of the
people, there are few large towns in which we do not
meet with some more or less learned natives — the
pandits, or, as they used to be called, pandins — men
who have passed through a regular apprenticeship in
Sanskrit grammar, and who generally devote themselves to the study of some special branch of Sanskrit
literature, whether law, or logic, or rhetoric, or astronomy, or anything else. These men, who formerly lived
on the liberality of the Rajahs and on the superstition
of the people, find it more and more difficult to make a
living among their own countrymen, and are glad to be
employed by any civilian or officer who takes an interest in their ancient lore. Though not scholars in

---

[1] Essays on the Sacred Language, Writings, and Religion of the Parsees.
By Martin Haug, Dr. Phil. Bombay, 1862.

our sense of the word, and therefore of little use as teachers of the language, they are extremely useful to more advanced students, who are able to set them to do that kind of work for which they are fit, and to check their labors by judicious supervision. All our great Sanskrit scholars, from Sir William Jones to H. H. Wilson, have fully acknowledged their obligations to their native assistants. They used to work in Calcutta, Benares, and Bombay with a pandit at each elbow, instead of the grammar and the dictionary which European scholars have to consult at every difficult passage. Whenever an English Sahib undertook to edit or translate a Sanskrit text, these pandits had to copy and to collate MSS., to make a verbal index, to prepare parallel passages from other writers, and, in many cases, to supply a translation into Hindustani, Bengali, or into their own peculiar English. In fact, if it had not been for the assistance thus fully and freely rendered by native scholars, Sanskrit scholarship would never have made the rapid progress which, during less than a century, it has made, not only in India, but in almost every country of Europe.

With this example to follow, it is curious that hardly any attempt should have been made by English residents, particularly in the Bombay Presidency, to avail themselves of the assistance of the Parsis for the purpose of mastering the ancient language and literature of the worshippers of Ormuzd. If it is remembered that, next to Sanskrit, there is no more ancient language than Zend, — and that, next to the Veda, there is, among the Aryan nations, no more primitive religious code than the Zend-Avesta, it is surprising that so little should have been done by the members of the

Indian Civil Service in this important branch of study. It is well known that such was the enthusiasm kindled in the heart of Anquetil Duperron by the sight of a fac-simile of a page of the Zend-Avesta, that in order to secure a passage to India, he enlisted as a private soldier, and spent six years (1754-1761) in different parts of Western India, trying to collect MSS. of the sacred writings of Zoroaster, and to acquire from the Dustoors a knowledge of their contents. His example was followed, though in a less adventurous spirit, by Rask, a learned Dane, who after collecting at Bombay many valuable MSS. for the Danish Government, wrote in 1826 his essay "On the Age and Genuineness of the Zend Language." Another Dane, at present one of the most learned Zend scholars in Europe, Westergaard, likewise proceeded to India (1841-1843), before he undertook to publish his edition of the religious books of the Zoroastrians. (Copenhagen, 1852.) During all this time, while French and German scholars, such as Burnouf, Bopp, and Spiegel, were hard at work in deciphering the curious remains of the Magian religion, hardly anything was contributed by English students living in the very heart of Parsiism at Bombay and Poona.

We are all the more pleased, therefore, that a young German scholar, Dr. Haug, — who through the judicious recommendation of Mr. Howard, Director of Public Instruction in the Bombay Presidency, was appointed to a Professorship of Sanskrit in the Poona College, — should have grasped the opportunity, and devoted himself to a thorough study of the sacred literature of the Parsis. He went to India well prepared for his task, and he has not disappointed the

hopes which those who knew him entertained of him
on his departure from Germany. Unless he had been
master of his subject before he went to Poona, the
assistance of the Dustoors would have been of little
avail to him. But knowing all that could be known
in Europe of the Zend language and literature, he
knew what questions to ask, he could check every
answer, and he could learn with his eyes what it is
almost impossible to learn from books, namely, the
religious ceremonial and the ritual observances which
form so considerable an element in the Vendidad and
Vispered. The result of his studies is now before us
in a volume of "Essays on the Sacred Language,
Writings, and Religion of the Parsees," published at
Bombay, 1862. It is a volume of only three hundred
and sixty-eight pages, and sells in England for one
guinea. Nevertheless, to the student of Zend it is one
of the cheapest books ever published. It contains four
Essays: 1. History of the Researches into the Sacred
Writings and Religion of the Parsees from the earliest
times down to the present; 2. Outline of a Grammar of the Zend Language; 3. The Zend-Avesta, or
the Scripture of the Parsees; 4. Origin and Development of the Zoroastrian Religion. The most important portion is the Outline of the Zend Grammar; for,
though a mere outline, it is the first systematic grammatical analysis of that curious language. In other
languages, we generally begin by learning the grammar, and then make our way gradually through the
literature. In Zend the grammatical terminations had
first to be discovered by a careful anatomy of the literature. The Parsis themselves possessed no such work.
Even their most learned priests are satisfied with

learning the Zend-Avesta by heart, and with acquiring
some idea of its import by means of a Pehlevi translation, which dates from the Sassanian period, or of a
Sanskrit translation of still later date. Hence the
translation of the Zend-Avesta published by Anquetil
Duperron, with the assistance of Dustoor Dârâb, was
by no means trustworthy. It was, in fact, a French
translation of a Persian rendering of a Pehlevi version
of the Zend original. It was Burnouf who, aided by
his knowledge of Sanskrit, and his familiarity with the
principles of comparative grammar, approached, for the
first time, the very words of the Zend original. He
had to conquer every inch of ground for himself;
and his "Commentaire sur le Yasna" is, in fact, like the
deciphering of one long inscription, only surpassed in
difficulty by his later decipherments of the cuneiform
inscriptions of the Achæmenian monarchs of Persia.
Aided by the labors of Burnouf and others, Dr. Haug
has at last succeeded in putting together the *disjecta
membra poetæ*, and we have now in his Outline, not
indeed a grammar like that of Pânini for Sanskrit, yet
a sufficient skeleton of what was once a living language,
not inferior, in richness and delicacy, even to the
idiom of the Vedas.

There are, at present, five editions, more or less
complete, of the Zend-Avesta. The first was litho-
graphed under Burnouf's direction, and published at
Paris 1829-1843. The second edition of the text,
transcribed into Roman characters, appeared at Leip-
zig, 1850, published by Professor Brockhaus. The
third edition, in Zend characters, was given to the
world by Professor Spiegel, 1851; and about the same
time a fourth edition was undertaken by Professor

Westergaard, at Copenhagen, 1852 to 1854. There are one or two editions of the Zend-Avesta, published in India, with Guzerati translations, which we have not seen, but which are frequently quoted by native scholars. A German translation of the Zend-Avesta was undertaken by Professor Spiegel, far superior in accuracy to that of Anquetil Duperron, yet in the main based on the Pehlevi version. Portions of the ancient text had been minutely analyzed and translated by Dr. Haug, even before his departure for the East.

The Zend-Avesta is not a voluminous work. We still call it the Zend-Avesta, though we are told that its proper title is " Avesta Zend," nor does it seem at all likely that the now familiar name will ever be surrendered for the more correct one. Who speaks of Cassius Dio, though we are told that Dio Cassius is wrong? Nor do we feel at all convinced that the name of " Avesta Zend " is the original and only correct name. According to the Parsis, Avesta means sacred text, Zend its Pehlevi translation. But in the Pehlevi translations themselves, the original work of Zoroaster is spoken of as " Avesta Zend." Why it is so called by the Pehlevi translators, we are nowhere told by themselves, and many conjectures have, in consequence, been started by almost every Zend scholar. Dr. Haug supposes that the earliest portions of the Zend-Avesta ought to be called " Avesta," the later portions " Zend,"—Zend meaning, according to him, commentary, explanation, gloss. Neither the word " Avesta " nor " Zend," however, occurs in the original Zend texts ; and though " Avesta " seems to be the Sanskrit avasthâ, the Pehlevi apestak, in the sense of " authorized text," the etymology of " Zend,' as derived from a supposed *zanti*, Sanskrit *gnati*, knowledge, is not free from serious objections. *Avesta Zend* was most likely a traditional name, hardly understood even at the time of the Pehlevi translators, who retained it in their writings. It was possibly misinterpreted by them, as many other Zend words have been at their hands, and may have been originally the Sanskrit word "*khandas*," [1] which is applied by the Brahmans to the sacred hymns of the Veda. Certainty on such a point is impossible; but as it is but fair to give a preference to the conjectures of those who are most familiar with the subject, we quote the following explanation of Dr. Haug : —

"The meaning of the term 'Zend' varied at different periods. Originally it meant the interpretation of the sacred texts descended from Zarathustra and his disciples by the successors of the prophet. In the course of time, these interpretations being regarded as equally sacred with the original texts, both were then called Avesta. Both having become unintelligible to the majority of the Zoroastrians, in consequence of their language having died out, they required a Zend or explanation again. This new Zend was furnished by the most learned priests of the Sassanian period in the shape of a translation into the vernacular language of Persia (Pehlevi) in those days, which translation being the only source to the priests of the present time whence to derive any knowledge of the old texts, is therefore the only Zend or explanation they know of. . . . . The name Pazend, to be met with frequently in connection with Avesta and Zend, denotes the further explanation of the Zend doctrine. . . . .

[1] See page 62.

The Pazend language is the same as the so-called Parsi, i. e. the ancient Persian, as written till about the time of Firdusi, 1000 A. D."

Whatever we may think of the nomenclature thus advocated by Dr. Haug, we must acknowledge in the fullest manner his great merit in separating for the first time the more ancient from the more modern parts of the Zend-Avesta. Though the existence of different dialects in the ancient texts was pointed out by Spiegel, and although the metrical portions of the Yasna had been clearly marked by Westergaard, it is nevertheless Haug's great achievement to have extracted these early relics, to have collected them, and to have attempted a complete translation of them, as far as such an attempt could be carried out at the present moment. His edition of the "Gâthâs"—for this is the name of the ancient metrical portions—marks an epoch in the history of Zend scholarship, and the importance of the recovery of these genuine relics of Zoroaster's religion has been well brought out by Bunsen in the least known of his books, "Gott in der Geschichte." We by no means think that the translations here offered by Dr. Haug are final. We hope, on the contrary, that he will go on with the work he has so well begun, and that he will not rest till he has removed every dark speck that still covers the image of Zoroaster's primitive faith. Many of the passages as translated by him are as clear as daylight, and carry conviction by their very clearness. Others, however, are obscure, hazy, meaningless. We feel that they must have been intended for something else, something more definite and forcible, though we cannot tell what to do with the words as they stand.

Sense, after all, is the great test of translation. We must feel convinced that there was good sense in these ancient poems, otherwise mankind would not have taken the trouble to preserve them: and if we cannot discover good sense in them, it must be either our fault, or the words as we now read them were not the words uttered by the ancient prophets of the world. The following are a few specimens of Dr. Haug's translations, in which the reader will easily discover the different lines of certainty and uncertainty, of sense and mere verbiage:—

"1. That I will ask Thee, tell me it right, thou living God! whether your friend (Sraosha) be willing to recite his own hymn as prayer to my friend (Frashaostra or Vistāspa), thou Wise! and whether he should come to us with the good mind, to perform for us true actions of friendship.

"2. That I will ask Thee, tell me it right, thou living God! How arose the best present life (this world)? By what means are the present things (the world) to be supported? That spirit, the holy (Vohu mano), O true wise spirit! is the guardian of the beings to ward off from them every evil; He is the promoter of all life.

"3. That I will ask Thee, tell me it right, thou living God! Who was in the beginning the Father and Creator of truth? Who made the sun and stars? Who causes the moon to increase and wane if not Thou? This I wish to know, except what I already know.

"4. That I will ask Thee, tell me it right, thou living God! Who is holding the earth and the skies above it? Who made the waters and the trees of the

field? Who is in the winds and storms that they so
quickly run? Who is the Creator of the good-minded
beings, thou Wise?"

This is a short specimen of the earliest portion of the
Zend-Avesta. The following is an extract from one
of the latest, the so-called "Ormuzd Yasht":—

"Zarathustra asked Ahuramazda after the most ef-
fectual spell to guard against the influence of evil
spirits. He was answered by the Supreme Spirit,
that the utterance of the different names of Ahuramazda protects best from evil. Thereupon Zarathustra
begged Ahuramazda to communicate to him those
names. He then enumerates twenty. The first is
'Ahmi,' i. e. 'I am;' the fourth, 'Asha - vahista,'
i. e. 'the best purity;' the sixth, 'I am wisdom;'
the eighth, 'I am knowledge;' the twelfth, 'Ahura,'
i. e. 'living;' the twentieth, 'I am who I am, Mazdao.'"

Ahuramazda says then further:—

"'If you call me at day or at night by these names,
I shall come to assist and help you; the angel Serosh
will then come, the genii of the waters and the trees.'
For the utter defeat of the evil spirits, bad men, witches,
Peris, a series of other names are suggested to Zarathustra, such as protector, guardian, spirit, the holiest,
the best fire-priest," etc.

Whether the striking coincidence between one of the
suggested names of Ahuramazda, namely, "I am who
I am," and the explanation of the name Jehovah, Exodus iii. 14, "I am that I am," is accidental or not, must
depend on the age that can be assigned to the Ormuzd
Yasht. The chronological arrangement, however, of
the various portions of the Zend-Avesta is as yet merely
tentative, and these questions must remain for future

consideration.   Dr. Haug points out other similarities between the doctrines of Zoroaster and the Old and New Testaments.   "The Zoroastrian religion," he writes, " exhibits a very close affinity to, or rather identity with, several important doctrines of the Mosaic religion and Christianity, such as the personality and attributes of the devil, and the resurrection of the dead."   Neither of those doctrines, however, would seem to be characteristic of the Old or New Testament, and the resurrection of the dead is certainly to be found by implication only, and is nowhere distinctly asserted, in the religious books of Moses.

There are other points on which we should join issue with Dr. Haug — as, for instance, when, on page 17, he calls the Zend the elder sister of Sanskrit.   This seems to us in the very teeth of the evidence so carefully brought together by himself in his Zend grammar.   If he means the modern Sanskrit, as distinguished from the Vedic, his statement would be right to some extent; but even thus, it would be easy to show many grammatical forms in the later Sanskrit more primitive than their corresponding forms in Zend.   These, however, are minor points compared with the great results of his labors which Dr. Haug has brought together in these four Essays; and we feel certain that all who are interested in the study of ancient language and ancient religion will look forward with the greatest expectations to Dr. Haug's continued investigations of the language, the literature, the ceremonial, and the religion of the descendants of Zoroaster.

December, 1862.

VI.

PROGRESS OF ZEND SCHOLARSHIP.[1]

THERE are certain branches of philological research
which seem to be constantly changing, shifting, and, we
hope, progressing. After the key to the interpretation
of ancient inscriptions has been found, it by no means
follows that every word can at once be definitely explained, or every sentence correctly construed. Thus
it happens that the same hieroglyphic or cuneiform text
is rendered differently by different scholars; nay, that
the same scholar proposes a new rendering not many
years after his first attempt at a translation has been
published. And what applies to the decipherment of
inscriptions applies with equal force to the translation
of ancient texts. A translation of the hymns of the
Veda, or of the Zend-Avesta, and, we may add, of the
Old Testament too, requires exactly the same process
as the deciphering of an inscription. The only safe way
of finding the real meaning of words in the sacred texts
of the Brahmans, the Zoroastrians, or the Jews, is to
compare every passage in which the same word occurs,
and to look for a meaning that is equally applicable to
all, and can at the same time be defended on grammatical and etymological grounds. This is no doubt a

[1] *A Lecture on an Original Speech of Zoroaster.* By Martin Haug. Bombay, 1865.

tedious process, nor can it be free from uncertainty; but it is an uncertainty inherent in the subject itself, for which it would be unfair to blame those by whose genius and perseverance so much light has been shed on the darkest pages of ancient history. To those who are not acquainted with the efforts by which Grotefend, Burnouf, Lassen, and Rawlinson unraveled the inscriptions of Cyrus, Darius, and Xerxes, it may seem inexplicable, for instance, how any inscription which at one time was supposed to confirm the statement, known from Herodotus, that Darius obtained the sovereignty of Persia by the neighing of his horse, should now yield so very different a meaning. Herodotus relates that after the assassination of Smerdis, the six conspirators agreed to confer the royal dignity on him whose horse should neigh first at sunrise. The horse of Darius neighed first, and he was accordingly elected king of Persia. After his election, Herodotus states that Darius erected a stone monument containing the figure of a horseman, with the following inscription: "Darius, the son of Hystaspes, obtained the kingdom of the Persians by the virtue of his horse (giving its name), and of Oibarus, his groom." Lassen translated one of the cuneiform inscriptions, copied originally by Niebuhr from a huge slab built in the southern wall of the great platform at Persepolis, in the following manner: " Auramazdis magnus est. Is maximus est deorum. Ipse Darium regem constituit, benevolens imperium obtulit. Ex voluntate Auramazdis Darius rex sum. Generosus sum Darius rex hujus regionis Persicæ; hanc mihi Auramazdis obtulit ' hoc pomœrio ope equi (Choaspis) claræ virtutis.' " This translation was published in 1844, and the arguments by which Lassen supported it, in the sixth volume of the "Zeitschrift für die Kunde des Morgenlandes," may be read with interest and advantage even now when we know that this eminent scholar was mistaken in his analysis. The first step towards a more correct translation was made by Professor Holtzmann, who in 1845 pointed out that Smerdis was murdered at Susa, not at Persepolis; and that only six days later Darius was elected king of Persia, which happened again at Susa, and not at Persepolis. The monument, therefore, which Darius erected in the *spadeium*, or suburb, in the place where the fortunate event which led to his elevation occurred, and the inscription recording the event in *two*, could not well be looked for at Persepolis. But far more important was the evidence derived from a more careful analysis of the words of the inscription itself. "Niba," which Lassen translated as *pomærium*, occurs in three other places, where it certainly cannot mean suburb. It seems to be an adjective meaning splendid, beautiful. Besides, nibâ is a nominative singular in the feminine, and so is the pronoun hyâ which precedes, and the two words which follow it — "uvaspâ" and "umartiyâ." Professor Holtzmann translated therefore the same sentence which Professor Lassen had rendered by "hoc pomœrio opo oqui (Chœspis) claræ virtutis," by "quæ nitida, herbosa, celebris est," a translation which is in the main correct, and has been adopted afterwards both by Sir H. Rawlinson and M. Oppert. Sir H. Rawlinson translates the whole passage as follows: "This Province of Persia which Ormazd has granted to me, which is illustrious, abounding in good horses, producing good men." Thus vanished the horse of Darius, and the curious confirmation which the

cuneiform inscription was at one time supposed to
lend to the Persian legend recorded by Herodotus.

It would be easy to point out many passages of this
kind, and to use them in order to throw discredit on
the whole method by which these and other inscriptions have lately been deciphered. It would not require any great display of forensic or parliamentary
eloquence, to convince the public at large, by means of
such evidence, that all the labors of Grotefend, Burnouf, Lassen, and Rawlinson had been in vain, and to
lay down once for all the general principle that the
original meaning of inscriptions written in a dead language, of which the tradition is once lost, can never be
recovered. Fortunately, questions of this kind are not
settled by eloquent pleading or by the votes of majorities, but, on the contrary, by the independent judgment of the few who are competent to judge. The
fact that different scholars should differ in their interpretations, or that the same scholar should reject his
former translation, and adopt a new one that possibly
may have to be surrendered again as soon as new light
can be thrown on points hitherto doubtful and obscure,
—all this, which in the hands of those who argue for
victory and not for truth, constitutes so formidable a
weapon, and appeals so strongly to the prejudices of
the many, produces very little effect on the minds of
those who understand the reason of these changes, and
to whom each new change represents but a new step
in advance in the discovery of truth.

Nor should the fact be overlooked that, if there
seems to be less change in the translation of the books
of the Old Testament for instance, or of Homer, it is
due in a great measure to the absence of that critical

exactness at which the decipherers of ancient inscriptions and the translators of the Veda and Zend-Avesta aim in rendering each word that comes before them. If we compared the translation of the Septuagint with the Authorized Version of the Old Testament, we should occasionally find discrepancies nearly as startling as any that can be found in the different translations of the cuneiform inscriptions, or of the Veda and Zend-Avesta. In the Book of Job, the Vulgate translates the exhortation of Job's wife by "Bless God and die;" the English version by "Curse God and die;" the Septuagint by "Say some word to the Lord and die." Though, at the time when the Seventy translated the Old Testament, Hebrew could hardly be called a dead language, yet there were then many of its words the original meaning of which even the most learned rabbi would have had great difficulty in defining with real accuracy. The meaning of words changes imperceptibly and irresistibly. Even where there is a literature, and a printed literature like that of modern Europe, four or five centuries work such a change that few even of the most learned divines in England would find it easy to read and to understand accurately a theological treatise written in English four hundred years ago. The same happened, and happened to a far greater extent, in ancient languages. Nor was the sacred character attributed to certain writings any safeguard. On the contrary, greater violence is done by successive interpreters to sacred writings than to any other relics of ancient literature. Ideas grow and change, yet each generation tries to find its own ideas reflected in the sacred pages of their early prophets, and, in addition to the ordinary influences which blur and obscure the sharp features of old words, artificial influences are here at work distorting the natural expression of words which have been invested with a sacred authority. Passages in the Veda or Zend-Avesta which do not bear on religious or philosophical doctrines are generally explained simply and naturally, even by the latest of native commentators. But as soon as any word or sentence can be so turned as to support a doctrine, however modern, or a precept however irrational, the simplest phrases are tortured and mangled till at last they are made to yield their assent to ideas the most foreign to the minds of the authors of the Veda and Zend-Avesta.

To those who take an interest in these matters we may recommend a small Essay lately published by the. Rev. R. G. S. Browne, — the " Mosaic Cosmogony," —in which the author endeavors to establish a literal translation of the first chapter of Genesis. Touching the first verb that occurs in the Bible, he writes: " What is the meaning or scope of the Hebrew verb, in our Authorized Version, rendered by ' created ' ? To English ears and understandings the sound comes naturally, and by long use irresistibly, as the representation of an *ex nihilo* creation. But, in the teeth of all the Rabbinical and Cabalistic fancies of Jewish commentators, and with reverential deference to modern criticism on the Hebrew Bible, it is not so. R. D. Kimchi, in his endeavor to ascertain the shades of difference existing between the terms used in the Mosaic cosmogony, has assumed that our Hebrew verb " bará " has the full signification of *ex nihilo creavit*. Our own Castell, a profound and self-denying scholar, has entertained the same groundless notion. And even

our illustrious Bryan Walton was not inaccessible to
this oblique ray of Rabbinical *ignis fatuus.*"

Mr. Browne then proceeds to quote Gesenius, who
gives as the primary meaning of bara, "he cut, cut
out, carved, planed down, polished ;" and he refers to
Lee, who characterizes it as a silly theory that "bara"
meant to create *ex nihilo.* In Joshua xvii. 15 and 18,
the same verb is used in the sense of cutting down
trees ; in Psalm civ. 30 it is translated by "Thou re-
newest the face of the earth."   In Arabic, too, according to Lane, bara means properly, though not
always, to create out of pre-existing matter. All
this shows that the verb "bara," as in the Sanskrit
tvaksh or taksh,¹ there is no trace of the meaning
assigned to it by later scholars, of a creation out of
nothing.   That idea in its definiteness was a modern
idea, most likely called forth by the contact between
Jews and Greeks at Alexandria.   It was probably in
contradistinction to the Greek notion of matter as co-
eternal with the Creator, that the Jews, to whom Jehovah was all in all, asserted, for the first time
deliberately, that God had made all things out of
nothing.   This became afterwards the received and orthodox view of Jewish and Christian divines, though
the verb "bara," so far from lending any support to
this theory, would rather show that, in the minds of
those whom Moses addressed and whose language he
spoke, it could only have called forth the simple conception of fashioning or arranging — if, indeed, it called
forth any more definite conception than the general
and vague one conveyed by the κτίσις of the Septuagint.
To find out how the words of the Old Testament were

¹ See Jarmann, in Kuhn's *Zeitschrift,* xi. p. 500.

understood by those to whom they were originally addressed is a task attempted by very few interpreters of the Bible. The great majority of readers transfer without hesitation the ideas which they connect with words as used in the nineteenth century to the mind of Moses or his contemporaries, forgetting altogether the distance which divides their language and their thoughts from the thoughts and language of the wandering tribes of Israel.

How many words, again, there are in Homer which have indeed a traditional interpretation, as given by our dictionaries and commentaries, but the exact purport of which is completely lost, is best known to Greek scholars. It is easy enough to translate γεφύρας by the bridges of war, but what Homer really meant by these γεφύραι has never been explained. It is extremely doubtful whether bridges, in our sense of the word, were known at all at the time of Homer; and even if it could be proved that Homer used γέφυρα in the sense of a dam, the etymology, i.e. the earliest history of the word, would still remain obscure and doubtful. It is easy, again, to see that ἱερός in Greek means something like the English sacred. But how, if it did so, the same adjective could likewise be applied to a fish or to a chariot, is a question which, if it is to be answered at all, can only be answered by an etymological analysis of the word.[1] To say that sacred may mean marvellous, and therefore big, is saying nothing, particularly as Homer does not speak of catching big fish, but of catching fish in general.

These considerations — which might be carried

1 On ἱερός, the Sanskrit ishira, lively, see Kuhn's Zeitschrift, vol. II. p. 275; vol. III. p. 134.

much further, but which, we are afraid, have carried us
away too far from our original subject — were suggested
to us while reading a lecture lately published by Dr.
Haug, and originally delivered by him at Bombay, in
1864, before an almost exclusive Parsi audience. In that
lecture Dr. Haug gives a new translation of ten short
paragraphs of the Zend-Avesta, which he had explained
and translated in his "Essays on the Sacred Language
of the Parsees," published in 1862. To an ordinary
reader the difference between the two translations,
published within the space of two years, might certainly be perplexing, and calculated to shake his faith
in the soundness of a method that can lead to such varying results. Nor can it be denied that, if scholars
who are engaged in these researches are bent on representing their last translation as final and as admitting
of no further improvement, the public has a right to
remind them that "finality" is as dangerous a thing
in scholarship as in politics. Considering the difficulty
of translating the pages of the Zend-Avesta, we can
never hope to have every sentence of it rendered into
clear and intelligible English. Those who for the
first time reduced the sacred traditions of the Zoroastrians to writing were separated by more than a thousand years from the time of their original composition.
After that came all the vicissitudes to which manu-
scripts are exposed during the process of being copied
by more or less ignorant scribes. The most ancient
MSS. of the Zend-Avesta date from the beginning of
the fourteenth century. It is true there is an early
translation of the Zend-Avesta, the Pehlevi translation, and a later one in Sanskrit by Neriosengh. But
the Pehlevi translation, which was made under the

auspices of the Sassanian kings of Persia, served only to show how completely the literal and grammatical meaning of the Zend-Avesta was lost even at that time, in the third century after Christ; while the Sanskrit translation was clearly made, not from the original, but from the Pehlevi.   It is true also, that even in more modern times the Parsis of Bombay were able to give to Anquetil Duperron and other Europeans what they considered as a translation of the Zend-Avesta in modern Persian.   But a scholar like Burnouf, who endeavored for the first time to give an account of every word in the Zend text, to explain each grammatical termination, to parse every sentence, and to establish the true meaning of each term by an etymological analysis and by a comparison of cognate words in Sanskrit, was able to derive but scant assistance from these traditional translations.   Professor Spiegel, to whom we owe a complete edition and translation of the Zend-Avesta, and who has devoted the whole of his life to the elucidation of the Zoroastrian religion, attributes a higher value to the tradition of the Parsis than Dr. Haug.   But he also is obliged to admit that he could ascribe no greater authority to these traditional translations and glosses than a Biblical scholar might allow to Rabbinical commentaries.   All scholars are agreed in fact on this, that whether the tradition be right or wrong, it requires in either case to be confirmed by an independent grammatical and etymological analysis of the original text. Such an analysis is no doubt as liable to error as the traditional translation itself, but it possesses this advantage, that it gives reasons for every word that has to be translated, and for every sentence that has to be construed. It is an excellent discipline to the mind even where the results at which we arrive are doubtful or erroneous, and it has imparted to these studies a scientific value and general interest which they could not otherwise have acquired.

We shall give a few specimens of the translations proposed by different scholars of one or two verses of the Zend-Avesta. We cannot here enter into the grammatical arguments by which each of these translations is supported. We only wish to show what is the present state of Zend scholarship, and though we would by no means disguise the fact of its somewhat chaotic character, yet we do not hesitate to affirm that, in spite of the conflict of the opinions of different scholars, and in spite of the fluctuation of systems apparently opposed to each other, progress may be reported, and a firm hope expressed that the essential doctrines of one of the earliest forms of religion may in time be recovered and placed before us in their original purity and simplicity. We begin with the Pehlevi translation of a passage in Yasna, 45 : —

" Thus the religion is to be proclaimed ; now give an attentive hearing, and now listen, that is, keep your ear in readiness, make your works and speeches gentle. Those who have wished from nigh and far to study the religion, may now do so. For now all is manifest, that Anhuma (Ormazd) created, that Anhuma created all these beings ; that at the second time, at the (time of the) future body, Aharman does not destroy (the life of) the worlds. Aharman made evil desire and wickedness to spread through his tongue."

Professor Spiegel, in 1859, translated the same passage, of which the Pehlevi is a running commentary rather than a literal rendering, as follows : —

" Now I will tell you, lend me your ear, now hear what you desired, you that came from near and from afar ! It is clear, the wise (spirits) have created all things; evil doctrine shall not for a second time destroy the world. The Evil One has made a bad choice with his tongue."

Next follows the translation of the passage as published by Dr. Haug in 1862 : —

" All ye, who have come from nigh and far, listen now and hearken to my speech. Now I will tell you all about that pair of spirits how it is known to the wise. Neither the ill-speaker (the devil) shall destroy the second (spiritual) life, nor that man who, being a liar with his tongue, professes the false (idolatrous) belief."

The same scholar, in 1865, translates the same passage somewhat differently : —

" All you that have come from near and far should now listen and hearken to what I shall proclaim. Now the wise have manifested this universe as a duality. Let not the mischief-maker destroy the second life, since he, the wicked, chose with his tongue the pernicious doctrine."

The principal difficulty in this paragraph consists in the word which Dr. Haug translated by " duality," namely, " dûm," and which he identifies with Sanskrit " dvam," i. e. dvandvam, pair. Such a word, as far as we are aware, does not occur again in the Zend-Avesta, and hence it is not likely that the uncertainty attaching to its meaning will ever be removed. Other interpreters take it as a verb in the second person plural, and hence the decided difference of interpretation.

The sixth paragraph of the same passage is explained by the Pehlevi translator as follows:—

"Thus I proclaimed that among all things the greatest is to worship God. The praise of purity is (due) to him who has a good knowledge, (to those) who depend on Ormazd. I hear Spentâmainyu (who is) Ormazd; listen to me, to what I shall speak (unto you). Whose worship is intercourse with the Good Mind; one can know (experience) the divine command to do good through inquiry after what is good. That which is in the intellect they teach me as the best, namely, the inborn (heavenly) wisdom (that is, that the divine wisdom is superior to the human)."

Professor Spiegel translates:—

"Now I will tell you of all things the greatest. It is praise with purity of Him who is wise from those who exist. The holiest heavenly being, Ahuramazda, may hear it. He for whose praise inquiry is made from the holy spirit, may He teach me the best by his intelligence."

Dr. Haug in 1862:—

"Thus I will tell you of the greatest of all (Sraosha), who is praising the truth, and doing good, and of all who are gathered round him (to assist him), by order of the holy spirit (Ahuramazda). The living Wise may hear me; by means of his goodness the good mind increases (in the world). He may lead me with the best of his wisdom."

Dr. Haug in 1865:—

"I will proclaim as the greatest of all things that one should be good, praising only truth. Ahuramazda will hear those who are bent on furthering (all that is good). May he whose goodness is communicated by the Good Mind instruct me in his best wisdom."

To those who are interested in the study of Zend, and wish to judge for themselves of the trustworthiness of these various translations, we can recommend a most useful work lately published in Germany by Dr. F. Justi, " Handbuch der Zendsprache," containing a complete dictionary, a grammar, and selections from the Zend-Avesta.

September, 1862.

VII.

GENESIS AND THE ZEND-AVESTA.[1]

O THAT scholars could have the benefit of a little
legal training, and learn at least the difference between
what is probable and what is proven! What an advantage also, if they had occasionally to address a jury
of respectable tradespeople, and were forced to acquire
the art, or rather not to shrink from the effort, of putting the most intricate and delicate points in the simplest and clearest form of which they admit! What a
lesson again it would be to men of independent research, if, after having amassed ever so many bags full
of evidence, they had always before their eyes the fear
of an impatient judge who wants to hear nothing but
what is important and essential, and hates to listen to
anything that is not to the point, however carefully it
may have been worked out, and however eloquently it

[1] Erân, das Land zwischen dem Indus und Tigris. Beiträge zur Kenntniss des Landes und seiner Geschichte. Von Dr. Friedrich Spiegel. Berlin, 1863.

Professor Spiegel has published a reply to my article in the Ausland, 16th March, 1863. His chief argument is, that other scholars, such as Haldun, Gosenius, Ewald, Delitzsch, Knobel, Windischmann, have held the same or very similar opinions. This is perfectly true, but Dr. Spiegel will for- give me for saying that the opinions of these scholars are, as he says they ought to be, well known even in England, and that we want to know what he has to say on these questions, not what others have thought before him, who were far less competent to form an opinion than the editor and trans- lator of the Avesta.

may be laid before him! There is hardly one book
published nowadays which, if everything in it that is
not to the purpose were left out, could not be reduced
to half its size. If authors could make up their minds
to omit everything that is only meant to display their
learning, to exhibit the difficulties they had to overcome, or to call attention to the ignorance of their predecessors, many a volume of thirty sheets would col-
lapse into a pamphlet of fifty pages, though in that form
it would probably produce a much greater effect than
in its more inflated appearance.

Did the writers of the Old Testament borrow anything from the Egyptians, the Babylonians, the Persians, or the Indians, is a simple enough question. It
is a question that may be treated quite apart from any
theological theories; for the Old Testament, whatever
view the Jews may take of its origin, may surely be
regarded by the historian as a really historical book,
written at a certain time in the history of the world, in
a language then spoken and understood, and proclaiming certain facts and doctrines meant to be accepta-
ble and intelligible to the Jews, such as they were at
that time, an historical nation, holding a definite place
by the side of their more or less distant neighbors,
whether Egyptians, Assyrians, Persians, or Indians.
It is well known that we have in the language of the
New Testament the clear vestiges of Greek and Roman
influences, and if we knew nothing of the historical intercourse between those two nations and the writers of
the New Testament, the very expressions used by them
— not only their language, but their thoughts, their
allusions, illustrations, and similes — would enable us
to say that some historical contact had taken place be

tween the philosophers of Greece, the lawgivers of
Rome, and the people of Judea. Why, then, should
not the same question be asked with regard to more
ancient times? Why should there be any hesitation
in pointing out in the Old Testament an Egyptian
custom, or a Greek word, or a Persian conception?
If Moses was learned in all the wisdom of the Egyptians, nothing surely would stamp his writings as more
truly historical than traces of Egyptian influences that
might be discovered in his laws. If Daniel prospered
in the reign of Cyrus the Persian, every Persian word
that could be discovered in Daniel would be most
valuable in the eyes of a critical historian. The only
thing which we may fairly require in investigations of
this kind is that the facts should be clearly established.
The subject is surely an important one, — important
historically, quite apart from any theological consequences that may be supposed to follow. It is as important to find out whether the authors of the Old
Testament had come in contact with the language and
ideas of Babylon, Persia, or Egypt, as it is to know
that the Jews, at the time of our Lord's appearance,
had been reached by the rays of Greek and Roman
civilization, — that in fact our Lord, his disciples, and
many of his followers, spoke Greek as well as Hebrew
(i. e. Chaldee), and were no strangers to that sphere
of thought in which the world of the Gentiles, the
Greeks, and Romans had been moving for centuries.

Hints have been thrown out from time to time by
various writers that certain ideas in the Old Testament
might be ascribed to Persian influences, and be traced
back to the Zend-Avesta, the sacred writings of Zoroaster. Much progress has been made in the decipher-

ing of these ancient documents, since Anquetil Duperron brought the first instalment of MSS. from Bombay, and since the late Eugène Burnouf, in his " Commentaire sur le Yasna," succeeded in establishing the grammar and dictionary of the Zend language upon a safe basis. Several editions of the works of Zoroaster have been published in France, Denmark, and Germany; and after the labors of Spiegel, Westergaard, Haug, and others, it might be supposed that such a question as the influence of Persian ideas on the writers of the Old Testament might at last be answered either in the affirmative or in the negative. We were much pleased, therefore, on finding that Professor Spiegel, the learned editor and translator of the Avesta, had devoted a chapter of his last work, " Erân, das Land zwischen dem Indus und Tigris," to the problem in question. We read his chapter, " Avesta und die Genesis, oder die Beziehungen der Eranier zu den Semiten," with the warmest interest, and when we had finished it, we put down the book with the very exclamation with which we began our article.

We do not mean to say anything disrespectful to Professor Spiegel, a scholar brimful of learning, and one of the two or three men who know the Avesta by heart. He is likewise a good Semitic scholar, and knows enough of Hebrew to form an independent opinion on the language, style, and general character of the different books of the Old Testament. He brings together in his Essay a great deal of interesting information, and altogether would seem to be one of the most valuable witnesses to give evidence on the point in question. Yet suppose him for a moment in a court of justice where, as in a patent case, some great issue depends on the question whether certain ideas had first been enunciated by the author of Genesis or the author of the Avesta; suppose him subjected to a cross-examination by a brow-beating lawyer, whose business it is to disbelieve and make others disbelieve every assertion that the witness makes, and we are afraid the learned Professor would break down completely. Now it may be said that this is not the spirit in which learned inquiries should be conducted, that authors have a right to a certain respect, and may reckon on a certain amount of willingness on the part of their readers. Such a plea may, perhaps, be urged when all preliminary questions in a contest have been disposed of, when all the evidence has been proved to lie in one direction, and when even the most obstinate among the gentlemen of the jury feel that the verdict is as good as settled. But in a question like this, where everything is doubtful, or, we should rather say, where all the prepossessions are against the view which Dr. Spiegel upholds, it is absolutely necessary for a new witness to be armed from top to toe, to lay himself open to no attack, to measure his words, and advance step by step in a straight line to the point that has to be reached. A writer like Dr. Spiegel should know that he can expect no mercy; nay, he should himself wish for no mercy, but invite the heaviest artillery against the floating battery which he has launched into the troubled waters of Biblical criticism. If he feels that his case is not strong enough, the wisest plan surely is to wait, to accumulate new strength if possible, or, if no new evidence is forthcoming, to acknowledge openly that there is no use.

M. Bréal — who, in his interesting Essay " Hercule et Cacus," has lately treated the same problem, the influence of Persian ideas on the writers of the Old Testament — gives an excellent example of how a case of this kind should be argued. He begins with the apocryphal books, and he shows that the name of an evil spirit like Asmodeus, which occurs in Tobit, could be borrowed from Persia only. It is a name inexplicable in Hebrew, and it represents very closely the Parsi Eshem-dev, the Zend Aêshma daêva, the spirit of concupiscence, mentioned several times in the Avesta (Vendidad, c. 10), as one of the *deva* or evil spirits. Now this is the kind of evidence we want for the Old Testament. We can easily discover a French word in English, nor is it difficult to tell a Persian word in Hebrew. Are there any Persian words in Genesis, words of the same kind as Asmodeus in Tobit? No such evidence has been brought forward, and the only words we can think of which, if not Persian, may be considered of Aryan origin, are the names of such rivers as Tigris and Euphrates; and of countries such as Ophir and Havilah among the descendants of Shem, Javan, Meshech, and others among the descendants of Japhet. These names are probably foreign names, and as such naturally mentioned by the author of Genesis in their foreign form. If there are other words of Aryan or Iranian origin in Genesis, they ought to have occupied the most prominent place in Dr. Spiegel's pleading.

We now proceed, and we are again quite willing to admit that, even without the presence of Persian words, the presence of Persian ideas might be detected by careful analysis. No doubt this is a much more

delicate process, yet, as we can discover Jewish and
Christian ideas in the Koran, there ought to be no in-
surmountable difficulty in pointing out any Persian ingredients in Genesis, however disguised and assimilated.   Only, before we look for such ideas, it is
necessary to show the channel through which they
could possibly have flowed either from the Avesta into
Genesis, or from Genesis into the Avesta.   History
shows us clearly how Persian words and ideas could
have found their way into such late works as Tobit, or
even into the book of Daniel, whether he flourished in
the reign of Darius, or in the reign of Cyrus the
Persian.   But how did Persians and Jews come in
contact, previously to the age of Cyrus?   Dr. Spiegel
says that Zoroaster was born in Arran.   This name is
given by mediæval Mohammedan writers to the plain
washed by the Araxes, and was identified by Anquetil
Duperron with the name " Airyana vaëga," which the
Zend-Avesta gives to the first created land of Ormuzd.
The Parsis place this sacred country in the vicinity of
Atropatene, and it is clearly meant as the northern-
most country known to the author or authors of the
Zend-Avesta.   We think that Dr. Spiegel is right in
defending the geographical position assigned by tradition to Airyana vaëga, against modern theories that
would place it more eastward in the plain of Pamer,
nor do we hesitate to admit that the name (" Airyana
vaëga," i. e. the seed of the Aryan) might have been
changed into Arran.   We likewise acknowledge the
force of the arguments by which he shows that the
books now called Zend-Avesta were composed in the
eastern, and not in the western, provinces of the
Persian monarchy, though we are hardly prepared to

subscribe at once to his conclusion (p. 270) that, because Zoroaster is placed by the Avesta and by later traditions in Arran, or the western provinces, he could not possibly be the author of the Avesta, a literary production which would appear to belong exclusively to the eastern provinces. The very tradition to which Dr. Spiegel appeals represents Zoroaster as migrating from Arran to Balkh, to the court of Gustasp, the son of Lohrasp; and, as one tradition has as much value as another, we might well admit that the work of Zoroaster, as a religious teacher, began in Balkh, and from thence extended still further east. But admitting that Arran, the country washed by the Araxes, was the birthplace of Zoroaster, can we possibly follow Dr. Spiegel when he says, Arran seems to be identical with Haran, the starting-point of the Hebrew people?[1] Does he mean the names to be identical? Then how are the aspirate and the double r to be explained? how is it to be accounted for that the late mediæval corruption of Airyana vaêga, namely, Arran, should appear in Genesis? And if the dissimilarity of the two names is waived, is it possible in two lines to settle the much contested situation of Haran, and thus to determine the ancient watershed between the Semitic and Aryan nations? The Abbé Banier, more than a hun-

1 See Spiegel, Erân, p. 374. "Der Ausgangspunct des Hebräischen Volkes, auf den seine Geschichte selbst hinweist, ist Haran, welches Land mit Arran, d. L. Airyana vaêjscha identisch zu sein scheint." Professor Spiegel, in answer to my remarks, has declared that by Haran he did not mean the land of Haran, or more correctly Charan, where Terah died (supposed to be the same as the Greek Karjai), but Haran, the son of Terah, the father of Lot, who died in the land of his nativity, in Ur of the Chaldees (Genesis xi. 28). That some of the personal names in Genesis represent towns or places rather than individuals, is clear enough, but with regard to Haran, the son of Terah, the case is more than doubtful.

dred years ago, pointed out that Haran, whither Abraham repaired, was the metropolis of Sabism, and that Magism was praticed in Ur of the Chaldees ("Mythology explained by History,' vol. i. book iii. cap. 3), but the time for such vague identifications has surely passed. Dr. Spiegel having, as he believes, established the most ancient meeting-point between Abraham and Zoroaster, proceeds to argue that whatever ideas are shared in common by Genesis and the Avesta must be referred to that very ancient period when personal intercourse was still possible between Abraham and Zoroaster, the prophets of the Jews and the Iranians. Now here the counsel for the defense would remind Dr. Spiegel that Genesis was not the work of Abraham, nor, according to Dr. Spiegel's view, was Zoroaster the author of the Zend-Avesta; and that therefore the neighborly intercourse between Zoroaster and Abraham in the country of Arran had nothing to do with the ideas shared in common by Genesis and the Avesta. But even if we admitted, for argument's sake, that as Dr. Spiegel puts it, the Avesta contains Zoroastrian and Genesis Abrahamitic ideas, surely there was ample opportunity for Jewish ideas to find admission into what we call the Avesta, or for Iranian ideas to find admission into Genesis, after the date of Abraham and Zoroaster, and before the time when we find the first MSS. of Genesis and the Avesta. The Zend MSS. of the Avesta are very modern, so are the Hebrew MSS. of Genesis, which do not carry us beyond the tenth century after Christ. The text of the Avesta, however, can be checked by the Pehlevi translation, which was made under the Sassanian dynasty (226–651 A. D.), just as the text of Genesis can be checked by the Septuagint translation, which was made in the third century before Christ. Now, it is known that about the same time and in the same place — namely at Alexandria — where the Old Testament was rendered into Greek, the Avesta also was translated into the same language, so that we have at Alexandria in the third century B. C. a well established historical contact between the believers in Genesis and the believers in the Avesta, and an easy opening for that exchange of ideas which, according to Dr. Spiegel, could have taken place nowhere but in Arran, and at the time of Abraham and Zoroaster. It might be objected that this was wrangling for victory, and not arguing for truth, and that no real scholar would admit that the Avesta, in its original form, did not go back to a much earlier date than the third century before Christ. Yet, when such a general principle is to be laid down, that all that Genesis and the Avesta share in common must belong to a time before Abraham had started for Canaan, and Zoroaster for Balkh, other possible means of later intercourse should surely not be entirely lost sight of.

For what happens? The very first tradition that is brought forward as one common to both these ancient works — namely, that of the Four Ages of the World — is confessedly found in the later writings only of the Parsis, and cannot be traced back in its definite shape beyond the time of the Sassanians ("Erân," p. 275)[1]. Indications of it are said to be found in the

1 Professor Spiegel in his latest essay (1863) writes: "It is an error if Müller believes that the division into four ages cannot be traced in the ancient writings. The period of 12,000 years is mentioned several times, and it is easy to show that the Avesta conceives the distribution of that period into four ages exactly in the same manner as the later heroic legend, or

earlier writings, but these indications are extremely vague. But we must advance a step further, and after reading very carefully the three pages devoted to this subject by Dr. Spiegel, we must confess we see no similarity whatever on that point between Genesis and the Avesta. In Genesis, the Four Ages have never assumed the form of a theory, as in India, Persia, or perhaps in Greece. If we say that the period from Adam to Noah is the first, that from Noah to Abraham the second, that from Abraham to the death of Jacob the third, that beginning with the exile in Egypt the fourth, we are transferring our ideas to Genesis; but we cannot say that the writer of Genesis himself laid a peculiar stress on this fourfold division. The Parsis, on the contrary, have a definite system. According to them the world is to last 12,000 years. During the first period of 3,000 years, the world was created. During the second period Gayo-maratan, the first man, lived by himself, without suffering from the attacks of evil. During the third period of 3,000 years the war between good and evil, between Ormuzd and Ahriman, began with the utmost fierceness; and it will gradually abate during the fourth period of 3,000 years which is still to elapse before the final victory of good. Where here is the similarity between Genesis and the Avesta? We are referred by Dr. Spiegel to Dr. Windischmann's " Zoroastrian Studies," and to his discovery that there are ten generations between Adam and Noah, as there are ten generations between Yima and Thraêtaona; that there are twelve generations between Shem and Isaac, as there are twelve be-

_____

can so conceive it." All depends on chapter and verse in the Zend-Avesta where Dr. Spiegel can show that the four ages are definitely mentioned.

tween Thraêtaona and Manuskitra; and that there
are thirteen generations between Isaac and David, as
there are thirteen between Manuskitra and Zarathustra. What has the learned counsel for the defense to
say to this? First, that the name of Shem is put by
mistake for that of Noah. Secondly, that Yima, who
is here identified with Adam, is never represented in
the Avesta as the first man, but is preceded there
by numerous ancestors, and surrounded by numerous
subjects, who are not his offspring. Thirdly, that
in order to establish in Genesis three periods of
ten, twelve, and thirteen generations, it is necessary
to count Isaac, who clearly belongs to the third, as
a member of the second, so that in reality the
number of generations is the same in one only out of
the three periods, which surely proves nothing.[1] As to
any similarity between the *Four Yugas* of the Brahmans and the *Four Ages* of the Parsis, we can only
say that, if it exists, no one has as yet brought it out.
The Greeks, again, who are likewise said to share the
primitive doctrine of the Four Ages, believe really in
five, and not in four, and separate them in a manner
which does not in the least remind us of Hindu Yugas,
Hebrew patriarchs, or the battle between Ormuzd and
Ahriman.

We proceed to a second point — the Creation as related in Genesis and the Avesta. Here we certainly
find some curious coincidences. The world is created
in six days in Genesis, and in six periods in the Avesta,
which six periods together form one year. In Genesis

the creation ends with the creation of man, so it does in the Avesta. On all other points Dr. Spiegel admits the two accounts differ, but they are said to agree again in the temptation and the fall. As Dr. Spiegel has not given the details of the temptation and the fall from the Avesta, we cannot judge of the points which he considers to be borrowed by the Jews from the Persians; but if we consult M. Bréal, who has treated the same subject more fully in his "Hercule et Cacus," we find there no more than this, that the Dualism of the Avesta, the struggle between Ormuzd and Ahriman, or the principles of light and darkness, is to be considered as the distant reflex of the grand struggle between Indra, the god of the sky, and Vritra, the demon of night and darkness, which forms the constant burden of the hymns of the Rig-veda. In this view there is some truth, but we doubt whether it fully exhibits the vital principle of the Zoroastrian religion, which is founded on a solemn protest against the whole worship of the powers of nature invoked in the Vedas, and on the recognition of one supreme power, the God of Light, in every sense of the word — the spirit Ahura, who created the world and rules it, and defends it against the power of evil. That power of evil which in the most ancient portions of the Avesta has not yet received the name of "Ahriman" (i. e. angro mainyus), may afterwards have assumed some of the epithets which in an early period were bestowed on Vritra and other enemies of the bright gods, and among them, it may have assumed the name of serpent. But does it follow, because the principle of evil in the Avesta is called serpent, or "azhi dahâka," that therefore the serpent mentioned in the third chapter of Genesis must be borrowed from Persia? Neither in the Veda nor in the Avesta does the serpent ever assume that subtile and insinuating form which it wears in Genesis; and the curse pronounced on it, "to be cursed above all cattle, and above every beast of the field," is not in keeping with the relation of Vritra to Indra, or Ahriman to Ormuzd, who face each other almost as equals. In later books, such as 1 Chronicles xxi. 1, where Satan is mentioned as provoking David to number Israel (the very same provocation which in 2 Samuel xxiv. 1 is ascribed to the anger of the Lord moving David to number Israel and Judah), and in all the passages of the New Testament where the power of evil is spoken of as a person, we may admit the influence of Persian ideas and Persian expressions, though even here strict proof is by no means easy. As to the serpent in Paradise, it is a conception that might have sprung up among the Jews as well as among the Brahmans; and the serpent that beguiled Eve seems hardly to invite comparison with the much grander conceptions of the terrible power of Vritra and Ahriman in the Veda and Avesta.

Dr. Spiegel next discusses the similarity between the garden of Eden and the Paradise of the Zoroastrians, and though he admits that here again he relies chiefly on the Bundehesh, a work of the Sassanian period, he maintains that that work may well be compared to Genesis, because it contains none but really ancient traditions. We do not for a moment deny that this may be so, but in a case like the present, where everything depends on exact dates, we decline to listen to such a plea. We value Dr. Spiegel's translations from the Bundehesh most highly, and we believe with him (p. 283) that there is little doubt as to the Pishon being the Indus, and the Gihon the Jaxartes. The identification, too, of the Persian river-name Ranha (the Vedic Rasâ) with the Araxes, the name given by Herodotus (i. 202) to the Jaxartes, seems very ingenious and well established. But we should still like to know why and in what language the Indus was first called Pishon, and the Jaxartes, or, it may be, the Oxus, Gihon.

We next come to the two trees in the garden of Eden, the tree of knowledge and the tree of life. Dr. Windischmann has shown that the Iranians, too, were acquainted with two trees, one called " Gaokerena," bearing the white Haoma, the other called the Painless tree. We are told first that these two trees are the same as the one fig-tree out of which the Indians believe the world to have been created. Now, first of all, the Indians believed no such thing, and secondly, there is the same difference between one and two trees as there is between North and South. But we confess that until we know a good deal more about these two trees of the Iranians, we feel no inclination whatever to compare the Painless tree and the tree of knowledge of good and evil, though perhaps the white Haoma tree might remind us of the tree of life, considering that Haoma, as well as the Indian Soma, was supposed to give immortality to those who drank its juice. We likewise consider the comparison of the Cherubim who keep the way of the tree of life and the guardians of the Soma in the Veda and Avesta, as deserving attention, and we should like to see the etymological derivation of " Cherubim " from γρύψ, Greifen, and of " Seraphim " from the Sanskrit " sarpa," serpents, either confirmed or refuted.

The Deluge is not mentioned in the sacred writings of the Zoroastrians, nor in the hymns of the Rig-veda. It is mentioned, however, in one of the latest Bráhmanas, and the carefully balanced arguments of Burnouf, who considered the traditions of the Deluge as borrowed by the Indians from Semitic neighbours, seem to us to be strengthened, rather than weakened, by the isolated appearance of the story of the Deluge in this one passage out of the whole of the Vedic literature. Nothing, however, has yet been pointed out to force us to admit a Semitic origin for the story of the Flood, as told in the Satapatha-bráhmana, and afterwards repeated in the Mahábhárata and the Puránas: the number of days being really the only point on which the two accounts startle us by their agreement.

That Noah's ark rested upon the mountain of Ararat, and that Ararat may admit of a Persian etymology, is nothing to the point. The etymology itself is ingenious, but no more. The same remark applies to all the rest of Dr. Spiegel's arguments. Thraétaona, who has before been compared to Noah, divided his land among his three sons, and gave Iran to the youngest, an injustice which exasperated his brothers, who murdered him. Now it is true that Noah, too, had three sons, but here the similarity ends; for that Terah had three sons, and that one of them only, Abram, took possession of the land of promise, and that of the two sons of Isaac, the youngest became the heir, is again of no consequence for our immediate purpose, though it may remind Dr. Spiegel and others of the history of Thraétaona. We agree with Dr. Spiegel, that Zoroaster's character resembles most closely the true Semitic notion of a prophet. He is considered worthy of per-

some. intercourse with Ormuzd: he receives from Ormuzd every word, though not, as Dr. Spiegel says,
every letter of the law. But if Zoroaster was a real
character, so was Abraham, and their being like each
other proves in no way that they lived in the same
place, or at the same time, or that they borrowed
aught one from the other. What Dr. Spiegel says of
the Persian name of the Deity, "Ahura," is very
doubtful. Ahura, he says, as well as ahu, means
lord, and must be traced back to the root ah, the
Sanskrit as, which means to be, so that Ahura would
signify the same as Jehovah, "he who is." The root
"as" no doubt means to be, but it has that meaning
became it originally meant to breathe. From it, in its
original sense of breathing, the Hindus formed "asu,"
breath, and "asura," the name of God, whether it meant
the breathing one, or the giver of breath. This asura
became in Zend "ahura," and if it assumed the general
meaning of Lord, this is as much a secondary meaning as the meaning of demon or evil spirit, which asura
assumed in the later Sanskrit of the Brâhmanas.

After this, Dr. Spiegel proceeds to sum up his evidence. He has no more to say, but he believes that he
has proved the following points: a very early intercourse between Semitic and Aryan nations; a common
belief shared by both in a paradise situated near the
sources of the Oxus and Jaxartes; the dwelling together of Abraham and Zoroaster in Haran, Arran, or
Airyana vaêga. Semitic and Aryan nations, he tells
us, still live together in those parts of the world, and so
it was from the beginning. As the form of the Jewish
traditions comes nearer to the Persian than to the Indian traditions, we are asked to believe that these two

races lived in the closest contact before, from this ancient hearth of civilization, they started towards the West and the East — that is to say, before Abraham migrated to Canaan, and before India was peopled by the Brahmans.

We have given a fair account of Dr. Spiegel's arguments, and we need not say that we should have hailed with equal pleasure any solid facts by which to establish either the dependence of Genesis on the Zend-Avesta, or the dependence of the Zend-Avesta on Genesis. It would be absurd to resist facts where facts exist; nor can we imagine any reason why, if Abraham came into personal contact with Zoroaster, the Jewish patriarch should have learnt nothing from the Iranian prophet, or *vice versâ*. If such an intercourse could be established, it would but serve to strengthen the historical character of the books of the Old Testament, and would be worth more than all the elaborate theories that have been started on the purely miraculous origin of these books. But though we by no means deny that some more tangible points of resemblance may yet be discovered between the Old Testament and the Zend-Avesta, we must protest against having so interesting and so important a matter handled in such an unbusiness-like manner.

April, 1864.

VIII.

THE MODERN PARSIS.[1]

I.

It is not fair to speak of any religious sect by a name to which its members object. Yet the fashion of speaking of the followers of Zoroaster as Fire-worshippers is so firmly established that it will probably continue long after the last believers in Ormuzd have disappeared from the face of the earth. At the present moment, the number of the Zoroastrians has dwindled down so much that they hardly find a place in the religious statistics of the world. Berghaus in his "Physical Atlas" gives the following division of the human race according to religion : —

Buddhists	31.2	per cent.
Christians	30.7	"
Mohammedans	15.7	"
Brahmanists	13.4	"
Heathens	8.7	"
Jews	0.3	"

He nowhere states the number of the Fire-worshippers, nor does he tell us under what head they are comprised in his general computation. The difficulties

[1] *The Manners and Customs of the Parsees.* By Dadabhai Naoroji Esq. Liverpool, 1861.
The Parsee Religion. By Dadabhai Naoroji, Esq. Liverpool, 1861.

of a religious census are very great, particularly when
we have to deal with Eastern nations. About two
hundred years ago, travellers estimated the Gabars (as
they are called in Persia) at eighty thousand families,
or about 400,000 souls. At present the Parsis in
Western India amount to about 100,000, to which, if
we add 5,500 in Yezd and Kirman, we get a total of
105,500. The number of the Jews is commonly estimated at 3,600,000 ; and if they represent 0.3 per cent.
of mankind, the Fire-worshippers could not claim at
present more than about 0.01 per cent. of the whole
population of the earth. Yet there were periods in the
history of the world when the worship of Ormuzd
threatened to rise triumphant on the ruins of the temples of all other gods. If the battles of Marathon and
Salamis had been lost, and Greece had succumbed to
Persia, the state religion of the empire of Cyrus,
which was the worship of Ormuzd, might have become
the religion of the whole civilized world. Persia had
absorbed the Assyrian and Babylonian empires ; the
Jews were either in Persian captivity or under Persian
sway at home ; the sacred monuments of Egypt had
been mutilated by the hands of Persian soldiers. The
edicts of the great king, the king of kings, were sent
to India, to Greece, to Scythia, and to Egypt ; and if
"by the grace of Ahuramazda" Darius had crushed the
liberty of Greece, the purer faith of Zoroaster might
easily have superseded the Olympian fables. Again,
under the Sassanian dynasty (226–651 A. D.) the revived national faith of the Zoroastrians assumed such
rigor that Shapur II., like another Diocletian, could
aim at the extirpation of the Christian faith. The
sufferings of the persecuted Christians in the East

were as terrible as they had ever been in the West;
nor was it by the weapons of Roman emperors or by
the arguments of Christian divines that the fatal blow
was dealt to the throne of Cyrus and the altars of
Ormuzd. The power of Persia was broken at last by
the Arabs; and it is due to them that the religion of
Ormuzd, once the terror of the world, is now, and has
been for the last thousand years, a mere curiosity in the
eyes of the historian.

The sacred writings of the Zoroastrians, commonly
called the Zend-Avesta, have for about a century
occupied the attention of European scholars, and,
thanks to the adventurous devotion of Anquetil Duperron, and the careful researches of Rask, Burnouf,
Westergaard, Spiegel, and Haug, we have gradually
been enabled to read and interpret what remains of the
ancient language of the Persian religion. The problem was not an easy one, and had it not been for
the new light which the science of language has shed
on the laws of human speech, it would have been as
impossible to Burnouf as it was to Hyde, the celebrated
Professor of Hebrew and Arabic at Oxford, to interpret with grammatical accuracy the ancient remnants
of Zoroaster's doctrine. How that problem was solved
is well known to all who take an interest in the ad-
vancement of modern scholarship. It was as great an
achievement as the deciphering of the cuneiform edicts
of Darius; and no greater compliment could have been
paid to Burnouf and his fellow-laborers than that
scholars, without inclination to test their method, and
without leisure to follow these indefatigable pioneers
through all the intricate paths of their researches,
should have pronounced the deciphering of the ancient

Zend as well as of the ancient Persian of the Achæmenian period to be impossible, incredible, and next to miraculous.

While the scholars of Europe are thus engaged in disinterring the ancient records of the religion of Zoroaster, it is of interest to learn what has become of that religion in those few settlements where it is still professed by small communities. Though every religion is of real and vital interest in its earliest state only, yet its later development too, with all its misunderstandings, faults, and corruptions, offers many an instructive lesson to the thoughtful student of history. Here is a religion, one of the most ancient of the world, once the state religion of the most powerful empire, driven away from its native soil, deprived of political influence, without even the prestige of a powerful or enlightened priesthood, and yet professed by a handful of exiles—men of wealth, intelligence, and moral worth in Western India—with an unhesitating fervor such as is seldom to be found in larger religious communities. It is well worth the earnest endeavor of the philosopher and the divine to discover, if possible, the spell by which this apparently effete religion continues to command the attachment of the enlightened Parsis of India, and makes them turn a deaf ear to the allurements of the Brahmanic worship and the earnest appeals of Christian missionaries. We believe that to many of our readers the two pamphlets, lately published by a distinguished member of the Parsi community, Mr. Dadabhai Naoroji, Professor of Guzerati at University College, London, will open many problems of a more than passing interest. One is a Paper read before the Liverpool Philomathic Society, "On

the Manners and Customs of the Parsees ;" the other
is a Lecture delivered before the Liverpool Literary
and Philosophical Society, "On the Parsee Religion."

In the first of these pamphlets, we are told that the
small community of Parsis, in Western India, is at the
present moment divided into two parties, the Conservatives and the Liberals. Both are equally attached to
the faith of their ancestors, but they differ from each
other in their modes of life: the Conservatives cling-
ing to all that is established and customary, however
absurd and mischievous ; the Liberals desiring to throw
off the abuses of former ages, and to avail themselves,
as much as is consistent with their religion and their
oriental character, of the advantages of European civilization. " If I say," writes our informant, " that the
Parsees use tables, knives and forks, etc., for taking
their dinners, it would be true with regard to one portion, and entirely untrue with regard to another. In
one house you see in the dining-room the dinner table
furnished with all the English apparatus for its agreeable
purposes ; next door, perhaps, you see the gentleman
perfectly satisfied with his primitive good old mode of
squatting on a piece of mat, with a large brass or
copper plate (round, and of the size of an ordinary
tray) before him, containing all the dishes of his dinner, spread on it in small heaps, and placed upon a stool
about two or three inches high, with a small tinned
copper cup at his side for his drinks, and his fingers for
his knives and forks. He does this, not because he
cannot afford to have a table, etc., but because he
would not have them in preference to his ancestral
mode of life, or, perhaps, the thought has not occurred
to him that he need have anything of the kind."

Instead, therefore of giving a general description of Parsi life at present, Mr. Dadabhai Naoroji gives us two distinct accounts — first of the old, secondly of the new school. He describes the incidents in the daily life of a Parsi of the old school, from the moment he gets out of bed to the time of his going to rest, and the principal ceremonies from the hour of his birth to the hour of his burial. Although we can gather from the tenor of his writings that the author himself belongs to the Liberals, we must give him credit for the fairness with which he describes the party to which he is opposed. There is no sneer, no expression of contempt anywhere, even when, as in the case of the Nirang, the temptation must have been considerable. What this Nirang is we may best state in the words of the writer:

" The Nirang is the urine of cow, ox, or she-goat, and the rubbing of it over the face and hands is the second thing a Parsee does after getting out of bed. Either before applying the Nirang to the face and hands, or while it remains on the hands after being applied, he should not touch anything directly with his hands ; but, in order to wash out the Nirang, he either asks somebody else to pour water on his hands, or resorts to the device of taking hold of the pot through the intervention of a piece of cloth, such as a handkerchief or his Sudrá, i. e. his *blouse*. He first pours water on one hand, then takes the pot in that hand and washes his other hand, face, and feet."

Strange as this process of purification may appear, it becomes perfectly disgusting when we are told that women, after childbirth, have not only to undergo this sacred ablution, but have actually to drink a little of the Nirang, and that the same rite is imposed on chil-

dren at the time of their investiture with the Sudrá and
Kusti, the budges of the Zoroastrian faith. The Liberal
party have completely surrendered this objectionable
custom, but the old school still keep it up, though their
faith, as Dadabhai Naoroji says, in the efficacy of Nirang to drive away Satan may be shaken. "The Reformers," our author writes, "maintain, that there is
no authority whatever in the original books of Zar-
thosht for the observance of this dirty practice, but
that it is altogether a later introduction. The old
adduce the authority of the works of some of the
priests of former days, and say the practice ought to
be observed. They quote one passage from the Zend-
Avesta corroborative of their opinion, which their opponents deny as at all bearing upon the point." Here,
whatever our own feelings may be about the Nirang,
truth obliges us to side with the old school, and if our
author had consulted the ninth Fasgard of the Vendidad
(page 120, line 21, in Brockhaus' edition), he would
have seen that both the drinking and the rubbing in of
the so-called " Gaomaezo "— i. e. Nirang —are clearly
enjoined by Zoroaster in certain purificatory rites.
The custom rests, therefore, not only on the authority
of a few priests of former days, but on the *ipsissima
verba* of the Zend-Avesta, the revealed word of Ormuzd ; and if, as Dadabhai Naoroji writes, the Reformers of the day will not go beyond abolishing and dis-
avowing the ceremonies that have no authority in the
original Zend-Avesta, we are afraid that the washing
with Nirang, and even the drinking of it, will have to
be maintained. A pious Parsi has to say his prayers
sixteen times at least every day — first on getting out
of bed, then during the Nirang operation, again when

he takes his bath, again when he cleanses his teeth, and when he has finished his morning ablutions. The same prayers are repeated whenever, during the day, a Parsi has to wash his hands. Every meal — and there are three — begins and ends with prayer, besides the grace, and before going to bed the work of the day is closed by a prayer. The most extraordinary thing is that none of the Parsis — not even their priests — understand the ancient language in which these prayers are composed. We must quote the words of our author, who is himself of the priestly caste, and who says : —

" All prayers, on every occasion, are said, or rather recited, in the old original Zend language, neither the reciter nor the people around intended to be edified, understanding a word of it. There is no pulpit among the Parsees. On several occasions, as on the occasion of the Ghumbars, the bimestral holidays, the third day's ceremonies for the dead, and other religious or special holidays, there are assemblages in the temple ; prayers are repeated, in which more or less join, but there is no discourse in the vernacular of the people. Ordinarily, every one goes to the fire-temple whenever he likes, or, if it is convenient to him, recites his prayers himself, and as long as he likes, and gives, if so inclined, something to the priests to pray for him."

In another passage our author says : —

" Far from being the teachers of the true doctrines and duties of their religion, the priests are generally the most bigoted and superstitious, and exercise much injurious influence over the women especially, who, until lately, received no education at all. The priests have, however, now begun to feel their degraded posi-tion. Many of them, if they can do so, bring up their sons in any other profession but their own. There are, perhaps, a dozen among the whole body of professional priests who lay claim to a knowledge of the Zend-Avesta; but the only respect in which they are superior to their brethren is, that they have learnt the meanings of the words of the books as they are taught, without knowing the language, either philosophically or grammatically."

Mr. Dadabhai Naoroji proceeds to give a clear and graphic description of the ceremonies to be observed at the birth and the investiture of children, at the betrothal of children, at marriages and at funerals; and he finally discusses some of the distinguishing features of the national character of the Parsis. The Parsis are monogamists. They do not eat anything cooked by a person of another religion; they object to beef, pork, or ham. Their priesthood is hereditary. None but the son of a priest can be a priest, but it is not obligatory for the son of a priest to take orders. The high-priest is called Dustoor, the others are called Mobed.

The principal points for which the Liberals among the Parsis are, at the present moment, contending, are the abolition of the filthy purifications by means of Nirang, the reduction of the large number of obligatory prayers; the prohibition of early betrothal and marriage; the suppression of extravagance at weddings and funerals; the education of women, and their admission into general society. A society has been formed, called " the Rahanumaee Mazdiashna," i. e. the Guide of the Worshippers of God. Meetings are held, speeches made, tracts distributed. A counter society, too, has been started called " the True Guides;" and we readily believe what Mr. Dadabhai Naoroji tells us — that, as in Europe, so in India, the Reformers have found themselves strengthened by the intolerant bigotry and the weakness of the arguments of their opponents. The Liberals have made considerable progress, but their work is as yet but half done, and they will never be able to carry out their religious and social reforms successfully, without first entering on a critical study of the Zend-Avesta, to which, as yet, they profess to appeal as the highest authority in matters of faith, law, and morality.

We propose, in another article, to consider the state of religion among the Parsis of the present day.

August, 1862.

II.

THE so-called Fire-worshippers certainly do not worship the fire, and they naturally object to a name which seems to place them on a level with mere idolaters. All they admit is that in their youth they are taught to face some luminous object while worshipping God (p. 7), and that they regard the fire, like other great natural phenomena, as an emblem of the Divine power (p. 26). But they assure us that they never ask assistance or blessings from an unintelligent material object, nor is it even considered necessary to turn the face to any emblem whatever in praying to Ormuzd. The most honest, however, among the Parsis, and those who would most emphatically protest against the idea of their ever paying divine honors to the sun or the fire, admit the existence of some kind of national instinct — an indescribable awe felt by every Parsi with regard to light and fire. The fact that the Parsis are the only Eastern people who entirely abstain from smoking is very significant; and we know that most of them would rather not blow out a candle, if they could help it. It is difficult to analyze such a feeling, but it seems, in some respects, similar to that which many Christians have about the cross. They do not worship the cross, but they have peculiar feelings of reverence for it, and it is intimately connected with some of their most sacred rites.

But although most Parsis would be very ready to tell us what they do not worship, there are but few who could give a straightforward answer if asked what they do worship and believe. Their priests, no doubt, would say that they worship Ormuzd and believe in Zoroaster, his prophet; and they would appeal to the Zend-Avesta, as containing the Word of God, revealed by Ormuzd to Zoroaster. If more closely pressed, however, they would have to admit that they cannot understand one word of the sacred writings in which they profess to believe, nor could they give any reason why they believe Zoroaster to have been a true prophet, and not an impostor. "As a body," says Mr. Dadabhai Naoroji, "the priests are not only ignorant of the duties and objects of their own profession, but are entirely uneducated, except that they are able to read and write, and that, also, often very imperfectly. They do not understand a single word of their prayers and recitations, which are all in the old Zend language."

What, then, do the laity know about religion? What makes the old teaching of Zoroaster so dear to them that, in spite of all differences of opinion among them-

selves, young and old seem equally determined never
to join any other religious community? Incredible as
it may sound, we are told by the best authority, by an
enlightened yet strictly orthodox Parsi, that there is
hardly a man or a woman who could give an account of
the faith that is in them. "The whole religious education of a Parsi child consists in preparing by rote
a certain number of prayers in Zend, without understanding a word of them — the knowledge of the doctrines of their religion being left to be picked up from
casual conversation." A Parsi, in fact, hardly knows
what his faith is. The Zend-Avesta is to him a sealed
book: and though there is a Gujerati translation of it,
that translation is not made from the original, but from
a Pehlevi paraphrase, nor is it recognized by the priests
as an authorized version. Till about five-and-twenty
years ago, there was no book from which a Parsi of an
inquiring mind could gather the principles of his religion. At that time, and, as it would seem, chiefly in
order to counteract the influence of Christian missionaries, a small Dialogue was written in Gujerati — a
kind of Catechism, giving, in the form of questions and
answers, the most important tenets of Parsiism. We
shall quote some passages from this Dialogue, as translated by Mr. Dadabhai Naoroji. The subject of it is
thus described: —

A few Questions and Answers to acquaint the Children of
the holy Zarthosti Community with the Subject of the
Mazdiasnee Religion, i. e. the Worship of God.

Question. Whom do we, of the Zarthosti community,
believe in?
Answer. We believe in only one God, and do not
believe in any besides Him.

Q. Who is that one God?

A. The God who created the heavens, the earth, the angels, the stars, the sun, the moon, the fire, the water, or all the four elements, and all things of the two worlds; that God we believe in. Him we worship, him we invoke, him we adore.

Q. Do we not believe in any other God?

A. Whoever believes in any other God but this, is an infidel, and shall suffer the punishment of hell.

Q. What is the form of our God?

A. Our God has neither face nor form, color nor shape, nor fixed place. There is no other like him. He is himself singly such a glory that we cannot praise or describe him; nor our mind comprehend him.

So far, no one could object to this Catechism, and it must be clear that the Dualism, which is generally mentioned as the distinguishing feature of the Persian religion — the belief in two Gods, Ormuzd, the principle of good, and Ahriman, the principle of evil — is not countenanced by the modern Parsis. Whether it exists in the Zend-Avesta is another question, which, however, cannot be discussed at present.[1]

The Catechism continues: —

Q. What is our religion?

A. Our religion is " Worship of God."

Q. Whence did we receive our religion?

A. God's true prophet — the true Zurthost (Zoroaster) Asphantamân Anoshirwân — brought the religion to us from God.

Here it is curious to observe that not a single question is asked us to the claim of Zoroaster to be considered a true prophet. He is not treated as a divine being, nor even as the son of Ormuzd. Plato, indeed, speaks of Zoroaster as the son of Oromazes ("Alc." i. p. 122 a), but this is a mistake, not countenanced, as far as we are aware, by any of the Parsi writings, whether ancient or modern. With the Parsis, Zoroaster is simply a wise man, a prophet favored by God, and admitted into God's immediate presence; but all this, on his own showing only, and without any supernatural credentials, except some few miracles recorded of him in books of doubtful authority. This shows, at all events, how little the Parsis have been exposed to controversial discussions; for as this is so weak a point in their system that it would have invited the attacks of every opponent, we may be sure that the Dasturs would have framed some argument in defense, if such defense had ever been needed.

The next extract from the Catechism treats of the canonical books:—

Q. What religion has our prophet brought us from God?

A. The disciples of our prophet have recorded in several books that religion. Many of these books were destroyed during Alexander's conquest; the remainder of the books were preserved with great care and respect by the Sassanian kings. Of these again, the greater portion were destroyed at the Mohammedan conquest by Khalif Omar, so that we have now very few books remaining; namely, the Vendidad, the Yazashné, the Vispered, the Khordeh Avesta, the Vistasp Nusk, and a few Pehlevi books. Resting our faith upon these few books, we now remain devoted to our good Mazdiashan religion. We consider these books as heavenly books, because God sent the tidings of these books to us through the holy Zurthost.

Here, again, we see theological science in its infancy. " We consider these books as heavenly books because God sent the tidings of these books to us through the holy Zurthost," is not very powerful logic. It would have been more simple to say, " We consider them heavenly books because we consider them heavenly books." However, whether heavenly or not, these few books exist. They form the only basis of the Zoroastrian religion, and the principal source from which it is possible to derive any authentic information as to its origin, its history, and its real character.

That the Parsis are of a tolerant character with regard to such of their doctrines as are not of vital importance, may be seen from the following extract : —

Q. Whose descendants we are ?

A. Of Gayomars. By his progeny was Persia populated.

Q. Was Gayomars the first man ?

A. According to our religion he was so, but the wise men of our community, of the Chinese, the Hindus, and several other nations, dispute the assertion, and say that there was human population on the earth before Gayomars.

The moral precepts which are embodied in this Catechism do the highest credit to the Parsis : —

Q. What commands has God sent us through his prophet, the exalted Zurthost ?

A. To know God as one; to know the prophet, the exalted Zerthost, as the true prophet; to believe the religion and the Avesta brought by him as true beyond all manner of doubt; to believe in the goodness of God; not to disobey any of the commands of the Mazdiasnn religion; to avoid evil deeds; to exert oneself in good deeds; to pray five times in the day; to believe on the reckoning and justice on the fourth morning after death; to hope for heaven and to fear hell; to consider doubtless the day of general destruction and resurrection; to remember always that God has done what he willed, and shall do what he wills; to face some luminous object while worshipping God.

Then follow several paragraphs which are clearly directed against Christian missionaries, and more particularly against the doctrine of vicarious sacrifice and prayer : —

"Some deceivers [the Catechism says], with the view of acquiring exaltation in this world, have set themselves up as prophets, and, going among the laboring and ignorant people, have persuaded them that, 'If you commit sin, I shall intercede for you, I shall plead for you, I shall save you,' and thus deceive them; but the wise among the people know the deceit."

This clearly refers to Christian missionaries, but whether Roman Catholic or Protestant is difficult to say. The answer given by the Parsis is curious and significant : —

"If any one commit sin," they reply, "under the belief that he shall be saved by somebody, both the deceiver as well as the deceived shall be damned to the day of Rastâ Khez. . . . . There is no savior. In the other world you shall receive the return according to your actions. . . . . Your savior is your deeds, and God himself. He is the pardoner and the giver. If you repent your sins and reform, and if the Great Judge consider you worthy of pardon, or would be merciful to you, He alone can and will save you."

It would be a mistake to suppose that the whole doctrine of the Parsis is contained in the short Guzerati Catechism, translated by Mr. Dadabhai Naoroji; still less can it be comprised in the fragmentary extracts here given. Their sacred writings, the Yasna, Vispered, and Vendidad, the productions of much earlier ages, contain many ideas, both religious and mythological, which belong to the past, to the childhood of our race, and which no educated Parsi could honestly profess to believe in now. This difficulty of reconciling the more enlightened faith of the present generation with the mythological phraseology of their old sacred writings is solved by the Parsis in a very simple manner. They do not, like Roman Catholics, prohibit the reading of the Zend-Avesta; nor do they, like Protestants, encourage a critical study of their sacred texts. They simply ignore the originals of their sacred writings. They repeat them in their prayers without attempting to understand them, and they acknowledge the insufficiency of every translation of the Zend-Avesta that has yet been made, either in Pehlevi, Sanskrit, Guzerati, French, or German. Each Parsi has to pick up his religion as best he may. Till lately, even the Catechism did not form a necessary part of a child's religious education. Thus the religious belief of the present Parsi communities is reduced to two or three fundamental doctrines; and these, though professedly resting on the teaching of Zoroaster, receive their real sanction from a much higher authority. A Parsi believes in one God, to whom he addresses his prayers. His morality is comprised in these words, — pure thoughts, pure words, pure deeds. Believing in the punishment of vice and the reward of virtue, he trusts for pardon to the mercy of God. There is a charm, no doubt, in so short a creed; and if the whole of Zoroaster's teaching were confined to this, there would be some truth in what his followers say of their religion, namely, that "it is for all, and not for any particular nation."

If now we ask again, how it is that neither Christians, nor Hindus, nor Muhammedans have had any considerable success in converting the Parsis, and why even the more enlightened members of that small community, though fully aware of the many weak points of their own theology, and deeply impressed with the excellence of the Christian religion, morals, and general civilization, scorn the idea of ever migrating from the sacred ruins of their ancient faith, we are able to discover some reasons; though they are hardly sufficient to account for so extraordinary a fact.

First, the very compactness of the modern Parsi creed accounts for the tenacity with which the exiles of Western India cling to it. A Parsi is not troubled with many theological problems or difficulties. Though he professes a general belief in the sacred writings of

Zoroaster, he is not asked to profess any belief in the stories incidentally mentioned in the Zend-Avesta. If it is said in the Yasna that Zoroaster was once visited by Homa, who appeared before him in a brilliant supernatural body, no doctrine is laid down as to the exact nature of Homa. It is said that Homa was worshipped by certain ancient sages, Vivanhvat, Athwya, and Thrita, and that, as a reward for their worship, great heroes were born as their sons. The fourth who worshipped Homa was Pourushaspa, and he was rewarded by the birth of his son Zoroaster. Now the truth is, that Homa is the same as the Sanskrit Soma, well known from the Veda as an intoxicating beverage used at the great sacrifices, and afterwards raised to the rank of a deity. The Parsis are fully aware of this, but they do not seem in the least disturbed by the occurrence of such "fables and endless genealogies." They would not be shocked if they were told, what is a fact, that most of these old wives' fables have their origin in the religion which they most detest, the religion of the Veda, and that the heroes of the Zend-Avesta are the same who, with slightly changed names, appear again as Jemshid, Feridun, Gershâsp, etc., in the epic poetry of Firdusi.

Another fact which accounts for the attachment of the Parsis to their religion is its remote antiquity and its former glory. Though age has little to do with truth, the length of time for which any system has lasted seems to offer a vague argument in favor of its strength. It is a feeling which the Parsi shares in common with the Jew and the Brahman, and which even the Christian missionary appeals to when confronting the systems of later prophets.

Thirdly, it is felt by the Parsis that in changing their religion, they would not only relinquish the heir-loom of their remote forefathers, but of their own fathers; and it is felt as a dereliction of filial piety to give up what was most precious to those whose memory is most precious and almost sacred to themselves.

If in spite of all this, many people, most competent to judge, look forward with confidence to the conversion of the Parsis, it is because, in the most essential points, they have already, though unconsciously, approached as near as possible to the pure doctrines of Christianity. Let them but read the Zend-Avesta, in which they profess to believe, and they will find that their faith is no longer the faith of the Yasna, the Vendidad, and the Vispered. As historical relics, these works, if critically interpreted, will always retain a prominent place in the great library of the ancient world. As oracles of religious faith, they are defunct, and a mere anachronism in the age in which we live.

On the other hand, let missionaries read their Bible, and let them preach that Christianity which once conquered the world,—the genuine and unshackled gospel of Christ and the Apostles. Let them respect native prejudices, and be tolerant with regard to all that can be tolerated in a Christian community. Let them consider that Christianity is not a gift to be pressed on unwilling minds, but the highest of all privileges which natives can receive at the hands of their present rulers. Natives of independent and honest character cannot afford at present to join the ranks of converts without losing that true caste which no man ought to lose, namely, self-respect. They are driven to prop up their tottering religions, rather than profess a faith which seems dictated to them by their conquerors. Such feelings ought to be respected. Finally, let missionaries study the sacred writings on which the faith of the Parsis is professedly founded. Let them examine the bulwarks which they mean to overthrow. They will find them less formidable from within than from without. But they will also discover that they rest on a foundation which ought never to be touched,—a faith in one God, the Creator, the Ruler, and the Judge of the world.

August, 1843.

IX.

BUDDHISM.[1]

IF the words of St. Paul, "Prove all things, hold fast that which is good," may be supposed to refer to spiritual things, and, more especially, to religious doctrines, it must be confessed that few only, whether theologians or laymen, have ever taken to heart the Apostle's command. How many candidates for holy orders are there who could give a straightforward answer if asked to enumerate the principal religions of the world, or to state the names of their founders, and the titles of the works which are still considered by millions of human beings as the sacred authorities for their religious belief? To study such books as the Koran of the Mohammedans, the Zend-Avesta of the Parsis, the Kings of the Confucians, the Tao-te-King of the Taoists, the Vedas of the Brahmans, the Tripitaka of the Buddhists, the Sûtras of the Jains, or the Granth of the Sikhs, would be considered by many mere waste of time. Yet St. Paul's command is very clear and simple; and to maintain that it referred to the heresies of his own time only, or to the philosophical systems of the Greeks and Romans, would be to narrow

[1] Le Bouddha et sa Religion. Par J. Barthélemy Saint-Hilaire, Membre de l'Institut. Paris. 1860.

the horizon of the Apostle's mind, and to destroy the general applicability of his teaching to all times and to all countries. Many will ask what possible good could be derived from the works of men who must have been either deceived or deceivers, nor would it be difficult to quote some passages in order to show the utter absurdity and worthlessness of the religious books of the Hindus and Chinese. But this was not the spirit in which the Apostle of the Gentiles addressed himself to the Epicureans and Stoics, nor is this the feeling with which a thoughtful Christian and a sincere believer in the divine government of the world is likely to rise from a perusal of any of the books which he knows to be or to have been the only source of spiritual light and comfort to thousands and thousands among the dwellers on earth.

Many are the advantages to be derived from a careful study of other religions, but the greatest of all is that it teaches us to appreciate more truly what we possess in our own. When do we feel the blessings of our own country more warmly and truly than when we return from abroad? It is the same with regard to religion. Let us see what other nations have had and still have in the place of religion; let us examine the prayers, the worship, the theology even of the most highly civilized races,—the Greeks, the Romans, the Hindus, the Persians,—and we shall then understand more thoroughly what blessings are vouchsafed to us in being allowed to breathe from the first breath of life the pure air of a land of Christian light and knowledge. We are too apt to take the greatest blessings as matters of course, and even religion forms no exception. We have done so little to gain our religion, we have suffered so little in the cause of truth, that however highly we prize our own Christianity, we never prize it highly enough until we have compared it with the religions of the rest of the world.

This, however, is not the only advantage; and we think that M. Barthélemy Saint-Hilaire has formed too low an estimate of the benefits to be derived from a thoughtful study of the religions of mankind when he writes of Buddhism. " Lo seul, mais immense service que le Bouddhisme puisse nous rendre, c'est par son triste contraste de nous faire apprécier mieux encore la valeur inestimable de nos croyances en nous montrant tout ce qu'il en coûte à l'humanité qui ne les partage point." This is not all. If a knowledge of other countries, and a study of the manners and customs of foreign nations, teach us to appreciate what we have at home, they likewise form the best cure of that national conceit and want of sympathy with which we are too apt to look on all that is strange and foreign. The feeling which led the Hellenic race to divide the whole world into Greeks and Barbarians is so deeply engrained in human nature that not even Christianity has been able altogether to remove it. Thus when we cast our first glance into the labyrinth of the religions of the world, all seems to us darkness, self-deceit, and vanity. It sounds like a degradation of the very name of religion to apply it to the wild ravings of Hindu Yogins or the blank blasphemies of Chinese Buddhists. But as we slowly and patiently wend our way through the dreary prisons, our own eyes seem to expand, and we perceive a glimmer of light where all was darkness at first. We learn to understand the saying of one who more than anybody had a right to speak with authority

on this subject, that "there is no religion which does
not contain a spark of truth." Those who would limit
the riches of God's goodness and forbearance and long
suffering, and would hand over the largest portion of
the human race to inevitable perdition, have never adduced a tittle of evidence from the gospel or from any
other trustworthy source in support of so unhallowed a
belief. They have generally appealed to the devilries
and orgies of heathen worship; they have quoted the
blasphemies of oriental Sufis and the immoralities
sanctioned by the successors of Mohammed; but they
have seldom, if ever, endeavored to discover the true
and original character of the strange forms of faith and
worship which they call the work of the devil. If the
Indians had formed their notions of Christianity from
the soldiers of Cortez and Pizarro, or if the Hindus had
studied the principles of Christian morality in the lives
of Clive and Warren Hastings; or, to take a less extreme case, if a Mohammedan, settled in England,
were to test the practical working of Christian charity
by the spirit displayed in the journals of our religious
parties, their notions of Christianity would be about
as correct as the ideas which thousands of educated
Christians entertain of the diabolical character of
heathen religion. Even Christianity has been de-
praved into Jesuitism and Mormonism, and if we, as
Protestants, claim the right to appeal to the gospel as
the only test by which our faith is to be judged, we
must grant a similar privilege to Mohammedans and
Buddhists, and to all who possess a written and, as they
believe, revealed authority for the articles of their faith.

But though no one is likely to deny the necessity of
studying each religion in its most ancient form and

from its original documents, before we venture to pronounce our verdict, the difficulties of this task are such
that in them more than in anything else, must be
sought the cause why so few of our best thinkers and
writers have devoted themselves to a critical and historical study of the religions of the world. All important religions have sprung up in the East. Their
sacred books are written in Eastern tongues, and some
of them are of such ancient date that those even who
profess to believe in them, admit that they are unable
to understand them without the help of translations and
commentaries. Until very lately the sacred books of
three of the most important religions, those of the
Brahmans, the Buddhists, and the Parsis, were totally
unknown in Europe. It was one of the most important results of the study of Sanskrit, or the ancient
language of India, that through it the key, not only to
the sacred books of the Brahmans, the Vedas, but likewise to those of the Buddhists and Zoroastrians, was recovered. And nothing shows more strikingly the rapid
progress of Sanskrit scholarship than that even Sir
William Jones, whose name has still, with many, a
more familiar sound than the names of Colebrook,
Burnouf, and Lassen, should have known nothing of
the Vedas; that he should never have read a line of
the canonical books of the Buddhists, and that he actually expressed his belief that Buddha was the same
as the Teutonic deity Wodan or Odin, and Sâkya,
another name of Buddha, the same as Shishac, king of
Egypt. The same distinguished scholar never perceived the intimate relationship between the language
of the Zend-Avesta and Sanskrit, and he declared the
whole of the Zoroastrian writings to be modern for-
geries.

Even at present we are not yet in possession of a complete edition, much less of any trustworthy translation, of the Vedas; we only possess the originals of a few books of the Buddhist canon; and though the text of the Zend-Avesta has been edited in its entirety, its interpretation is beset with greater difficulties than that of the Vedas or the Tripitaka. A study of the ancient religions of China, those of Confucius and Laotse, presupposes an acquaintance with Chinese, a language which it takes a life to learn thoroughly; and even the religion of Mohammed, though more accessible than any other Eastern religion, cannot be fully examined except by a master of Arabic. It is less surprising, therefore, than it might at first appear, that a comprehensive and scholarlike treatment of the religions of the world should still be a desideratum. Scholars who have gained a knowledge of the language, and thereby free access to original documents, find so much work at hand which none but themselves can do, that they grudge the time for collecting and arranging, for the benefit of the public at large, the results which they have obtained. Nor need we wonder that critical historians should rather abstain from the study of the religions of antiquity than trust to mere translations and second-hand authorities.

Under these circumstances we feel all the more thankful if we meet with a writer like M. Barthélemy Saint-Hilaire, who has acquired a knowledge of Eastern languages sufficient to enable him to consult original texts and to control the researches of other scholars, and who at the same time commands that wide view of the history of human thought which enables him to assign to each system its proper place, to perceive its most salient features, and to distinguish between what is really important and what is not, in the lengthy lucubrations of ancient poets and prophets. M. Barthélemy Saint-Hilaire is one of the most accomplished scholars of France; and his reputation as the translator of Aristotle has made us almost forget that the Professor of Greek Philosophy at the Collège de France[1] is the same as the active writer in the "Globe" of 1827, and the "National" of 1830; the same who signed the protest against the July "ordonnances," and who in 1848 was Chief Secretary of the Provisional Government. If such a man takes the trouble to acquire a knowledge of Sanskrit, and to attend, in the same college where he was professor, the lectures of his own colleague, the late Eugène Burnouf, his publications on Hindu philosophy and religion will naturally attract a large amount of public interest. The Sanskrit scholar by profession works and publishes chiefly for the benefit of other Sanskrit scholars. He is satisfied with bringing to light the ore which he has extracted by patient labor from among the dusty MSS. of the East India House. He seldom takes the trouble to separate the metal from the ore, to purify or to strike it into current coin. He is but too often apt to forget no lasting addition is ever made to the treasury of human knowledge unless the results of special research are translated into the universal language of science, and rendered available to every person of intellect and education. A division of labor seems most conducive to this end. We want a class of in-

[1] M. Barthélemy Saint-Hilaire resigned the chair of Greek literature at the Collège de France after the coup d'état of 1851, declining to take the oath of allegiance to the existing government.

terpreters, men such as M. Barthélemy Saint-Hilaire, who are fully competent to follow and to control the researches of professional students, and who at the same time have not forgotten the language of the world.

In his work on Buddhism, of which a second edition has just appeared, M. Barthélemy Saint-Hilaire has undertaken to give to the world at large the really trustworthy and important results which have been obtained by the laborious researches of oriental scholars, from the original documents of that interesting and still mysterious religion. It was a task of no ordinary difficulty, for although these researches are of very recent date, and belong to a period of Sanskrit scholarship posterior to Sir W. Jones and Colebrook, yet such is the amount of evidence brought together by the combined industry of Hodgson, Turnour, Csoma de Körös, Stanislas Julien, Foucaux, Fausböll, Spence Hardy, but above all, of the late Eugène Burnouf, that it required no common patience and discrimination to compose from such materials so accurate, and at the same time so lucid and readable a book on Buddhism as that which we owe to M. Barthélemy Saint-Hilaire. The greater part of it appeared originally in the " Journal des Savants," the time-honored organ of the French Academy, which counts on its staff the names of Cousin, Flourens, Villemain, Biot, Mignet, Littré, etc.. and admits as contributors sixteen only of the most illustrious members of that illustrious body, *la crème de la crème.*

Though much had been said and written about Buddhism, — enough to frighten priests by seeing themselves anticipated in auricular confession, beads, and tonsure by the Lamas of Thibet,[1] and to discomfort philosophers by finding themselves outbid in positivism and nihilism by the inmates of Chinese monasteries, — the real beginning of an historical and critical study of the doctrines of Buddha dates from the year 1824. In that year Mr. Hodgson announced the fact that the original documents of the Buddhist canon had been preserved in Sanskrit in the monasteries of Nepal. Before that time our information on Buddhism had been derived at random from China, Japan, Burmah, Thibet, Mongolia, and Tartary; and though it was known that the Buddhist literature in all these countries professed itself to be derived, directly or indirectly, from India, and that the technical terms of that religion, not excepting the very name of Buddha, had their etymology in Sanskrit only, no hope was entertained that the originals of these various translations could ever be recovered. Mr. Hodgson, who settled in Nepal in 1821, as political resident of the East India Company, and whose eyes were always open, not only to the natural history of that little-explored country, but likewise to its antiquities, its languages, and traditions, was not long before he discovered that his friends, the priests of Nepal, possessed a complete literature of their own. That literature was not written in the spoken dialects of the country, but in Sanskrit. Mr. Hodgson procured a catalogue of all the works, still in existence, which formed the Buddhist canon. He afterwards succeeded in procuring copies of these works, and he was able in 1824 to send about sixty volumes to the Asiatic Society of Bengal. As no member of that society seemed inclined to devote himself to the study of these MSS., Mr. Hodgson sent two complete collections of the same MSS. to the Asiatic Society of London and the Société Asiatique of Paris. Before alluding to the brilliant results which the last-named collection produced in the hands of Eugène Burnouf, we must mention the labors of other students which preceded the publication of Burnouf's researches.

Mr. Hodgson himself gave to the world a number of valuable essays written on the spot, and afterwards collected under the title of "Illustrations of the Literature and Religion of the Buddhists," Serampore, 1841. He established the important fact, in accordance with the traditions of the priests of Nepal, that some of the Sanskrit documents which he recovered had existed in the monasteries of Nepal ever since the second century of our era, and that the whole of that collection had, five or six hundred years later, when Buddhism became definitely established in Thibet, been translated into the language of that country. As the art of printing had been introduced from China into Thibet, there was less difficulty in procuring complete copies of the Thibetan translation of the Buddhist canon. The real difficulty was to find a person acquainted with the

language. By a fortunate concurrence of circumstances,
however, it so happened that about the same time when
Mr. Hodgson's discoveries began to attract the attention of oriental scholars at Calcutta, a Hungarian, of
the name of Alexander Csoma de Körös, arrived there.
He had made his way from Hungary to Thibet on foot,
without any means of his own, and with the sole object of discovering somewhere in Central Asia the native home of the Hungarians. Arrived in Thibet, his
enthusiasm found a new vent in acquiring a language
which no European before his time had mastered, and
in exploring the vast collection of the canonical books
of the Buddhists, preserved in that language. Though
he arrived at Calcutta almost without a penny, he met
with a hearty welcome from the members of the Asiatic
Society, and was enabled with their assistance to publish the results of his extraordinary researches. People
have complained of the length of the sacred books of
other nations, but there are none that approach in bulk
to the sacred canon of the Thibetans. It consists of two
collections, commonly called the "Kanjur" and "Tanjur." The proper spelling of their names is Bkah-
hgyur, pronounced Kah-gyur, and Bstan-hgyur, pronounced Tan-gyur. The Kanjur consists, in its different editions, of 100, 102, or 108 volumes folio. It
comprises 1,083 distinct works. The Tanjur consists
of 225 volumes folio, each weighing from four to five
pounds in the edition of Peking. Editions of this
colossal code were printed at Peking, Lhassa, and
other places. The edition of the Kanjur published at
Peking, by command of the Emperor Khian-Lung,
sold for £600. A copy of the Kanjur was bartered
for 7,000 oxen by the Buriates, and the same tribe paid

1,200 silver rubles for a complete copy of the Kanjur
and Tanjur together.[1] Such a jungle of religious
literature — the most excellent hiding-place we should
think, for Lamas and Dalai-Lamas — was too much
even for a man who could travel on foot from Hungary to Thibet.   The Hungarian enthusiast, however,
though he did not translate the whole, gave a most valuable analysis of this immense bible, in the twentieth
volume of the " Asiatic Researches," sufficient to
establish the fact that the principal portion of it was a
translation from the same Sanskrit originals which had
been discovered in Nepal by Mr. Hodgson. Csoma
de Körös died soon after he had given to the world
the first fruits of his labors, — a victim to his heroic
devotion to the study of ancient languages and religions.

It was another fortunate coincidence that, contem-
poraneously with the discoveries of Hodgson and
Csoma de Körös, another scholar, Schmidt of St.
Petersburg, had so far advanced in the study of the
Mongolian language, as to be able to translate portions
of the Mongolian version of the Buddhist canon, and
thus forward the elucidation of some of the problems
connected with the religion of Buddha.

It never rains but it pours.   Whereas for years,
nay, for centuries, not a single original document of
the Buddhist religion had been accessible to the
scholars of Europe, we witness, in the small space of
ten years, the recovery of four complete Buddhist literatures.   In addition to the discoveries of Hodgson
in Nepal, of Csoma de Körös in Thibet, and of Schmidt
'n Mongolia, the Honorable George Turnour suddenly

[1] Die Religion des Buddha, von Köppen, vol. II. p. 282.

presented to the world the Buddhist literature of Ceylon, composed in the sacred language of that island, the ancient Páli. The existence of that literature had been known before. Since 1826 Sir Alexander Johnston had been engaged in collecting authentic copies of the Mahávansa, the Rágávali, and the Rájaratnákari. These copies were translated at his suggestion from Páli into modern Singhalese and thence into English. The publication was intrusted to Mr. Edward Upham, and the work appeared in 1833, under the title of "Sacred and Historical Works of Ceylon," dedicated to William IV. Unfortunately, whether through fraud or through misunderstanding, the priests who were to have procured an authentic copy of the Páli originals and translated them into the vernacular language, appear to have formed a compilation of their own from various sources. The official translators by whom this mutilated Singhalese abridgment was to have been rendered into English, took still greater liberties; and the "Sacred and Historical Books of Ceylon" had hardly been published before Burnouf, then a mere beginner in the study of Páli, was able to prove the utter uselessness of that translation. Mr. Turnour, however, soon made up for this disappointment. He set to work in a more scholarlike spirit, and after acquiring himself a knowledge of the Páli language, he published several important essays on the Buddhist canon, as preserved in Ceylon. These were followed by an edition and translation of the Mahávansa, or the history of Ceylon, written in the fifth century after Christ, and giving an account of the island from the earliest times to the beginning of the fourth century A. D. Several continuations of that history are in existence, but Mr. Turnour was prevented by an early death from continuing his edition beyond the original portion of that chronicle. The exploration of the Ceylonese literature has since been taken up again by the Rev. D. J. Gogerly (died 1862), whose essays are unfortunately scattered about in Singhalese periodicals and little known in Europe; and by the Rev. Spence Hardy, for twenty years Wesleyan missionary in Ceylon. His two works, " Eastern Monachism" and " Manual of Buddhism," are full of interesting matter, but as they are chiefly derived from Singhalese, and even more modern sources, they require to be used with caution.[1]

In the same manner as the Sanskrit originals of Nepal were translated by Buddhist missionaries into Thibetan, Mongolian, and, as we shall soon see, into Chinese and Mandshu,[2] the Pâli originals of Ceylon were carried to Burmah and Siam, and translated there into the languages of these countries. Hardly anything has as yet been done for exploring the literature of these two countries, which open a promising field for any one ambitious to follow in the footsteps of Hodgson, Csoma, and Turnour.

A very important collection of Buddhist MSS. has lately been brought from Ceylon to Europe by M. Grimblot, and is now deposited in the Imperial Library at Paris. This collection, to judge from a report published in 1866 in the " Journal des Savants," by M. Barthélemy Saint-Hilaire, consists of no less than

---

[1] The same author has lately published another valuable work, *The Legends and Theories of the Buddhists*. London, 1866. He died in 1868.

[2] *Mélanges Asiatiques*, vol. II. p. 571.

eighty-seven works; and, as some of them are represented by more than one copy, the total number of MSS. amounts to one hundred and twenty-one. They fill altogether 14,000 palm leaves, and are written partly in Singhalese, partly in Burmese characters. Next to Ceylon, Burmah and Siam would seem to be the two countries most likely to yield large collections of Páli MSS., and the MSS. which now exist in Ceylon may, to a considerable extent, be traced back to these two countries. At the beginning of the sixteenth century, the Tamil conquerors of Ceylon are reported to have burnt every Buddhist book they could discover, in the hope of thus destroying the vitality of that detested religion. Buddhism, however, though persecuted, —or, more probably, because persecuted, — remained the national religion of the island, and in the eighteenth century it had recovered its former ascendency. Missions were then sent to Siam to procure authentic copies of the sacred documents; priests properly ordained were imported from Burmah; and several libraries, which contain both the canonical and the profane literature of Buddhism, were founded at Dadala, Ambagapitya, and other places.

The sacred canon of the Buddhists is called the "Tripitaka," i. e. the three baskets. The first basket contains all that has reference to morality, or Vinaya; the second contains the Sútras, i. e. the discourses of Buddha; the third includes all works treating of dogmatic philosophy or metaphysics. The second and third baskets are sometimes comprehended under the general name of "Dharma," or law, and it has become usual to apply to the third basket the name of "Abhidharma," or by-law. The first and second pitakas

contain each five separate works; the third contains
seven.   M. Grimblot has secured MSS. of nearly every
one of these works, and he has likewise brought home
copies of the famous commentaries of Buddhaghosha.
These commentaries are of great importance; for although Buddhaghosha lived as late as 430 A. D., he is
supposed to have been the translator of more ancient
commentaries, brought in 318 B. C. to Ceylon from
Magadha by Mahinda, the son of Asoka, translated by
him from Pâli into Singhalese, and retranslated by
Buddhaghosha into Pâli, the original language both
of the canonical books and of their commentaries.
Whether historical criticism will allow to the commentaries of Buddhaghosha the authority due to documents
of the fourth century before Christ, is a question that
has yet to be settled.   But even as a collector of earlier traditions and as a writer of the fifth century after
Christ, his authority would be considerable with regard
to the solution of some of the most important problems
of Indian history and chronology.   Some scholars who
have written on the history of Buddhism have clearly
shown too strong an inclination to treat the statements
contained in the commentaries of Buddhaghosha as
purely historical, forgetting the great interval of time
by which he is separated from the events which he
relates.   No doubt if it could be proved that Buddhaghosha's works were literal translations of the so-called
"Attakathâs" or commentaries brought by Mahinda to
Ceylon, this would considerably enhance their historical value.   But the whole account of these translations rests on tradition, and if we consider the extraordinary precautions taken, according to tradition, by the
LXX. translators of the Old Testament, and then ob-

serve the discrepancies between the chronology of the Septuagint and that of the Hebrew text, we shall be better able to appreciate the risk of trusting to oriental translations, even to those that pretend to be literal. The idea of a faithful literal translation seems altogether foreign to oriental minds. Granted that Mahinda translated the original Pâli commentaries into Singhalese, there was nothing to restrain him from inserting anything that he thought likely to be useful to his new converts. Granted that Buddhaghosha translated these translations back into Pâli, why should he not have incorporated any facts that were then believed and had been handed down by tradition from generation to generation? Was he not at liberty, — nay, would he not have felt it his duty, to explain apparent difficulties, to remove contradictions, and to correct palpable mistakes? In our time, when even the contemporaneous evidence of Herodotus, Thucydides, Livy, or Jornandes is sifted by the most uncompromising skepticism, we must not expect a more merciful treatment for the annals of Buddhism. Scholars engaged in special researches are too willing to acquiesce in evidence, particularly if that evidence has been discovered by their own efforts and comes before them with all the charms of novelty. But, in the broad daylight of historical criticism, the prestige of such a witness as Buddhaghosha soon dwindles away, and his statements as to kings and councils eight hundred years before his time are in truth worth no more than the stories told of Arthur by Geoffrey of Monmouth, or the accounts we read in Livy of the early history of Rome.

One of the most important works of M. Grimblot's

collection, and one that we hope will soon be published, is a history of Buddhism in Ceylon, called the "Dipavansa." The only work of the same character which has hitherto been known is the "Mahávansa," published by the Honorable George Turnour. But this is professedly based on the "Dipavansa," and is probably of a much later date. Mahánáma, the compiler of the "Mahávansa," lived about 500 A. D. His work was continued by later chroniclers to the middle of the eighteenth century. Though Mahánáma wrote towards the end of the fifth century after Christ, his own share of the chronicle seems to have ended with the year 302 A. D., and a commentary which he wrote on his own chronicle likewise breaks off at that period. The exact date of the "Dipavansa" is not yet known; but as it also breaks off with the death of Máhasena in 302 A. D., we cannot ascribe to it, for the present, any higher authority than could be commanded by a writer of the fourth century after Christ.

We now return to Mr. Hodgson. His collections of Sanskrit MSS. had been sent, as we saw, to the Asiatic Society of Calcutta from 1824 to 1839, to the Royal Asiatic Society in London in 1835, and to the Société Asiatique of Paris in 1837. They remained dormant at Calcutta and in London. At Paris, however, these Buddhist MSS. fell into the hands of Burnouf. Unappalled by their size and tediousness, he set to work, and was not long before he discovered their extreme importance. After seven years of careful study, Burnouf published, in 1844, his "Introduction à l'Histoire du Buddhisme." It is this work which laid the foundation for a systematic study of the religion of Buddha. Though acknowledging the great value of the researches made in the Buddhist literatures of Thibet, Mongolia, China, and Ceylon, Burnouf showed that Buddhism, being of Indian origin, ought to be studied first of all in the original Sanskrit documents, preserved in Nepal. Though he modestly called his work an "Introduction to the History of Buddhism," there are few points of importance on which his industry has not brought together the most valuable evidence, and his genius shed a novel and brilliant light. The death of Burnouf in 1851 put an end to a work which, if finished according to the plan sketched out by the author in the preface, would have been the most perfect monument of oriental scholarship. A volume published after his death, in 1852, contains a translation of one of the canonical books of Nepal, with notes and appendices, the latter full of the most valuable information on some of the more intricate questions of Buddhism. Though much remained to be done, and though a very small breach only had been made in the vast pile of Sanskrit MSS. presented by Mr Hodgson to the Asiatic Societies of Paris and London, no one has been bold enough to continue what Burnouf left unfinished. The only important additions to our knowledge of Buddhism since his death are an edition of the "Lalita-Vistara," or the life of Buddha, prepared by a native, the learned Babu Rajendralal Mittra; an edition of the Pâli original of the "Dhammapadam," by Dr. Fausböll, a Dane; and last, not least, the excellent translation by M. Stanislas Julien, of the life and travels of Hiouen-Thsang. This Chinese pilgrim had visited India from 629 to 645 A. D., for the purpose of learning Sanskrit, and translating from Sanskrit into Chinese some important works on the religion

and philosophy of the Buddhists; and his account of
the geography, the social, religious, and political state
of India at the beginning of the seventh century is in-
valuable for studying the practical working of that religion at a time when its influence began to decline, and
when it was soon to be supplanted by modern Brahmanism and Mohammedanism.

It was no easy task for M. Barthélemy Saint-Hilaire
to make himself acquainted with all these works. The
study of Buddhism would almost seem to be beyond
the power of any single individual, if it required a
practical acquaintance with all the languages in which
the doctrines of Buddha have been written down.
Burnouf was probably the only man who, in addition
to his knowledge of Sanskrit, did not shrink from acquiring a practical knowledge of Thibetan, Pâli, Singhalese, and Burmese, in order to prepare himself for
such a task. The same scholar had shown, however,
that though it was impossible for a Thibetan, Mongolian,
or Chinese scholar to arrive, without a knowledge of
Sanskrit, at a correct understanding of the doctrines
of Buddha, a knowledge of Sanskrit was sufficient for
entering into their spirit, for comprehending their origin
and growth in India, and their modification in the different countries where they took root in later times.
Assisted by his familiarity with Sanskrit, and bringing
into the field, as a new and valuable auxiliary, his intimate acquaintance with nearly all the systems of philosophy and religion of both the ancient and modern
worlds, M. Barthélemy Saint-Hilaire has succeeded in
drawing a picture, both lively and correct, of the origin,
the character, the strong as well as weak points, of the
religion of Buddha. He has become the first historian

of Buddhism. He has not been carried away by a temptation which must have been great for one who is able to read in the past the lessons for the present or the future. He has not used Buddhism either as a bugbear or as a *beau idéal*. He is satisfied with stating in his preface that many lessons might be learned by modern philosophers from a study of Buddhism, but in the body of the work he never perverts the chair of the historian into the pulpit of the preacher.

"This book may offer one other advantage," he writes, "and I regret to say that at present it may seem to come opportunely. It is the misfortune of our times that the same doctrines which form the foundation of Buddhism meet at the hands of some of our philosophers with a favor which they ill deserve. For some years we have seen systems arising in which metempsychosis and transmigration are highly spoken of, and attempts are made to explain the world and man without either a God or a Providence, exactly as Buddha did. A future life is refused to the yearnings of mankind, and the immortality of the soul is replaced by the immortality of works. God is dethroned, and in His place they substitute man, the only being, we are told, in which the Infinite becomes conscious of itself. These theories are recommended to us sometimes in the name of science, or of history, or philology, or even of metaphysics; and though they are neither new or very original, yet they can do much injury to feeble hearts. This is not the place to examine these theories, and their authors are both too learned and too sincere to deserve to be condemned summarily and without discussion. But it is well that they should know by the example, too little known, of Buddhism, what becomes of man if he depends on himself alone, and if his meditations, misled by a pride of which he is hardly conscious, bring him to the precipice where Buddha was lost. I am well aware of all the differences, and I am not going to insult our contemporary philosophers by confounding them indiscriminately with Buddha, although addressing to both the same reproof. I acknowledge willingly all their additional merits, which are considerable. But systems of philosophy must always be judged by the conclusions to which they lead, whatever road they may follow in reaching them; and their conclusions, though obtained by different means, are not therefore less objectionable. Buddha arrived at his conclusions 2,400 years ago. He proclaimed and practiced them with an energy which is not likely to be surpassed, even if it be equaled. He displayed a childlike intrepidity which no one can exceed, nor can it be supposed that any system in our days could again acquire so powerful an ascendency over the souls of men. It would be useful, however, if the authors of these modern systems would just cast a glance at the theories and destinies of Buddhism. It is not philosophy in the sense in which we understand this great name, nor is it religion in the sense of ancient Paganism, of Christianity, or of Mohammedanism; but it contains elements of all worked up into a perfectly independent doctrine which acknowledges nothing in the universe but man, and obstinately refuses to recognize anything else, though confounding man with nature in the midst of which he lives. Hence all those aberrations of Buddhism which ought to be a warning to others. Unfortunately, if people rarely profit by their own faults, they profit yet more rarely by the faults of others." ("Introduction," p. vii.)

But though M. Barthélemy Saint-Hilaire does not write history merely for the sake of those masked batteries which French writers have used with so much skill at all times, but more particularly during the late years of Imperial sway, it is clear, from the remarks just quoted, that our author is not satisfied with simply chronicling the dry facts of Buddhism, or turning into French the tedious discourses of its founder. His work is an animated sketch, giving too little rather than too much. It is just the book which was wanted to dispel the erroneous notions about Buddhism, which are still current among educated men, and to excite an interest which may lead those who are naturally frightened by the appalling proportions of Buddhist literature, and the uncouth sounds of Buddhist terminology, to a study of the quartos of Burnouf, Turnour, and others. To those who may wish for more detailed information on Buddhism, than could be given by M. Barthélemy Saint-Hilaire, consistently with the plan of his work, we can strongly recommend the work of a German writer, "Die Religion des Buddha," von Köppen, Berlin, 1857. It is founded on the same materials as the French work, but being written by a scholar and for scholars, it enters on a more minute examination of all that has been said or written on Buddha and Buddhism. In a second volume the same learned and industrious student has lately published a history of Buddhism in Thibet.

M. Barthélemy Saint-Hilaire's work is divided into three portions. The first contains an account of the origin of Buddhism, a life of Buddha, and an examination of Buddhist ethics and metaphysics. In the second he describes the state of Buddhism in India in the seventh century of our era, from the materials supplied by the travels of Hiouen-Thsang. The third gives a description of Buddhism as actually existing in Ceylon, and as lately described by an eyewitness, the Rev. Spence Hardy. We shall confine ourselves chiefly to the first part, which treats of the life and teaching of Buddha.

M. Barthélemy Saint-Hilaire, following the example of Burnouf, Lassen, and Wilson, accepts the date of the Ceylonese era 543 B. C. as the date of Buddha's death. Though we cannot enter here into long chronological discussions, we must remark, that this date was clearly obtained by the Buddhists of Ceylon by calculation, not by historical tradition, and that it is easy to point out in that calculation a mistake of about seventy years. The more plausible date of Buddha's death is 477 B. C. For the purposes, however, which M. Barthélemy Saint-Hilaire had in view, this difference is of small importance. We know so little of the history of India during the sixth and fifth centuries B. C., that the stage on which he represents Buddha as preaching and teaching would have had very much the same background, the same costume and accessories, for the sixth as for the fifth century B. C.

In the life of Buddha, which extends from pp. 1 to 79, M. Barthélemy Saint-Hilaire follows almost exclusively the "Lalita-Vistara." This is one of the most popular works of the Buddhists. It forms part of the Buddhist canon; and as we know of a translation into Chinese, which M. Stanislas Julien ascribes to the year 76 A. D., we may safely refer its original composition to an ante-Christian date. It has been published in San-

skrit by Babu Rajendralal Mittra, and we owe to M.
Foucaux an edition of the same work in its Thibetan
translation, the first Thibetan text printed in Europe.
From specimens that we have seen, we should think it
would be highly desirable to have an accurate translation of the Chinese text, such as M. Stanislas Julien
alone is able to give us.[1] Few people, however, except
scholars, would have the patience to read this work
either in its English or French translation, as may be
seen from the following specimen, containing the beginning of Babu Rajendralal Mittra's version:—

"Om! Salutation to all Buddhas, Bodhisattvas,
Áryas, Srávakas, and Pratyeka Buddhas of all times,
past, present, and future; who are adored throughout
the furthest limits of the ten quarters of the globe.
Thus hath it been heard by me, that once on a time
Bhagavat sojourned in the garden of Anáthapindada,

[1] The advantages to be derived from these Chinese translations have
been pointed out by M. Stanislas Julien. The analytical structure of that
language imparts to Chinese translations the character almost of a gloss;
and though we need not follow implicitly the interpretations of the Buddhist originals, adopted by the Chinese translators, still their antiquity would
naturally impart to them a considerable value and interest. The following
specimens were kindly communicated to me by M. Stanislas Julien:—

"Je me suis si je vous ai communiqué autrefois les curieux passages qui
suivent: On lit dans le Lotus français, p. 271, l. 14, [ ] que c'est une
chose difficile à rencontrer que la naissance d'un bouddha, aussi difficile à
rencontrer que la fleur de l'Udumbara, que l'introduction de col d'une tortue dans l'ouverture d'un joug formé par le grand océan.

"Il y a eu ailleurs un bouddha est difficile à rencontrer, comme les fleurs
Udumbara et l'allégorie; et en outre comme si une tortue borgne voulait rencontrer au trou dans un trou flottant (lit. le trou d'un bois flottant.)

"Lotus français, p. 39, l. 119 (les créatures), exclues par la concupiscence comme par la queue du Yak, perpétuellement aveuglées et au monde
par les désirs, elles ne cherchent pas le Buddha.

"Il y a un chinois. Profondément attachées aux cinq désirs — Elles
les aiment comme le Yak aime sa queue. Par la concupiscence et l'amour
elles s'aveuglent elles-mêmes." etc.

at Getavana, in Srâvastî, accompanied by a venerable body of 12,000 Bhikshukas. There likewise accompanied him 32,000 Bodhisattvas, all linked together by unity of caste, and perfect in the virtues of pâramitâ; who had made their command over Bodhisattva knowledge a pastime, were illumined with the light of Bodhisattva dhâranis, and were masters of the dhâranis themselves; who were profound in their meditations, all submissive to the lord of Bodhisattvas, and possessed absolute control over samâdhi; great in self-command, refulgent in Bodhisattva forbearance, and replete with the Bodhisattva element of perfection. Now then, Bhagavat arriving in the great city of Srâvastî, sojourned therein, respected, venerated, revered, and adored, by the fourfold congregation; by kings, princes, their counselors, prime ministers, and followers; by retinues of kshatriyas, brâhmanas, householders, and ministers; by citizens, foreigners, srâmanas, brâhmanas, recluses, and ascetics; and although regaled with all sorts of edibles and sauces, the best that could be prepared by purveyors, and supplied with cleanly mendicant apparel, begging pots, couches, and pain-assuaging medicaments, the benevolent lord, on whom had been showered the prime of gifts and applauses, remained unattached to them all, like water on a lotus leaf; and the report of his greatness as the venerable, the absolute Buddha, the learned and well-behaved, the god of happy exit, the great knower of worlds, the valiant, the all-controlling charioteer, the teacher of gods and men, the quinocular lord Buddha fully manifest spread far and wide in the world. And Bhagavat, having by his own power acquired all knowledge regarding this world and the next, comprising devas, mâras, brâhmaṇas (followers of Brahmâ), ṡrâmaṇas, and brâhmaṇas, as subjects, that is both gods and men, sojourned here, imparting instructions in the true religion, and expounding the principles of a brahmakarya, full and complete in its nature, holy in its import, pure and immaculate in its character, auspicious is its beginning, auspicious its middle, auspicious its end."

The whole work is written in a similar style, and where fact and legend, prose and poetry, sense and nonsense, are so mixed together, the plan adopted by M. Barthélemy Saint-Hilaire, of making two lives out of one, the one containing all that seems possible, the other what seems impossible, would naturally recommend itself. It is not a safe process, however, to distill history out of legend by simply straining the legendary through the sieve of physical possibility. Many things are possible, and may yet be the mere inventions of later writers; and many things which sound impossible have been reclaimed as historical, after removing from them the thin film of mythological phraseology. We believe that the only use which the historian can safely make of the "Lalita-Vistara," is to employ it, not as evidence of facts which actually happened, but in illustration of the popular belief prevalent at the time when it was committed to writing. Without therefore adopting the division of fact and fiction in the life of Buddha, as attempted by M. Barthélemy Saint-Hilaire, we yet believe that in order to avoid a repetition of childish absurdities, we shall best consult the interest of our readers if we follow his example, and give a short and rational abstract of the life of Buddha as handed down by tradition, and committed to writing not later than the first century A. C.

Buddha, or more correctly, the Buddha, — for Buddha is an appellative meaning Enlightened, — was born at Kapilavastu, the capital of a kingdom of the same name, situated at the foot of the mountains of Nepal, north of the present Oude. His father, the king of Kapilavastu, was of the family of the Śākyas, and belonged to the clan of the Gautamas. His mother was Māyādevi, daughter of king Suprabuddha, and need we say that she was as beautiful as he was powerful and just? Buddha was therefore by birth of the Kshatriya, or warrior caste, and he took the name of Śākya from his family, and that of Gautama from his clan, claiming a kind of spiritual relationship with the honored race of Gautmas. The name of Buddha, or the Buddha, dates from a later period of his life, and so probably does the name Siddhārtha (he whose objects have been accomplished), though we are told that it was given him in his childhood. His mother died seven days after his birth, and the father confided the child to the care of his deceased wife's sister, who, however, had been his wife even before the mother's death. The child grew up a most beautiful and most accomplished boy, who soon knew more than his masters could teach him. He refused to take part in the games of his playmates, and never felt so happy as when he could sit alone, lost in meditation, in the deep shadows of the forest. It was there that his father found him when he had thought him lost, and in order to prevent the young prince from becoming a dreamer, the king determined to marry him at once. When the subject was mentioned by the aged ministers to the future heir to the throne, he demanded seven days for reflection, and convinced at last that not even marriage could disturb the calm of his mind, he allowed the ministers to look out for a princess. The princess selected was the beautiful Gopâ, the daughter of Dandapâni. Though her father objected at first to her marrying a young prince who was represented to him as deficient in manliness and intellect, he gladly gave his consent when he saw the royal suitor distancing all his rivals, both in feats of arms and power of mind. Their marriage proved one of the happiest, but the prince remained, as he had been before, absorbed in meditation on the problems of life and death. "Nothing is stable on earth," he used to say, "nothing is real. Life is like the spark produced by the friction of wood. It is lighted and is extinguished,—we know not whence it came or whither it goes. It is like the sound of a lyre, and the wise man asks in vain from whence it came and whither it goes. There must be some supreme intelligence where we could find rest. If I attained it, I could bring light to man; if I were free myself, I could deliver the world." The king, who perceived the melancholy mood of the young prince, tried everything to divert him from his speculations: but all was in vain. Three of the most ordinary events that could happen to any man, proved of the utmost importance in the career of Buddha. We quote the description of these occurrences from M. Barthélemy Saint-Hilaire:—

"One day when the prince with a large retinue, was driving through the eastern gate of the city on the way to one of his parks, he met on the road an old man, broken and decrepit. One could see the veins and muscles over the whole of his body; his teeth chattered, he was covered with wrinkles, bald, and hardly able to utter hollow and unmelodious sounds. He was bent on his stick, and all his limbs and joints trembled. 'Who is that man?' said the prince to his coachman. 'He is small and weak, his flesh and his blood are dried up, his muscles stick to his skin, his head is white, his teeth chatter, his body is wasted away; leaning on his stick he is hardly able to walk, stumbling at every step. Is there something peculiar in his family, or is this the common lot of all created beings?'

" 'Sir,' replied the coachman, ' that man is sinking under old age: his senses have become obtuse, suffering has destroyed his strength, and he is despised by his relations. He is without support and useless, and people have abandoned him, like a dead tree in a forest. But this is not peculiar to his family. In every creature youth is defeated by old age. Your father, your mother, all your relations, all your friends, will come to the same state: this is the appointed end of all creatures.'

" ' Alas ! ' replied the prince, ' are creatures so ignorant, so weak and foolish, as to be proud of the youth by which they are intoxicated, not seeing the old age which awaits them ! As for me, I go away. Coachman, turn my chariot quickly. What have I, the future prey of old age, — what have I to do with pleasure?' And the young prince returned to the city without going to his park.

" Another time the prince was driving through the southern gate to his pleasure garden, when he perceived on the road a man suffering from illness, parched with fever, his body wasted, covered with mud, without a friend, without a home, hardly able to breathe, and frightened at the sight of himself and the approach of death. Having questioned his coachman, and received from him the answer which he expected, the young prince said, 'Alas! health is but the sport of a dream, and the fear of suffering must take this frightful form. Where is the wise man who, after having seen what he is, could any longer think of joy and pleasure?' The prince turned his chariot and returned to the city.

"A third time he was driving to his pleasure garden through the western gate, when he saw a dead body on the road, lying on a bier, and covered with a cloth. The friends stood about, crying, sobbing, tearing their hair, covering their heads with dust, striking their breasts, and uttering wild cries. The prince, again calling his coachman to witness this painful scene, exclaimed, 'O woe to youth, which must be destroyed by old age! Woe to health, which must be destroyed by so many diseases! Woe to this life, where a man remains so short a time! If there were no old age, no disease, no death; if these could be made captive forever!' Then betraying for the first time his intentions, the young prince said, 'Let us turn back, I must think how to accomplish deliverance.'

"A last meeting put an end to his hesitation. He was driving through the northern gate on the way to his pleasure gardens, when he saw a mendicant who appeared outwardly calm, subdued, looking downwards, wearing with an air of dignity his religious vestment, and carrying an alms-bowl.

"'Who is this man?' asked the prince.

"'Sir,' replied the coachman, 'this man is one of those who are called bhikshus, or mendicants. He has renounced all pleasures, all desires, and leads a life of austerity. He tries to conquer himself. He has become a devotee. Without passion, without envy, he walks about asking for alms.'

"'This is good and well said,' replied the prince. 'The life of a devotee has always been praised by the wise. It will be my refuge, and the refuge of other creatures; it will lead us to a real life, to happiness and immortality.'

"With these words the young prince turned his chariot and returned to the city."

After having declared to his father and his wife his intention of retiring from the world, Buddha left his palace one night when all the guards that were to have watched him were asleep. After travelling the whole night, he gave his horse and his ornaments to his groom, and sent him back to Kapilavastu. "A monument," remarks the author of the "Lalita-Vistara" (p. 270), "is still to be seen on the spot where the coachman turned back." Hiouen-Thsang (II. 320) saw the same monument at the edge of a large forest, on his road to Kusinágara, a city now in ruins, and situated about fifty miles E. S. E. from Gorakpur.[1]

Buddha first went to Vaisáli, and became the pupil of a famous Brahman, who had gathered round him 300 disciples. Having learnt all that the Brahman could teach him, Buddha went away disappointed. He had not found the road to salvation. He then tried another Brahman at Rájagriha, the capital of Magadha

---

[1] The geography of India at the time of Buddha, and later at the time of Fahian and Hiouen-Thsang, has been admirably treated by M. L. Vivien de Saint-Martin, in his *Mémoire Analytique sur la Carte de l'Asie Centrale et de l'Inde*, in the third volume of M. Stanislas Julien's *Pélerins Bouddhistes*.

or Behar, who had 700 disciples, and there too he looked in vain for the means of deliverance. He lost him, followed by five of his fellow-students, and for six years retired into solitude, near a village named Uruvilva, subjecting himself to the most severe penances, previous to his appearing in the world as a teacher. At the end of this period, however, he arrived at the conviction that asceticism, far from giving peace of mind and preparing the way to salvation, was a snare and a stumbling-block in the way of truth. He gave up his exercises, and was at once deserted as an apostate by his five disciples. Left to himself, he now began to elaborate his own system. He had learnt that neither the doctrines nor the austerities of the Brahmans were of any avail for accomplishing the deliverance of man, and freeing him from the fear of old age, disease, and death. After long meditations and ecstatic visions, he at last imagined that he had arrived at that true knowledge which discloses the cause, and thereby destroys the fear, of all the changes inherent in life. It was from the moment when he arrived at this knowledge, that he claimed the name of Buddha, the Enlightened. At that moment we may truly say that the fate of millions of millions of human beings trembled in the balance. Buddha hesitated for a time whether he should keep his knowledge to himself, or communicate it to the world. Compassion for the sufferings of man prevailed, and the young prince became the founder of a religion which, after more than 2,000 years, is still professed by 455,000,000 of human beings.[1]

[1] Though truth is not settled by majorities, it would be interesting to know which religion counts at the present moment the largest number of

The further history of the new teacher is very simple. He proceeded to Benares, which at all times was the principal seat of learning in India, and the first converts he made were the five fellow-students who had left him when he threw off the yoke of the Brahmanical observances. Many others followed; but as the "Lalita-Vistara" breaks off at Buddha's arrival at Benares, we have no further consecutive account of the rapid progress of his doctrine. From what we can gather from scattered notices in the Buddhist canon, he was invited by the king of Magadha, Bimbisâra, to his capital, Râgagriha. Many of his lectures are represented as having been delivered at the monastery of Kalantaka, with which the king or some rich merchant had presented him; others on the Vulture Peak, one of the five hills that surrounded the ancient capital.

Three of his most famous disciples, Sâriputra, Kâtyâyana, and Maudgalyâyana, joined him during his stay in Magadha, where he enjoyed for many years the friendship of the king. That king was afterwards as-

believers. Berghaus, in his *Physical Atlas* gives the following division of the human race according to religions: —

Buddhists	31.2 per cent.
Christians	30.7 "
Mahommedans	15.7 "
Brahmeists	13.4 "
Heathens	8.7 "
Jews	0.3 "

As Berghaus does not distinguish the Buddhists in China from the followers of Confucius and Laotse, the first place on the scale belongs really to Christianity. It is difficult in China to say to what religion a man belongs, as the same person may profess two or three. The emperor himself, after sacrificing according to the ritual of Confucius, visits a Taoïst temple, and afterwards bows before an image of Fo in a Buddhist chapel. *Mélanges Asiatiques de St. Pétersbourg*, vol. II. p. 374.

assinated by his son, Ajátasatru, and then we hear of
Buddha as settled for a time at Srávasti, north of the
Ganges, where Anáthapindada, a rich merchant, had
offered him and his disciples a magnificent building for
their residence. Most of Buddha's lectures or sermons
were delivered at Srávastí, the capital of Kosala; and
the king of Kosala himself, Prasénajit, became a convert to his doctrine. After an absence of twelve years
we are told that Buddha visited his father at Kapilavastu, on which occasion he performed several miracles, and converted all the Sákyas to his faith. His
own wife became one of his followers, and, with his
aunt, offers the first instance of female Buddhist dev-
otees in India. We have fuller particulars again of
the last days of Buddha's life. He had attained the
good age of three-score and ten, and had been on a
visit to Rájagriha, where the king, Ajátasatru, the
former enemy of Buddha, and the assassin of his own
father, had joined the congregation, after making a
public confession of his crimes. On his return he was
followed by a large number of disciples, and when on
the point of crossing the Ganges, he stood on a square
stone, and turning his eyes back towards Rájagriha,
he said, full of emotion, "This is the last time that I
see that city." He likewise visited Vaisáli, and after
taking leave of it, he had nearly reached the city of
Kusinágara, when his vital strength began to fail. He
halted in a forest, and while sitting under a sál tree,
he gave up the ghost, or, as a Buddhist would say,
entered into Nirvána.

This is the simple story of Buddha's life. It reads
much better in the eloquent pages of M. Barthélemy
Saint-Hilaire, than in the turgid language of the Bud

llists. If a critical historian, with the materials we
possess, entered at all on the process of separating
truth from falsehood, he would probably cut off much
of what our biographer has left. Professor Wilson,
in his Essay on Buddha and Buddhism, considers it
doubtful whether any such person as Buddha ever
actually existed. He dwells on the fact that there are
at least twenty different dates assigned to his birth,
varying from 2420 to 458 B. C. He points out that the
clan of the Śākyas is never mentioned by early Hindu
writers, and he lays much stress on the fact that
most of the proper names of the persons connected
with Buddha suggest an allegorical signification. The
name of his father means, he whose food is pure; that
of his mother signifies illusion; his own secular appellation, Siddhārtha, he by whom the end is accomplished. Buddha itself means, the Enlightened, or,
as Professor Wilson translates it less accurately, he
by whom all is known. The same distinguished
scholar goes even further, and maintaining that Kapilavastu, the birthplace of Buddha, has no place in the
geography of the Hindus, suggests that it may be rendered, the substance of Kapila; intimating, in fact, the
Sânkhya philosophy, the doctrine of Kapila Muni, upon
which the fundamental elements of Buddhism, the
eternity of matter, the principles of things, and the
final extinction, are supposed to be planned. "It
seems not impossible," he continues, "that Śākya
Muni is an unreal being, and that all that is related
of him is as much a fiction, as is that of his preceding
migrations, and the miracles that attended his birth,
his life, and his departure." This is going far beyond
Niebuhr, far even beyond Strauss. If an allegorical

name had been invented for the father of Buddha, one more appropriate than "Clean-food" might surely have been found. His mother is not the only queen known by the name of "Mâyâ," "Mâyâdêvi," or "Mâyâvatî." Why, if these names were invented, should his wife have been allowed to keep the prosaic name of "Gopâ" (cowherdess), and his father-in-law, that of "Dandapâni," "Stirk-hand?" As to his own name, "Siddhârtha," the Thibetans maintain that it was given him by his parent, whose wish (artha) had been fulfilled (siddha), as we hear of "Désiré" and "Dieudonné" in French. One of the ministers of Dasaratha had the same name. It is possible also that Buddha himself assumed it in after life, as was the case with many of the Roman surnames. As to the name of Buddha, no one ever maintained that it was more than a title, "the Enlightened," changed from an appellative into a proper name, just like the name of "Christos, the Anointed," or "Mohammed, the Expected." [1] "Kapilavastu" would be a most extraordinary compound to express "the substance of the Sânkhya philosophy." But all doubt on the subject is removed by the fact that both Fahian in the fifth, and Hionen-Thsang in the seventh centuries visited the real ruins of that city.

Making every possible allowance for the accumulation of fiction which is sure to gather round the life of the founder of every great religion, we may be satisfied that Buddhism, which changed the aspect, not only of India, but of nearly the whole of Asia, had a real founder; that he was not a Brahman by birth, but belonged to the second or royal caste: that being of a

[1] See Sprenger. Das Leben des Mohammed, 1851, vol. 1 p. 155.

meditative turn of mind, and deeply impressed with the
frailty of all created things, he became a recluse, and
sought for light and comfort in the different systems of
Bráhman philosophy and theology. Dissatisfied with
the artificial systems of their priests and philosophers,
convinced of the uselessness, nay of the pernicious influence, of their ceremonial practices and bodily penances, shocked, too, by their worldliness and pharisaical
conceit, which made the priesthood the exclusive property of one caste, and rendered every sincere approach
of man to his Creator impossible without their intervention, Buddha must have produced at once a powerful
impression on the people at large, when breaking
through all the established rules of caste, he assumed
the privileges of a Brahman, and throwing away the
splendor of his royal position, travelled about as a
beggar, not shrinking from the defiling contact of sin-
ners and publicans. Though when we now speak of
Buddhism, we think chiefly of its doctrines, the reform
of Buddha had originally much more of a social than of
a religious character. Buddha swept away the web
with which the Brahmans had encircled the whole of
India. Beginning as the destroyer of an old, he
became the founder of a new religion. We can hardly
understand how any nation could have lived under a
system like that of the Brahmanic hierarchy, which
coiled itself round every public and private act, and
would have rendered life intolerable to any who had
forfeited the favor of the priests. That system was
attacked by Buddha. Buddha might have taught
whatever philosophy he pleased, and we should hardly
have heard his name. The people would not have
minded him, and his system would only have been a

drop in the ocean of philosophical speculation, by which India was deluged at all times. But when a young prince assembled round him people of all castes, of all ranks; when he defeated the Brahmans in public disputations; when he declared the sacrifices by which they made their living not only useless but sinful; when, instead of severe penance or excommunications inflicted by the Brahmans sometimes for the most trifling offenses, he only required public confession of sin and a promise to sin no more; when the charitable gifts hitherto monopolized by the Brahmans began to flow into new channels, supporting hundreds and thousands of Buddhist mendicants, more had been achieved than probably Buddha himself had ever dreamt of; and he whose meditations had been how to deliver the soul of man from misery and the fear of death, had delivered the people of India from a degrading thralldom and from priestly tyranny.

The most important element of the Buddhist reform has always been its social and moral code, not its metaphysical theories. That moral code, taken by itself, is one of the most perfect which the world has ever known. On this point all testimonies from hostile and from friendly quarters agree. Spence Hardy, a Wesleyan missionary, speaking of the "Dhamma Padam," or the "Footsteps of the Law," admits that a collection might be made from the precepts of this work, which in the purity of its ethics could hardly be equaled from any other heathen author. M. Laboulaye, one of the most distinguished members of the French Academy, remarks in the "Débats" of the 4th of April, 1853: "It is difficult to comprehend how men not assisted by revelation could have soared so high, and approached so near to the truth." Besides the five great commandments not to kill, not to steal, not to commit adultery, not to lie, not to get drunk, every shade of vice, hypocrisy, anger, pride, suspicion, greediness, gossiping, cruelty to animals, is guarded against by special precepts. Among the virtues recommended, we find not only reverence of parents, care for children, submission to authority, gratitude, moderation in time of prosperity, submission in time of trial, equanimity at all times, but virtues unknown in any heathen system of morality, such as the duty of forgiving insults and not rewarding evil with evil. All virtues, we are told, spring from Maitri, and this Maitri can only be translated by charity and love. "I do not hesitate," says Burnouf,[1] "to translate by charity the word ' Maitri; ' it does not express friendship or the feeling of particular affection which a man has for one or more of his fellow-creatures, but that universal feeling which inspires us with good-will towards all men and constant willingness to help them." We add one more testimony from the work of M. Barthélemy Saint-Hilaire: —

"Je n'hésite pas à ajouter," he writes, "que, sauf le Christ tout seul, il n'est point, parmi les fondateurs de religion, de figure plus pure ni plus touchante que celle du Bouddha. Sa vie n'a point de tâche. Son constant héroïsme égale sa conviction; et si la théorie qu'il préconise est fausse, les exemples personnels qu'il donne sont irréprochables. Il est le modèle achevé de toutes les vertus qu'il prêcha; son abnégation, sa charité, son inaltérable douceur, ne se démentent point un seul instant; il abandonne à vingt-neuf ans la cour

---

[1] Burnouf, Lotus de la bonne Loi, p. 300.

du roi son père pour se faire religieux et mendiant ; il prépare silencieusement sa doctrine par six années de retraite et de méditation ; il la propage par la seule puissance de la parole et de la persuasion, pendant plus d'un demi-siècle ; et quand il meurt entre les bras de ses disciples, c'est avec la sérénité d'un sage qui a pratiqué le bien toute sa vie, et qui est assuré d'avoir trouvé le vrai." (Page v.)

There still remain, no doubt, some blurred and doubtful pages in the history of the prince of Kapilavastu ; but we have only to look at the works on ancient philosophy and religion published some thirty years ago, in order to perceive the immense progress that has been made in establishing the true historical character of the founder of Buddhism. There was a time when Buddha was identified with Christ. The Manichæans were actually forced to adjure their belief that Buddha, Christ, and Mani were one and the same person.[1] But we are thinking rather of the eighteenth and nineteenth centuries, when elaborate books were written, in order to prove that Buddha had been in reality the Thoth of the Egyptians, that he was Mercury, or Wodan, or Zoroaster, or Pythagoras. Even Sir W. Jones, as we saw, identified Buddha, first with Odin, and afterwards with Shishak, " who either in person or by a colony from Egypt imported into India the mild heresy of the ancient Bauddhas." Now we know that neither Egypt nor the Walhalla of Germany, neither Greece nor Persia, could have produced either the man himself or his doctrine. He is the offspring of India in mind and soul. His doctrine, by the very antago-

1 Neander, History of the Church, vol. I. p. 817; The Zapolis and Buddho on the Xyoto and the Manigada ἕν καὶ τὸ αὐτο εἶναι.

nism in which it stands to the old system of Brahmanism, shows that it could not have sprung up in any
country except India. The ancient history of Brahmanism leads on to Buddhism, with the same necessity
with which mediæval Romanism led to Protestantism.
Though the date of Buddha is still liable to small
chronological oscillations, his place in the intellectual
annals of India is henceforth definitely marked: Buddhism became the state religion of India at the time of
Asoka; and Asoka, the Buddhist Constantine, was
the grandson of Kandragupta, the contemporary of
Seleucus Nicator. The system of the Brahmans had
run its course. Their ascendency, at first purely intellectual and religious, had gradually assumed a political character. By means of the system of caste this
influence pervaded the whole social fabric, not as a
vivifying leaven, but as a deadly poison. Their in-
creasing power and self-confidence are clearly exhibited
in the successive periods of their ancient literature.
It begins with the simple hymns of the Veda. These
are followed by the tracts, known by the name of
Brâhmanas, in which a complete system of theology is
elaborated and claims advanced in favor of the Brahmans, such as were seldom conceded to any hierarchy.
The third period in the history of their ancient literature is marked by their Sûtras or Aphorisms, curt
and dry formularies, showing the Brahmans in secure
possession of all their claims. Such privileges as they
then enjoyed are never enjoyed for any length of
time. It was impossible for anybody to move or to assert his freedom of thought and action without finding himself impeded on all sides by the web of the
Brahmanic law; nor was there anything in their relig-

ice, to satisfy the natural yearnings of the human
heart after spiritual comfort. What was felt by Buddha, had been felt more or less intensely by thousands;
and this was the secret of his success. That success
was accelerated, however, by political events. Kandragupta had conquered the throne of Magadha, and
acquired his supremacy in India in defiance of the
Brahmanic law. He was of low origin, a mere adventurer, and by his accession to the throne an important mesh had been broken in the intricate system of casts. Neither he nor his successors could
count on the support of the Brahmans, and it is but
natural that his grandson, Asoka, should have been
driven to seek support from the sect founded by Buddha. Buddha, by giving up his royal station, had
broken the law of caste as much as Kandragupta by
usurping it. His school, though it had probably escaped open persecution until it rose to political importance, could never have been on friendly terms with
the Brahmans of the old school. The parvenu on the
throne saw his natural allies in the followers of Buddha, and the mendicants, who by their unostentatious
behavior had won golden opinions among the lower
and middle classes, were suddenly raised to an importance little dreamt of by their founder. Those who
see in Buddhism, not a social but chiefly a religious
and philosophical reform, have been deceived by the
later Buddhist literature, and particularly by the con-
troversies between Buddhists and Brahmans, which in
later times led to the total expulsion of the former from
India, and to the political reëstablishment of Brahmanism. These, no doubt, turn chiefly on philosophical
problems, and are of the most abstruse and intricate

character. But such was not the teaching of Buddha. If we may judge from "the four verities," which Buddha inculcated from the first day that he entered on his career as a teacher, his philosophy of life was very simple. He proclaims that there was nothing but sorrow in life; that sorrow is produced by our affections, that our affections must be destroyed in order to destroy the root of sorrow, and that he could teach mankind how to eradicate all the affections, all passions, all desires. Such doctrines were intelligible; and considering that Buddha received people of all castes, who, after renouncing the world and assuming their yellow robes, were sure of finding a livelihood from the charitable gifts of the people, it is not surprising that the number of his followers should have grown so rapidly. If Buddha really taught the metaphysical doctrines which are ascribed to him by subsequent writers—and this is a point which it is impossible to settle—not one in a thousand among his followers would have been capable of appreciating those speculations. They must have been reserved for a few of his disciples, and they would never have formed the nucleus for a popular religion.

Nearly all who have written on Buddhism, and M. Barthélemy Saint-Hilaire among the rest, have endeavored to show that these metaphysical doctrines of Buddha were borrowed from the earlier systems of Brahmanic philosophy, and more particularly from the Sânkhya system. The reputed founder of that system is Kapila; and we saw before how Professor Wilson actually changed the name of Kapilavastu, the birthplace of Buddha, into a mere allegory,—"Kapilavastu" meaning, according to him, the substance of Kapila or

of the Sânkhya philosophy. This is not all. Mr. Spence
Hardy (p. 132) quotes a legend in which it is said that
Buddha was in a former existence the ascetic Kapila;
that the Sâkya princes came to his hermitage, and that
he pointed out to them the proper place for founding a
new city, which city was named after him Kapilavastu.
But we have looked in vain for any definite similarities
between the system of Kapila, as known to us in the
Sânkhya-sûtras, and the Abhidharma, or the metaphysics of the Buddhists. Such similarities would be in-
valuable. They would probably enable us to decide
whether Buddha borrowed from Kapila or Kapila
from Buddha, and thus determine the real chronology
of the philosophical literature of India, as either prior
or subsequent to the Buddhist era. There are certain
notions which Buddha shares in common not only with
Kapila, but with every Hindu philosopher. The idea
of transmigration; the belief in the continuing effects
of our good and bad actions, extending from our former to our present and from our present to our
future lives; the sense that life is a dream or a burden;
the admission of the uselessness of religious observances after the attainment of the highest knowledge, —
all these belong, so to say, to the national philosophy of
India. We meet with these ideas everywhere, in the
poetry, the philosophy, the religion of the Hindus.
They cannot be claimed as the exclusive property of
any system in particular. But if we look for more
special coincidences between Buddha's doctrines and
those of Kapila or other Indian philosophers, we look
in vain. At first it might seem as if the very first
aphorism of Kapila, namely, "the complete cessation
of pain, which is of three kinds, is the highest aim of

man," was merely a philosophical paraphrase of the events which, as we saw, determined Buddha to renounce the world in search of the true road to salvation. But though the starting-point of Kapila and Buddha is the same, a keen sense of human misery and a yearning after a better state, their roads diverge so completely and their goals are so far apart, that it is difficult to understand how, almost by common consent, Buddha is supposed either to have followed in the footsteps of Kapila, or to have changed Kapila's philosophy into a religion. Some scholars imagine that there was a more simple and primitive philosophy, which was taught by Kapila, and that the Sûtras which are now ascribed to him are of later date. It is impossible either to prove or to disprove such a view. At present we know Kapila's philosophy from his Sûtras only,[1] and these Sûtras seem to us posterior, not anterior, to Buddha. Though the name of Buddha is not mentioned in the Sûtras, his doctrines are clearly alluded to and controverted in several parts of them.

It has been said that Buddha and Kapila were both atheists, and that Buddha borrowed his atheism from Kapila. But atheism is an indefinite term, and may mean very different things. In one sense every Indian philosopher was an atheist, for they all perceived that the gods of the populace could not claim the attributes that belong to a Supreme Being. But all the important philosophical systems of the Brahmans admit, in some form or other, the existence of an Absolute and

Supreme Being, the source of all that exists, or seems
to exist. Kapila, when accused of atheism, is not accused of denying the existence of an Absolute Being.
He is accused of denying the existence of Isvara,
which in general means the Lord, but which, in the
passage where it occurs, refers to the Isvara of the
Yogins, or mystic philosophers. They maintained that
in an ecstatic state man possesses the power of seeing
God face to face, and they wished to have this ecstatic
intuition included under the head of sensuous percep-
tions. To this Kapila demurred. "You have not
proved the existence of your Lord," he says, "and
therefore I see no reason why I should alter my definition, of sensuous preception in order to accommodate
your ecstatic visions." The commentator narrates that
this strong language was used by Kapila in order to silence the wild talk of the Mystics, and that, though he
taunted his adversaries with having failed to prove the
existence of their Lord, he himself did not deny the
existence of a Supreme Being. Kapila, however,
went further. He endeavored to show that all the
attributes which the Mystics ascribed to their Lord are
inappropriate. He used arguments very similar to
those which have lately been used with such ability by
a distinguished Bampton Lecturer. The supreme lord
of the Mystics, Kapila argued, — either absolute and
unconditioned ("mukta"), or he is bound and con-
ditioned ("baddha"). If he is absolute and unconditioned, he cannot enter into the condition of a
Creator; he would have no desires which could insti-
gate him to create. If, on the contrary, he is represented as active, and entering on the work of creation,
he would no longer be the absolute and unchangeable

Being which we are asked to believe in. Kapila, like the preacher of our own days, was accused of paving the road to atheism, but his philosophy was nevertheless admitted as orthodox, because, in addition to sensuous perception and inductive reasoning, Kapila professed emphatically his belief in revelation, i. e. in the Veda, and allowed to it a place among the recognized instruments of knowledge. Buddha refused to allow to the Vedas any independent authority whatever, and this constituted the fundamental difference between the two philosophers.

Whether Kapila's philosophy was really in accordance with the spirit of the Veda, is quite a different question. No philosophy, at least nothing like a definite system, is to be found in the sacred hymns of the Brahmans; and though the Vedânta philosophy does less violence to the passages which it quotes from the Veda, the authors of the Veda would have been as much surprised at the consequences deduced from their words by the Vedântin, as by the strange meaning attributed to them by Kapila. The Vedânta philosopher, like Kapila, would deny the existence of a Creator in the usual sense of the word. He explained the universe as an emanation from Brahman, which is all in all. Kapila admitted two principles, an absolute Spirit and Nature, and he looked upon the universe as produced by a reflection of Nature thrown on the mirror of the absolute Spirit. Both systems seem to regard creation, or the created world, as a misfortune, as an unfortunate accident. But they maintain that its effects can be neutralized, and that emancipation from the bonds of earthly existence is possible by means of philosophy. The Vedânta philosopher imagines he is free when he has arrived at the knowledge that nothing exists but Brahman; that all phenomena are merely the result of ignorance; that after the destruction of that ignorance, and of its effects, all is merged again in Brahman, the true source of being, thought, and happiness. Kapila taught that the spirit became free from all mundane fetters as soon as it perceived that all phenomena were only passing reflections produced by nature upon the spirit, and as soon as it was able to shut its eyes to those illusory visions. Both systems, therefore, and the same applies to all the other philosophical systems of the Brahmans, admitted an absolute or self-existing Being as the cause of all that exists or seems to exist. And here lies the specific difference between Kapila and Buddha. Buddha, like Kapila, maintained that this world had no absolute reality; that it was a snare and an illusion. The words, " All is perishable, all is miserable, all is void," must frequently have passed his lips. But we cannot call things unreal unless we have a conception of something that is real. Where, then, did Buddha find a reality in comparison with which this world might be called unreal? What remedy did he propose as an emancipation from the sufferings of this life? Difficult as it seems to us to conceive it, Buddha admits of no real cause of this unreal world. He denies the existence not only of a Creator, but of any Absolute Being. According to the metaphysical tenets, if not of Buddha himself, at least of his sect, there is no reality anywhere, neither in the past nor in the future. True wisdom consists in perceiving the nothingness of all things, and in a desire to become nothing, to be blown out, to enter into Nirvâna. Emancipation is obtained by total extinction, not by

absorption in Brahman, or by a recovery of the soul's
true estate. If to be is misery, not to be must be
felicity, and this felicity is the highest reward which
Buddha promised to his disciples. In reading the
Aphorisms of Kapila, it is difficult not to see in his
remarks on those who maintain that all is void, covert
attacks on Buddha and his followers. In one place
(I. 43) Kapila argues that if people believed in the
reality of thought only, and denied the reality of external objects, they would soon be driven to admit that
nothing at all exists, because we perceive our thoughts
in the same manner as we perceive external objects.
This naturally leads him to an examination of that extreme doctrine, according to which all that we perceive
is void, and all is supposed to perish, because it is the
nature of things that they should perish. Kapila
remarks in reference to this view (I. 45), that it is a
mere assertion of persons who are "not enlightened,"
in Sanskrit "a-buddha," a sarcastic expression in which
it is very difficult not to see an allusion to Buddha, or
to those who claimed for him the title of "the Enlightened." Kapila then proceeds to give the best
answer that could be given to those who taught that
complete annihilation must be the highest aim of man,
as the only means of a complete cessation of suffering.
"It is not so," he says; "for if people wish to be
free from suffering, it is they themselves who wish to
be free, just as in this life it is they themselves who
wish to enjoy happiness. There must be a permanent
soul in order to satisfy the yearnings of the human
heart, and if you deny that soul, you have no right to
speak of the highest aim of man."

Whether the belief in this kind of Nirvâna i. e. in a

total extinction of being, personality, and consciousness, was at any time shared by the large masses of the people, is difficult either to assert or deny. We know nothing in ancient times of the religious convictions of the millions. We only know what a few leading spirits believed, or professed to believe. That certain individuals should have spoken and written of total extinction as the highest aim of man, is intelligible. Job cursed the day on which he was born, and Solomon praised the "dead which are already dead, more than the living which are yet alive." "Yea, better is he than both they," he said, "which hath not yet been, who hath not seen the evil work that is done under the sun." Voltaire said in his own flippant way, "On aime la vie, mais le néant ne laisse pas d'avoir du bon;" and a modern German philosopher, who has found much favor with those who profess to despise Kant, Schelling, and Hegel, writes, "Considered in its objective value, it is more than doubtful that life is preferable to the Nothing. I should say even, that if experience and reflection could lift up their voices they would recommend to us the Nothing. We are what ought not to be, and we shall therefore cease to be." Under peculiar circumstances, in the agonies of despair, or under the gathering clouds of madness, such language is intelligible; but to believe, as we are asked to believe, that one half of mankind had yearned for total annihilation, would be tantamount to a belief that there is a difference in kind between man and man. Buddhist philosophers, no doubt, held this doctrine, and it cannot be denied that it found a place in the Buddhist canon. But even among the different schools of Buddhist philosophers, very different views are adopted as to the true meaning of "Nirvâna;" and with the modern Buddhists of Burmah, "Nigban," as they call it, is defined simply as freedom from old age, disease, and death. We do not find fault with M. Barthélemy Saint-Hilaire for having so emphatically pressed the charge of nihilism against Buddha himself. In one portion of the Buddhist canon the most extreme views of nihilism are put into his mouth. All we can say is that that canon is later than Buddha, and that in the same canon [1] the founder of Buddhism, after having entered into Nirvâna is still spoken of as living, nay, as showing himself to those who believe in him. Buddha, who denied the existence, or at least the divine nature of the gods worshipped by the Brahmans, was raised himself to the rank of a deity by some of his followers [2] (the Aisvarikas), and we need not wonder, therefore, if his Nirvâna too was gradually changed into an Elysian field. And finally, if we may argue from human nature, such as we find it at all times and in all countries, we confess that we cannot bring ourselves to believe that the reformer of India, the teacher of so perfect a code of morality, the young prince who gave up all he had in order to help those whom he saw afflicted in mind, body, or estate, should have cared much about speculations which he knew would either be misunderstood, or not understood at all, by those whom he wished to benefit; that he should have thrown away one of the most powerful weapons

---

[1] L'enfant égaré, par Th. Ed. Foucaux, p. 19.

[2] How early this took place, we see from Clemens of Alexandria, Strom. I. p. 305, A. B. (ed. Colon 1688), Μεγασθένης Indika, ed. Schwanbeck, p. 139, καὶ Ἰνδῶν Ἰνδοῖ οἱ τοῖς Βυττα (τῷ Βούτα) πειθόμενοι παραγγέλμασιν, δι᾽ ὑπερβολὴν σεμνότητος εἰς θεὸν τετιμήκασιν.

in the hands of every religious teacher, — the belief in
a future life ; and should not have seen, that if this life
was sooner or later to end in nothing, it was hardly
worth the trouble which he took himself, or the sacrifices which he imposed on his disciples.

April, 1852.

X.

BUDDHIST PILGRIMS.[1]

M. STANISLAS JULIEN has commenced the publication of a work entitled, "Voyages des Pèlerins Bouddhistes." The first volume, published in the year 1853, contains the biography of Hiouen-thsang, who, in the middle of the seventh century A. D., travelled from China through Central Asia to India. The second, which has just reached us, gives us the first portion of Hiouen-thsang's own diary.

There are not many books of travel which can be compared to these volumes. Hiouen-thsang passed through countries which few had visited before him. He describes parts of the world which no one has explored since, and where even our modern maps contain hardly more than the ingenious conjectures of Alexander von Humboldt. His observations are minute; his geographical, statistical, and historical remarks most accurate and trustworthy. The chief object of his travels was to study the religion of Buddha, the great reformer of India. Some Chinese pilgrims visited India before, several after, his time. Hiouen-thsang,

1 *Voyages des Pèlerins Bouddhistes.* Vol. I. *Histoire de la Vie de Hiouen-Thsang, et de ses Voyages dans l'Inde, depuis l'an 629 jusqu'en 645, par Hoeili et Yen Thsong; traduite du Chinois par Stanislas Julien.* Vol. II. *Mémoires sur les Contrées Occidentales, traduits du Sanscrit en Chinois, en l'an 648, par Hiouen-thsang, et du Chinois en Français, par Stanislas Julien.* Paris 1853-1857: B. Duprat. London and Edinburgh: Williams & Norgate.

however, is considered by the Chinese themselves as the most distinguished of these pilgrims, and M. Stanislas Julien has rightly assigned to him the first place in his collection.

In order to understand what Hiouen-thsang was, and to appreciate his life and his labors, we must first cast a glance at the history of a religion which, however unattractive and even mischievous it may appear to ourselves, inspired her votary with the true spirit of devotion and self-sacrifice. That religion has now existed for 2,400 years. To millions and millions of human beings it has been the only preparation for a higher life placed within their reach. And even at the present day it counts in Asia a more numerous array of believers than any other faith, not excluding Mohammedanism or Christianity. The religion of Buddha took its origin in India about the middle of the sixth century B. C., but it did not assume its political importance till about the time of Alexander's invasion. We know little, therefore, of its first origin and spreading, because the canonical works on which we must chiefly rely for information belong to a much later period, and are strongly tinged with a legendary character. The very existence of such a being as Buddha, the son of Suddhodana, king of Kapilavastu, has been doubted. But what can never be doubted is this, that Buddhism, such as we find it in Russia[1] and Sweden,[2]

[1] See W. Spottiswoode's *Tarantasse Journey*, p. 230, "Visit to the Buddhist Temple."

[2] The only trace of the influence of Buddhism among the Kælic races, the Finns, Laps, etc., is found in the name of their priests and sorcerers, the Shamans. "Shaman" is supposed to be a corruption of "Sramana," a name applied to Buddha, and to Buddhist priests in general. The ancient mythological religion of the Kælic races has nothing in common with Buddhism. See Castren's *Lectures on Finnish Mythology*, 1854. Finland

on the very threshold of European civilization, in the north of Asia, in Mongolia, Tartary, China, Thibet, Nepal, Siam, Burmah, and Ceylon, had its origin in India. Doctrines similar to those of Buddha existed in that country long before his time. We can trace them like meandering roots below the surface long before we reach the point where the roots strike up into a stem, and the stem branches off again into fruit-bearing branches. What was original and new in Buddha was his changing a philosophical system into a practical doctrine; his taking the wisdom of the few, and coining as much of it as he thought genuine for the benefit of the many; his breaking with the traditional formalities of the past, and proclaiming for the first time, in spite of castes and creeds, the equality of the rich and the poor, the foolish and the wise, the " twice-born " and the outcast. Buddhism, as a religion and as a political fact, was a reaction against Brahmanism, though it retained much of that more primitive form of faith and worship. Buddhism, in its historical growth, presupposes Brahmanism, and, however hostile the mutual relation of these two religions may have been at different periods of Indian history, it can be shown, without much difficulty, that the latter was but a natural consequence of the former

The ancient religion of the Aryan inhabitants of India had started, like the religion of the Greeks, the

Romans, the Germans, Slaves, and Celts, with a simple and intelligible mythological phraseology. In the Veda — for there is but one real Veda — the nature of all the so-called gods or Devas betray their original physical character and meaning without disguise. The fire was praised and invoked by the name of "Agni" (*ignis*); the earth by the name of "Prithvi" (the broad); the sky by the name of "Dyu" (Jupiter), and afterwards of "Indra;" the firmament and the waters by the name of "Varuna," or Oἰρανός. The sun was invoked by many names, such as "Sûrya," "Savitri," "Vishnu," or "Mitra;" and the dawn rejoiced in such titles as "Ushas," "Urvasi," "Ahanâ," and "Sûryâ." Nor was the moon forgotten. For though it is mentioned but rarely under its usual name of "Kandra," it is alluded to under the more sacred appellation of "Soma;" and each of its four phases had received its own denomination. There is hardly any part of nature, if it could impress the human mind in any way with the ideas of a higher power, of order, eternity, or beneficence, — whether the winds, or the rivers, or the trees, or the mountains, — without a name and representative in the early Hindu Pantheon. No doubt there existed in the human mind, from the very beginning, something, whether we call it a suspicion, an innate idea, an intuition, or a sense of the Divine. What distinguishes man from the rest of the animal creation is chiefly that ineradicable feeling of dependence and reliance upon some higher power, a consciousness of bondage, from which the very name of "religion" was derived. "It is He that hath made us, and not we ourselves." The presence of that power was felt everywhere, and nowhere more clearly and strongly than in the rising and setting of the sun, in the change of day and night, of spring and winter, of birth and death. But, although the Divine presence was felt everywhere, it was impossible in that early period of thought, and with a language incapable as yet of expressing anything but material objects, to conceive the idea of God in its purity and fullness, or to assign to it an adequate and worthy expression. Children cannot think the thoughts of men, and the poets of the Veda could not speak the language of Aristotle. It was by a slow process that the human mind elaborated the idea of one absolute and supreme Godhead ; and by a still slower process that the human language tortured a word to express that idea. A period of growth was inevitable, and those who, from a mere guess of their own, do not hesitate to speak authoritatively of a primæval revelation, which imparted to the Pagan world the idea of the Godhead in all its purity, forget that, however pure and sublime and spiritual that revelation might have been, there was no language capable as yet of expressing the high and immaterial conceptions of that Heaven-sent message. The real history of religion, during the earliest mythological period, represents to us a slow process of fermentation in thought and language, with its various interruptions, its overflowings, its coolings, its deposits, and its gradual clearing from all extraneous and foreign admixture. This is not only the case among the Indo-European or Aryan races in India, in Greece, and in Germany. In Peru, and wherever the primitive formations of the intellectual world crop out, the process is exactly the same. "The religion of the sun," as it has been boldly said by the author of the "Spanish

Conquest in America," " was inevitable." It was like
a deep furrow which that heavenly luminary drew, in
its silent procession from east to west, over the virgin
mind of the gazing multitude; and in the impression
left there by the first rising and setting of the sun, there
lay the dark seed of a faith in a more than human
being, the first intimation of a life without beginning,
of a world without end. Manifold seed fell afterwards
into the soil once broken. Something divine was discovered in everything that moved and lived. Names
were stammered forth in anxious haste, and no single
name could fully express what lay hidden in the human
mind and wanted expression — the idea of an absolute,
and perfect, and supreme, and immortal Essence.
Thus a countless host of nominal gods was called into
being, and for a time seemed to satisfy the wants of a
thoughtless multitude. But there were thoughtful
men at all times, and their reason protested against
the contradictions of a mythological phraseology,
though it had been hallowed by sacred customs and
traditions. That rebellious reason had been at work
from the very first, always ready to break the yoke of
names and formulas which no longer expressed what
they were intended to express. The idea which had
yearned for utterance was the idea of a supreme and
absolute Power, and that yearning was not satisfied by
such names as "Kronos," "Zeus," and "Apollon."
The very sound of such a word as "God," used in the
plural, jarred on the ear, as if we were to speak of
two universes, or of a single twin. There are many
words, as Greek and Latin grammarians tell us, which,
if used in the plural, have a different meaning from
what they have in the singular. The Latin "ædes"

means a temple; if used in the plural it means a house.
"Deus" and Θεός ought to be added to the same class
of words. The idea of supreme perfection excluded
limitation, and the idea of God excluded the possibility
of many gods. This may seem language too abstract
and metaphysical for the early times of which we are
speaking. But the ancient poets of the Vedic hymns
have expressed the same thought with perfect clearness and simplicity. In the Rig-veda (I. 164, 46)
we read : —

"That which is one the sages speak of in many ways
— they call it 'Agni,' 'Yama,' 'Mâtariśvan.' "

Besides the plurality of gods, which was sure to lead
to their destruction, there was a taint of mortality
which they could not throw off. They all derived
their being from the life of nature. The god who represented the sun was liable, in the mythological language of antiquity, to all the accidents which threatened the solar luminary. Though he might rise in
immortal youth in the morning, he was conquered by
the shadows of the night, and the powers of winter
seemed to overthrow his heavenly throne. There is
nothing in nature free from change, and the gods of
nature fell under the thralldom of nature's laws. The
sun must set, and the solar gods and heroes must die.
There must be one God, there must be one unchanging
Deity; this was the silent conviction of the human
mind. There are many gods, liable to all the vicissitudes of life; this was everywhere the answer of
mythological religion.

It is curious to observe in how many various ways
these two opposite principles were kept for a time from
open conflict, and how long the heathen temples re-

sisted the enemy which was slowly and imperceptibly undermining their very foundations. In Greece this mortal element, inherent in all gods, was eliminated to a great extent by the conception of heroes. Whatever was too human in the ancient legends told of Zeus and Apollon was transferred to so-called half-gods or heroes, who were represented as the sons or favorites of the gods, and who bore their fate under a slightly altered name. The twofold character of Herakles as a god and as a hero is acknowledged even by Herodotus, and some of his epithets would have been sufficient to indicate his solar and originally divine character. But, in order to make some of the legends told of the solar deity possible or conceivable, it was necessary to represent Herakles as a more human being, and to make him rise to the seat of the Immortals only after he had endured toils and sufferings incompatible with the dignity of an Olympian god. We find the same idea in Peru, only that there it led to different results. A thinking, or, as he was called, a freethinking Inca [1] remarked that this perpetual travelling of the sun was a sign of servitude,[2] and he threw doubts upon the divine nature of such an unquiet thing as that great luminary appeared to him to be. And this misgiving led to a tradition which, even should it be unfounded in history, had some truth in itself, that there was in Peru an earlier worship, that of an invisible Deity, the Creator of the world, Pachacamac. In Greece, also, there are signs of a similar craving after the " Unknown

[1] Helps, The Spanish Conquest, vol. iii. p. 303 ; " Que cosa tam inquieta non le parecia ser Dios."

[2] On the servitude of the gods, see the " Essay on Comparative Mythology," Oxford Essays, 1856, p. 60.

God." A supreme God was wanted, and Zeus, the stripling of Creta, was raised to that rank. He became God above all gods — ἄριστον ϑεῶν, as Pindar calls him. Yet more was wanted than a mere Zeus; and thus a supreme Fate or Spell was imagined before which all the gods, and even Zeus, had to bow. And even this Fate was not allowed to remain supreme, and there was something in the destinies of man which was called ὑπέρμορα, or "beyond Fate." The most awful solution, however, of the problem belongs to Teutonic mythology. Here, also, some heroes were introduced; but their death was only the beginning of the final catastrophe. "All gods must die." Such is the last word of that religion which had grown up in the forests of Germany, and found a last refuge among the glaciers and volcanoes of Iceland. The death of Sigurd, the descendant of Odin, could not avert the death of Balder, the son of Odin; and the death of Balder was soon to be followed by the death of Odin himself, and of all the immortal gods.

All this was inevitable, and Prometheus, the man of forethought, could safely predict the fall of Zeus. The struggles by which reason and faith overthrow tradition and superstition vary in different countries and at different times; but the final victory is always on their side. In India the same antagonism manifested itself, but what there seemed a victory of reason threatened to become the destruction of all religious faith. At first there was hardly a struggle. On the primitive mythological stratum of thought two new formations arose, — the Brahmanical philosophy and the Brahmanical ceremonial; the one opening the widest avenues of philosophical thought, the other fencing all

religious feeling within the narrowest barriers.	Both
derived their authority from the same source.	Both
professed to carry out the meaning and purpose of the
Veda.	Thus we see on the one side, the growth of a
numerous and powerful priesthood, and the establishment of a ceremonial which embraced every moment
of a man's life from his birth to his death.	There was
no event which might have moved the heart to a spontaneous outpouring of praise or thanksgiving, which
was not regulated by priestly formulas.	Every prayer
was prescribed, every sacrifice determined.	Every
god had his share, and the claims of each deity on the
adoration of the faithful were set down with such
punctiliousness, the danger of offending their pride was
represented in such vivid colors, that no one would
venture to approach their presence without the assistance of a well-paid staff of masters of divine ceremo-
nies.	It was impossible to avoid sin without the help
of the Brahmans.	They alone knew the food that
might properly be eaten, the air which might properly
be breathed, the dress which might properly be worn.
They alone could tell what god should be invoked,
what sacrifice be offered; and the slightest mistake of
pronunciation, the slightest neglect about clarified
butter, or the length of the ladle in which it was to be
offered, might bring destruction upon the head of the
unassisted worshipper.	No nation was ever so com-
pletely priest-ridden as the Hindus under the sway of
the Brahmanic law.	Yet, on the other side, the same
people were allowed to indulge in the most unrestrained
freedom of thought, and in the schools of their philosophy the very names of their gods were never men-
tioned.	Their existence was neither denied nor as-

serted; they were of no greater importance in the system of the world of thought than trees or mountains, men or animals; and to offer sacrifices to them with a hope of rewards, so far from being meritorious, was considered as dangerous to that emancipation to which a clear perception of philosophical truth was to lead the patient student. There was one system which taught that there existed but one Being, without a second; that everything else which seemed to exist was but a dream and illusion, and that this illusion might be removed by a true knowledge of the one Being. There was another system which admitted two principles,—one a subjective and self-existent mind, the other matter, endowed with qualities. Here the world, with its joys and sorrows, was explained as the result of the subjective Self, reflecting itself in the mirror of matter; and final emancipation was obtained by turning away the eyes from the play of nature, and being absorbed in the knowledge of the true and absolute Self. A third system started with the admission of atoms, and explained every effect, including the elements and the mind, animals, men, and gods, from the concurrence of these atoms. In fact, as M. Cousin remarked many years ago, the history of the philosophy of India is " un abrégé de l'histoire de la philosophie." The germs of all these systems are traced back to the Vedas, Bráhmanas, and the Upanishads, and the man who believed in any of them was considered as orthodox as the devout worshipper of the gods: the one was saved by knowledge and faith, the other by works and faith.

Such was the state of the Hindu mind when Buddhism arose; or, rather, such was the state of the

Hindu mind which gave rise to Buddhism. Buddha himself went through the school of the Brahmans. He performed their penances, he studied their philosophy, and he at last claimed the name of "the Buddha," or "the Enlightened," when he threw away the whole ceremonial, with its sacrifices, superstitions, penances, and castes, as worthless, and changed the complicated systems of philosophy into a short doctrine of salvation. This doctrine of salvation has been called pure Atheism and Nihilism, and it no doubt was liable to both charges in its metaphysical character, and in that form in which we chiefly know it. It was Atheistic, not because it denied the existence of such gods as Indra and Brahman. Buddha did not even condescend to deny their existence. But it was called Atheistic, like the Sânkhya philosophy, which admitted but one subjective Self, and considered creation as an illusion of that Self, imaging itself for a while in the mirror of nature. As there was no reality in creation, there could be no real Creator. All that seemed to exist was the result of ignorance. To remove that ignorance was to remove the cause of all that seemed to exist. How a religion which taught the annihilation of all existence, of all thought, of all individuality and personality, as the highest object of all endeavors, could have laid hold of the minds of millions of human beings, and how at the same time, by enforcing the duties of morality, justice, kindness, and self-sacrifice, it could have exercised a decided beneficial influence, not only on the natives of India, but on the lowest barbarians of Central Asia, is a riddle which no one has been able to solve. We must distinguish, it seems, between Buddhism as a religion, and Buddhism as a philosophy. The former addressed itself to millions, the latter to a few isolated thinkers It is from these isolated thinkers, however, and from their literary compositions, that we are apt to form our notions of what Buddhism was, while, as a matter of fact, not one in a thousand would have been capable of following these metaphysical speculations. To the people at large Buddhism was a moral and religious, not a philosophical reform. Yet even its morality has a metaphysical tinge. The morality which it teaches is not a morality of expediency and rewards. Virtue is not enjoined because it necessarily leads to happiness. No; virtue is to be practiced, but happiness is to be shunned, and the only reward for virtue is that it subdues the passions, and thus prepares the human mind for that knowledge which is to end in complete annihilation. There are ten commandments which Buddha imposes on his disciples.[1] They are —

1. Not to kill.
2. Not to steal.
3. Not to commit adultery.
4. Not to lie.
5. Not to get intoxicated.
6. To abstain from unseasonable meals.
7. To abstain from public spectacles.
8. To abstain from expensive dresses.
9. Not to have a large bed.
10. Not to receive silver or gold.

The duties of those who embraced a religious life were more severe. They were not allowed to wear any dress except rags collected in cemeteries, and these rags

[1] See Burnouf, *Lotus de la bonne Loi*, p. 444. Barthélemy Saint-Hilaire *Du Bouddhisme*, p. 183. Ch. F. Neumann, *Catechism of the Shamans*.

they had to sew together with their own hands. A
yellow cloak was to be thrown over these rags. Their
food was to be extremely simple, and they were not to
possess anything, except what they could get by collecting alms from door to door in their wooden bowls.
They had but one meal in the morning, and were not
allowed to touch any food after midday. They were to
live in forests, not in cities, and their only shelter was
to be the shadow of a tree. There they were to sit, to
spread their carpet, but not to lie down, even during
sleep. They were allowed to enter the nearest city or
village in order to beg, but they had to return to their
forest before night, and the only change which was
allowed, or rather prescribed, was when they had to
spend some nights in the cemeteries, there to meditate
on the vanity of all things. And what was the object
of all this asceticism? Simply to guide each individual towards that path which would finally bring him to
Nirvâna, to utter extinction or annihilation. The very
definition of virtue was that it helped man to cross
over to the other shore, and that other shore was
not death, but cessation of all being. Thus charity
was considered a virtue; modesty, patience, courage,
contemplation, and science, all were virtues, but they
were practised only as a means of arriving at deliverance. Buddha himself exhibited the perfection of all
these virtues. His charity knew no bounds. When he
saw a tigress starved, and unable to feed her cubs, he
is said to have made a charitable oblation of his body
to be devoured by them. Hiouen-thsang visited the
place on the banks of the Indus where this miracle was
supposed to have happened, and he remarks that the
soil is still red there from the blood of Buddha, and

that the trees and flowers have the same color.[1] As
to the modesty of Buddha, nothing could exceed it.
One day, king Prasenajit, the protector of Buddha,
called on him to perform miracles, in order to silence
his adversaries, the Brahmans. Buddha consented.
He performed the required miracles ; but he exclaimed,
"Great king, I do not teach the law to my pupils, telling them, Go, ye saints, and before the eyes of the
Brahmans and householders perform, by means of your
supernatural powers, miracles greater than any man
can perform. I tell them, when I teach them the
law, Live, ye saints, hiding your good works and showing your sins." And yet all this self-sacrificing charity,
all this self-sacrificing humility, by which the life of
Buddha was distinguished throughout, and which he
preached to the multitudes that came to listen to him,
had, we are told, but one object, and that object was
final annihilation. It is impossible almost to believe
it, and yet when we turn away our eyes from the
pleasing picture of that high morality which Buddha
preached for the first time to all classes of men, and
look into the dark pages of his code of religious metaphysics, we can hardly find another explanation. Fortunately, the millions who embraced the doctrines of
Buddha, and were saved by it from the depths of bar-
barism, brutality, and selfishness, were unable to fathom
the meaning of his metaphysical doctrines. With
them the Nirvâna to which they aspired, became only a
relative deliverance from the miseries of human life ;
nay, it took the bright colors of a paradise, to be re-
gained by the pious worshipper of Buddha. But was
this the meaning of Buddha himself? In his "Four

Verities" he does not, indeed, define "Nirvâna," except by cessation of all pain; but when he traces the cause of pain, and teaches the means of destroying not only pain itself, but the cause of pain, we shall see that his Nirvâna assumes a very different meaning. His "Four Verities" are very simple. The first asserts the existence of pain; the second asserts that the cause of pain lies in sin; the third asserts that pain may cease by Nirvâna; the fourth shows the way that leads to Nirvâna. This way to Nirvâna consists in eight things; right faith (orthodoxy), right judgment (logic), right language (veracity), right purpose (honesty), right practice (religious life), right obedience (lawful life), right memory, and right meditation. All these precepts might be understood as part of a simply moral code, closing with a kind of mystic meditation on the highest object of thought, and with a yearning after deliverance from all worldly ties. Similar systems have prevailed in many parts of the world, without denying the existence of an absolute Being, or of a something towards which the human mind tends, in which it is absorbed or even annihilated. Awful as such a mysticism may appear, yet it leaves still something that exists, it acknowledges a feeling of dependence in man. It knows of a first cause, though it may have nothing to predicate of it except that it is τὸ ἐνὸν δαιμόν. A return is possible from that desert. The first cause may be called to life again. It may take the names of " Creator," " Preserver," " Ruler; " and when the simplicity and helplessness of the child have reëntered the heart of man, the name of father will come back to the lips which had uttered in vain all the names of a philosophical despair. But from the

Nirvâna of the Buddhist metaphysician there is no return. He starts from the idea that the highest object is to escape pain. Life in his eyes is nothing but misery; birth the cause of all evil, from which even death cannot deliver him, because he believes in an eternal cycle of existence, or in transmigration. There is no deliverance from evil, except by breaking through the prison walls, not only of life, but of existence, and by extirpating the last cause of existence. What, then, is the cause of existence? The cause of existence, says the Buddhist metaphysician, is attachment—an inclination towards something; and this attachment arises from thirst or desire. Desire presupposes perception of the object desired; perception presupposes contact; contact, at least a sentient contact, presupposes the senses; and, as the senses can only perceive what has form and name, or what is distinct, distinction is the real cause of all the effects which end in existence, birth, and pain. Now, this distinction is itself the result of conceptions or ideas; but these ideas, so far from being, as in Greek philosophy, the true and everlasting forms of the Absolute, are here represented as mere illusions, the effects of ignorance ("avidyâ"). Ignorance, therefore, is really the primary cause of all that seems to exist. To know that ignorance, as the root of all evil, is the same as to destroy it, and with it all effects that flowed from it. In order to see how this doctrine affects the individual, let us watch the last moments of Buddha as described by his disciples. He enters into the first stage of meditation when he feels freedom from sin, acquires a knowledge of the nature of all things, and has no desire except that of Nirvâna. But he still feels pleasure; he even uses his reasoning and discriminating powers. The use of these powers ceases in the second stage of meditation, when nothing remains but a desire after Nirvána, and a general feeling of satisfaction, arising from his intellectual perfection. That satisfaction, also, is extinguished in the third stage. Indifference succeeds; yet there is still self-consciousness, and a certain amount of physical pleasure. These last remnants are destroyed in the fourth stage; memory fades away, all pleasure and pain are gone, and the doors of Nirvána now open before him. After having passed these four stages once, Buddha went through them a second time, but he died before he attained again to the fourth stage. We must soar till higher, and though we may feel giddy and disgusted, we must sit out this tragedy till the curtain falls. After the four stages of meditation [1] are passed, the Buddha (and every being is to become a Buddha) enters into the infinity of space; then into the infinity of intelligence; and thence he passes into the region of nothing. But even here there is no rest. There is still something left,— the idea of the nothing in which he rejoices. That also must be destroyed, and it is destroyed in the fourth and last region, where there is not even the idea of a nothing left, and where there is complete rest, undisturbed by nothing, or what is not nothing.[2] There are few persons who will take the trouble of reasoning out such hallucinations; least of all, persons who are accustomed to the sober language of

[1] These "four stages" are described in the same manner in the canonical books of Ceylon and Nepal, and may therefore safely be ascribed to that original form of Buddhism from which the Southern and the Northern schools branched off at a later period. See Burnouf, Lotus de la bonne Loi p. 811.

[2] See Burnouf, Lotus de la bonne Loi, p. 811.

Greek philosophy; and it is the more interesting to hear the opinion which one of the best Aristotelian scholars of the present day, after a patient examination of the authentic documents of Buddhism, has formed of its system of metaphysics. M. Barthélemy Saint-Hilaire, in a review on Buddhism, published in the "Journal des Savants," says: —

"Buddhism has no God; it has not even the confused and vague notion of a Universal Spirit in which the human soul, according to the orthodox doctrine of Brahmanism, and the Sânkhya philosophy, may be absorbed. Nor does it admit nature, in the proper sense of the word, and it ignores that profound division between spirit and matter which forms the system and the glory of Kapila. It confounds man with all that surrounds him, all the while preaching to him the laws of virtue. Buddhism, therefore, cannot unite the human soul, which it does not even mention, with a God, whom it ignores; nor with nature, which it does not know better. Nothing remained but to annihilate the soul; and in order to be quite sure that the soul may not reappear under some new form in this world, which has been cursed as the abode of illusion and misery, Buddhism destroys its elements, and never gets tired of glorying in this achievement. What more is wanted? If this is not the absolute nothing, what is Nirvâna?"

Such religion, we should say, was made for a mad-house. But Buddhism was an advance, if compared with Brahmanism; it has stood its ground for centuries, and if truth could be decided by majorities, the show of hands, even at the present day, would be in favor of Buddha. The metaphysics of Buddhism, like

the metaphysics of most religions, not excluding our
own Gnosticism and Mysticism, were beyond the reach
of all except a few hardened philosophers or ecstatic
dreamers. Human nature could not be changed. Out
of the very nothing it made a new paradise; and he
who had left no place in the whole universe for a Divine Being, was deified himself by the multitudes who
wanted a person whom they could worship, a king
whose help they might invoke, a friend before whom
they could pour out their most secret griefs. And
there remained the code of a pure morality, proclaimed by Buddha. There remained the spirit of
charity, kindness, and universal pity with which he
had inspired his disciples.[1] There remained the simplicity of the ceremonial he had taught, the equality of
all men which he had declared, the religious toleration
which he had preached from the beginning. There
remained much, therefore, to account for the rapid
strides which his doctrine made from the mountain
peaks of Ceylon to the Tundras of the Samoyedes,
and we shall see in the simple story of the life of
Hiouen-thsang that Buddhism, with all its defects, has
had its heroes, its martyrs, and its saints.

Hiouen-thsang, born in China more than a thousand
years after the death of Buddha, was a believer in
Buddhism. He dedicated his whole life to the study

[1] See the *Dhammapadam* a Pâli work on Buddhist ethics, lately edited
by V. Fausböll, a distinguished pupil of Professor Westergaard, of Copenhagen. The Rev. Spence Hardy (*Eastern Monachism*, p. 169) writes: "A
collection might be made from the precepts of this work, that in the purity
of its ethics could scarcely be equalled from any other heathen author."
Mr. Knighton, when speaking of the same work in his *History of Ceylon* (p.
71), remarks: "In it we have exemplified a code of morality, and a list of
precepts, which, for pureness, excellence, and wisdom, is only second to that
of the Divine Lawgiver himself."

of that religion; travelling from his native country to India, visiting every place mentioned in Buddhist history or tradition, acquiring the ancient language in which the canonical books of the Buddhists were written, studying commentaries, discussing points of difficulty, and defending the orthodox faith at public councils against disbelievers and schismatics. Buddhism had grown and changed since the death of its founder, but it had lost nothing of its vitality. At a very early period a proselytizing spirit awoke among the disciples of the Indian reformer, an element entirely new in the history of ancient religions. No Jew, no Greek, no Roman, no Brahman ever thought of converting people to his own national form of worship. Religion was looked upon as private or national property. It was to be guarded against strangers. The most sacred names of the gods, the prayers by which their favor could be gained, were kept secret. No religion, however, was more exclusive than that of the Brahmans. A Brahman was born, nay, twice-born. He could not be made. Not even the lowest caste, that of the Sûdras, would open its ranks to a stranger. Here lay the secret of Buddha's success. He addressed himself to castes and outcasts. He promised salvation to all; and he commanded his disciples to preach his doctrine in all places and to all men. A sense of duty, extending from the narrow limits of the house, the village, and the country to the widest circle of mankind; a feeling of sympathy and brotherhood towards all men; the idea, in fact, of humanity, was in India first pronounced by Buddha. In the third Buddhist Council, the acts of which have been preserved to us in the "Mahavansa,"[1] we hear of missionaries be-

---

[1] *Mahavansa*, ed. G. Turnour. Ceylon, 1837, p. 71.

ing sent to the chief countries beyond India. This Council, we are told, took place 308 b. c., 235 years after the death of Buddha, in the 17th year of the reign of the famous king Asoka, whose edicts have been preserved to us on rock inscriptions in various parts of India. There are sentences in these inscriptions of Asoka which might be read with advantage by our own missionaries, though they are now more than 2,000 years old. Thus it is written on the rocks of Girnar, Dhauli, and Kapurdigiri :—

"Piyadasi, the king beloved of the gods, desires that the ascetics of all creeds might reside in all places. All these ascetics profess alike the command which people should exercise over themselves, and the purity of the soul. But people have different opinions, and different inclinations."

And again :—

"A man ought to honor his own faith only; but he should never abuse the faith of others. It is thus that he will do no harm to anybody. There are even circumstances where the religion of others ought to be honored. And in acting thus, a man fortifies his own faith, and assists the faith of others. He who acts otherwise, diminishes his own faith, and hurts the faith of others."

Those who have no time to read the voluminous works of the late E. Burnouf on Buddhism, his "Introduction à l'Histoire du Buddhisme," and his translation of "Le Lotus de la bonne Loi," will find a very interesting and lucid account of these councils, and edicts, and missions, and the history of Buddhism in general, in a work lately published by Mrs. Speir, "Life in Ancient India." Buddhism spread in the

south to Ceylon, in the north to Kashmir, the Himalayan countries, Thibet, and China. One Buddhist missionary is mentioned in the Chinese annals as early as
217 B. C.;[1] and about the year 120 B. C. a Chinese
general, after defeating the barbarous tribes north of
the Desert of Gobi, brought back as a trophy a golden
statue, the statue of Buddha.[2] It was not, however,
till the year 66 A. D. that Buddhism was officially recognized by the Emperor Ming-ti[3] as a third state religion in China. Ever since, it has shared equal
honors with the doctrines of Confucius and Lao-tse, in
the celestial empire, and it is but lately that these three
established religions have had to fear the encroachments of a new rival in the creed of the Chief of the
rebels.

After Buddhism had been introduced into China,
the first care of its teachers was to translate the sacred
works from Sanskrit, in which they were originally
written, into Chinese. We read of the Emperor
Ming-ti,[4] of the dynasty of Han, sending Tsai-in and
other high officials to India, in order to study there the
doctrine of Buddha. They engaged the services of two
learned Buddhists, Matánga and Tchou-fa-lan, and
some of the most important Buddhist works were
translated by them into Chinese. "The Life of Buddha," the "Lalita-Vistara,"[5] a Sanskrit work which,
on account of its style and language, had been referred
by oriental scholars to a much more modern period of

[1] See Foe Koue Ki, p. 41, and xxxviii. preface.
[2] See Foe Koue Ki, p. 41.
[3] Lalita-Vistara, ed. Foucaux, p. xvii. n.
[4] Lalita-Vistara, p. 17.
[5] Two parts of the Sanskrit text have been published in the Bibliotheca Indica.

Indian literature, can now safely be ascribed to an ante-Christian era, if, as we are told by Chinese scholars, it was translated from Sanskrit into Chinese, as one of the canonical books of Buddhism, as early as the year 76 A. D. The same work was translated also into Thibetan; and an edition of it — the first Thibetan work printed in Europe — published in Paris by M. E. Foucaux, reflects high credit on that distinguished scholar, and on the Government which supports these studies in the most liberal and enlightened spirit. The intellectual intercourse between the Indian peninsula and the northern continent of Asia remained uninterrupted for many centuries. Missions were sent from China to India, to report on the political and geographical state of the country, but the chief object of interest which attracted public embassies and private pilgrims across the Himalayan mountains was the religion of Buddha. About three hundred years after the public recognition of Buddhism by the Emperor Ming-ti, the great stream of Buddhist pilgrims began to flow from China to India. The first account which we possess of these pilgrimages refers to the travels of Fahian, who visited India towards the end of the fourth century. His travels have been translated by Rémusat, but M. Julien promises a new and more correct translation. After Fahian, we have the travels of Hœi-seng and Song-yun, who were sent to India, in 518, by command of the Empress, with a view of collecting sacred books and relics. Of Hiouen-thsang, who follows next in time, we possess, at present, eight out of twelve books; and there is reason to hope that the last four books of his Journal will soon follow in M. Julien's translation.[1] After Hiouen-thsang, the chief works of

[1] They have since been published.

Chinese pilgrims are the "Itineraries" of the fifty-six monks, published in 730, and the travels of Khi-nie, who visited India in 964, at the head of three hundred pilgrims. India was for a time the Holy Land of China. There lay the scene of the life and death of the great teacher; there were the monuments commemorating the chief events of his life; there the shrines where his relics might be worshipped; there the monasteries where tradition had preserved his sayings and his doings; there the books where his doctrine might be studied in its original purity; there the schools where the tenets of different sects which had sprung up in the course of time might best be acquired.

Some of the pilgrims and envoys have left us accounts of their travels, and, in the absence of anything like an historical literature in India itself, these Chinese works are of the utmost importance for gaining an insight into the social, political, and religious history of that country from the beginning of our era to the time of the Mohammedan conquest. The importance of Mohammedan writers, so far as they treat on the history of India during the Middle Ages, was soon recognized, and in a memoir lately published by the most eminent Arabic scholar of France, M. Reinaud, new and valuable historical materials have been collected, — materials doubly valuable in India, where no native historian has ever noted down the passing events of the day. But, although the existence of similar documents in Chinese was known, and although men of the highest literary eminence — such as Humboldt, Biot, and others — had repeatedly urged the necessity of having a translation of the early travels of the Chinese Pil-

grims, it seemed almost as if our curiosity was never to
be satisfied. France has been the only country where
Chinese scholarship has ever flourished, and it was a
French scholar, Abel Rémusat, who undertook at last
the translation of one of the Chinese Pilgrims. Rémusat died before his work was published, and his
translation of the travels of Fahian, edited by M. Lan-
dresse, remained for a long time without being followed
up by any other. Nor did the work of that eminent
scholar answer all expectations. Most of the proper
names, the names of countries, towns, mountains, and
rivers, the titles of books, and the whole Buddhistic
phraseology, were so disguised in their Chinese dress
that it was frequently impossible to discover their
original form.

The Chinese alphabet was never intended to represent the sound of words. It was in its origin a hieroglyphic system, each word having its own graphic representative. Nor would it have been possible to write
Chinese in any other way. Chinese is a monosyllabic
language. No word is allowed more than one consonant
and one vowel, — the vowels including diphthongs and
nasal vowels. Hence the possible number of words is
extremely small and the number of significative sounds
in the Chinese language, is said to be no more than 450.
No language, however, could be satisfied with so small
a vocabulary, and in Chinese, as in other monosyllabic
dialects, each word, as it was pronounced with various
accents and intonations, was made to convey a large
number of meanings; so that the total number of
words, or rather of ideas, expressed in Chinese, is said
to amount to 43,496. Hence a graphic representation
of the mere sound of words would have been perfectly

useless, and it was absolutely necessary to resort to hieroglyphical writing, enlarged by the introduction of determinative signs. Nearly the whole immense dictionary of Chinese — at least twenty-nine thirtieths — consists of combined signs, one part indicating the general sound, the other determining its special meaning. With such a system of writing it was possible to represent Chinese, but impossible to convey either the sound or the meaning of any other language. Besides, some of the most common sounds — such as r, b, d, and the short a — are unknown in Chinese.

How, then, were the translators to render Sanskrit names in Chinese? The most rational plan would have been to select as many Chinese signs as there were Sanskrit letters, and to express one and the same letter in Sanskrit always by one and the same sign in Chinese; or, if the conception of a consonant without a vowel, and of a vowel without a consonant, was too much for a Chinese understanding, to express at least the same syllabic sound in Sanskrit, by one and the same syllabic sign in Chinese. A similar system is adopted at the present day, when the Chinese find themselves under the necessity of writing the names of Lord Palmerston or Sir John Bowring; but, instead of adopting any definite system of transcribing, each translator seems to have chosen his own signs for rendering the sounds of Sanskrit words, and to have chosen them at random. The result is that every Sanskrit word as transcribed by the Chinese Buddhists is a riddle which no ingenuity is able to solve. Who could have guessed that "Fo-to," or more frequently "Fo," was meant for Buddha? "Ko-lo-keou-lo" for Râhula, the son of Buddha? "Po-lo-nai" for Benares ? " Heng-ho " for Ganges ? " Niepan " for Nirvâna ? " Chamen " for Sramana ? " Feito " for Veda ? " Tcha-li " for Kshattriya ? " Siu-to-lo " for Sûdra ? " Fan " or " Fan-lou-mo " for Brahma ? Sometimes, it is true the Chinese endeavored to give, besides the sounds, a translation of the meaning of the Sanskrit words. But the translation of proper names is always very precarious, and it required an intimate knowledge of Sanskrit and Buddhist literature to recognise from these awkward translations the exact form of the proper names for which they were intended. If, in a Chinese translation of " Thukydides," we read of a person called " Leader of the people," we might guess his name to have been " Demagogos," or " Lao-egos," as well as " Agesilaos." And when the name of the town of Sravasti was written " Che-wei," which means in Chinese " where one hears," it required no ordinary power of combination to find that the name of Sravasti was derived from a Sanskrit noun, " sravas " (Greek κλέος, Lat. clue), which means " hearing," or " fame," and that the etymological meaning of the name of " Sravasti " was intended by the Chinese " Che-wei." Besides these names of places and rivers, of kings and saints, there was the whole strange phraseology of Buddhism, of which no dictionary gives any satisfactory explanation. How was even the best Chinese scholar to know that the words which usually mean " dark shadow " must be taken in the technical sense of " Nirvâna," or " becoming absorbed in the Absolute," that " return-purity " had the same sense, and that a third synonymous expression was to be recognized in a phrase which, in ordinary Chinese would have the sense of " transport-figure-crossing-age ? " A

monastery is called "origin-door," instead of "black-
door." The voice of Buddha is called "the voice of
the dragon;" and his doctrine goes by the name of
"the door of expedients."

Tedious as these details may seem, it was almost a
duty to state them, in order to give an idea of the
difficulties which M. Stanislas Julien had to grapple
with. Oriental scholars labor under great disadvan-
tages. Few people take an interest in their works, or,
if they do, they simply accept the results, but they are
unable to appreciate the difficulty with which these results were obtained. Many persons who have read the
translation of the cuneiform inscriptions are glad, no
doubt, to have the authentic and contemporaneous
records of Darius and Xerxes. But if they followed
the process by which scholars such as Grotefend, Burnouf, Lassen, and Rawlinson arrived at their results,
they would see that the discovery of the alphabet, the
language, the grammar, and the meaning of the inscriptions of the Achaemenian dynasty deserves to be classed
with the discoveries of a Kepler, a Newton, or a Fara-
day. In a similar manner, the mere translation of a
Chinese work into French seems a very ordinary performance; but M. Stanislas Julien, who has long been
acknowledged as the first Chinese scholar in Europe,
had to spend twenty years of incessant labor in order
to prepare himself for the task of translating the
"Travels of Hiouen-thsang." He had to learn Sanskrit, no very easy language; he had to study the Buddhist literature written in Sanskrit, Pâli, Thibetan,
Mongolian, and Chinese. He had to make vast in-
dices of every proper name connected with Buddhism.
Thus only could he shape his own tools, and accom-

plish what at last he did accomplish. Most persons
will remember the interest with which the travels of
M. M. Huc and Gabet were read a few years ago,
though these two adventurous missionaries were obliged to renounce their original intention of entering
India by way of China and Thibet, and were not allowed to proceed beyond the famous capital of Lhassa.
If, then it be considered that there was a traveller who
had made a similar journey twelve hundred years
earlier; who had succeeded in crossing the deserts
and mountain passes which separate China from India;
who had visited the principal cities of the Indian
Peninsula, at a time of which we have no information,
from native or foreign sources, as to the state of that
country; who had learned Sanskrit, and made a large
collection of Buddhist works: who had carried on
public disputations with the most eminent philosophers
and theologians of the day; who had translated the
most important works on Buddhism from Sanskrit into
Chinese, and left an account of his travels, which still
existed in the libraries of China,—nay, which had
been actually printed and published, —we may well
imagine the impatience with which all scholars interested in the ancient history of India, and in the subject of Buddhism, looked forward to the publication of
so important a work. Hiouen-thsang's name had first
been mentioned in Europe by Abel Rémusat and
Klaproth. They had discovered some fragments of his
travels in a Chinese work on foreign countries and foreign nations. Rémusat wrote to China to procure, if
possible, a complete copy of Hiouen-thsang's works.
He was informed by Morrison that they were out of
print. Still, the few specimens which he had given at

the end of his translation of the "Foe Koue ki" had whetted the appetite of oriental scholars. M. Stanislas Julien succeeded in procuring a copy of Hiouen-thsang in 1838; and after nearly twenty years spent in preparing a translation of the Chinese traveller, his version is now before us. If there are but few who know the difficulty of a work like that of M. Stanislas Julien, it becomes their duty to speak out, though, after all, perhaps the most intelligible eulogium would be that in a branch of study where there are no monopolies and no patents, M. Stanislas Julien is acknowledged to be the only man in Europe who could produce the article which he has produced in the work before us.

We shall devote the rest of our space to a short account of the life and travels of Hiouen-thsang. Hiouen-thsang was born in a provincial town of China, at a time when the empire was in a chronic state of revolution. His father had left the public service, and had given most of his time to the education of his four children. Two of them distinguished themselves at a very early age.—one of them was Hiouen-thsang, the future traveller and theologian. The boy was sent to school at a Buddhist monastery, and, after receiving there the necessary instruction, partly from his elder brother, he was himself admitted as a monk at the early age of thirteen. During the next seven years, the young monk travelled about with his brother from place to place, in order to follow the lectures of some of the most distinguished professors. The horrors of war frequently broke in upon his quiet studies, and forced him to seek refuge in the more distant provinces of the empire. At the age of twenty he took priest's orders, and had then already become famous by his ta.t knowledge. He had studied the chief canonical books of the Buddhist faith, the records of Buddha's life and teaching, the systems of ethics and metaphysics; and he was versed in the works of Confucius and Lao-tse. But still his own mind was agitated by doubts. Six years he continued his studies in the chief places of learning in China, and where he came to learn he was frequently asked to teach. At last, when he saw that none, even the most eminent theologians, were able to give him the information he wanted, he formed his resolve of travelling to India. The works of earlier pilgrims, such as Fahian and others, were known to him. He knew that in India he should find the originals of the works which in their Chinese translation left so many things doubtful in his mind; and though he knew from the same sources the dangers of his journey, yet, " the glory," as he says, " of recovering the Law, which was to be a guide to all men and the means of their salvation, seemed to him worthy of imitation." In common with several other priests, he addressed a memorial to the Emperor to ask leave for their journey. Leave was refused, and the courage of his companions failed. Not that of Hiouen-thsang. His own mother had told him that, soon before she gave birth to him, she had seen her child travelling to the Far West in search of the Law. He was himself haunted by similar visions, and having long surrendered worldly desires, he resolved to brave all dangers, and to risk his life for the only object for which he thought it worth while to live. He proceeded to the Yellow River, the Hoang-ho, and to the place where the caravans bound for India used to meet, and, though the Governor had sent strict orders not to allow any

one to cross the frontier, the young priest, with the
assistance of his co-religionists, succeeded in escaping
the vigilance of the Chinese "dominions." Spies were
sent after him. But so frank was his avowal, and so
firm his resolution, which he expressed in the presence
of the authorities, that the Governor himself tore his
hue and cry to pieces, and allowed him to proceed.
Hitherto he had been accompanied by two friends.
They now left him, and Hiouen-thsang found himself
alone, without a friend and without a guide. He
sought for strength in fervent prayer. The next
morning a person presented himself, offering his services as a guide. This guide conducted him safely for
some distance, but left him when they approached the
desert. There were still five watch-towers to be passed,
and there was nothing to indicate the road through the
desert, except the hoof-marks of horses, and skeletons.
The traveller followed this melancholy track, and,
though misled by the "mirage" of the desert, he
reached the first tower. Here the arrows of the
watchmen would have put an end to his existence and
his cherished expedition; but the officer in command,
himself a zealous Buddhist, allowed the courageous
pilgrim to proceed, and gave him letters of recommendation to the officers of the next towers. The last
tower, however, was guarded by men inaccessible to
bribes, and deaf to reasoning. In order to escape their
notice, Hiouen-thsang had to make a long détour. He
passed through another desert, and lost his way. The
bag in which he carried his water burst, and then even
the courage of Hiouen-thsang failed. He began to
retrace his steps. But suddenly he stopped. " I took
an oath," he said, " never to make a step backward till

I had reached India. Why, then, have I come here? It is better I should die proceeding to the West than return to the East and live." Four nights and five days he travelled through the desert without a drop of water. He had nothing to refresh himself except his prayers,—and what were they? Texts from a work which taught that there was no god, no Creator, no creation,—nothing but mind, minding itself. It is incredible in how exhausted an atmosphere the divine spark within us will glimmer on, and even warm the dark chambers of the human heart. Comforted by his prayers, Hiouen-thsang proceeded, and arrived after some time at a large lake. He was in the country of the Oigour Tartars. They received him well, nay, too well. One of the Tartar Khans, himself a Buddhist, sent for the Buddhist pilgrim, and insisted on his staying with him to instruct his people. Remonstrances proved of no avail. But Hiouen-thsang was not to be conquered. "I know," he said "that the king, in spite of his power, has no power over my mind and my will;" and he refused all nourishment in order to put an end to his life. Three days he persevered, and at last the Khan, afraid of the consequences, was obliged to yield to the poor monk. He made him promise to visit him on his return to China, and then to stay three years with him. At last, after a delay of one month, during which the Khan and his Court came daily to hear the lessons of their pious guest, the traveller continued his journey with a numerous escort, and with letters of introduction from the Khan to twenty-four princes whose territories the little caravan had to pass. Their way lay through what is now called Dsungary, across the

Musar-dabaghan mountains, the northern portion of
the Belur-tag, the Yaxartes valley, Bactria, and Kabulistan.   We cannot follow them through all the places
they passed, though the accounts which he gives of
their adventures are most interesting, and the description of the people most important.   Here is a description of the Musar-dabaghan mountains:—

   " The top of the mountain rises to the sky.   Since
the beginning of the world the snow has been accumu-
lating, and is now transformed into vast masses of ice,
which never melt, either in spring or summer.   Hard
and brilliant sheets of snow are spread out till they are
lost in the infinite, and mingled with the clouds.   If
one looks at them, the eyes are dazzled by the splendor.
Frozen peaks hang down over both sides of the road,
some hundred feet high, and twenty feet or thirty feet
thick.   It is not without difficulty and danger that the
traveller can clear them or climb over them.   Besides,
there are squalls of wind, and tornadoes of snow which
attack the pilgrims.   Even with double shoes, and in
thick furs, one cannot help trembling and shivering."

   During the seven days that Hiouen-thsang crossed
these Alpine passes he lost fourteen of his companions.

   What is most important, however, in this early portion of the Chinese traveller is the account which he
gives of the high degree of civilization among the
tribes of Central Asia.   We had gradually accustomed ourselves to believe in an early civilization of
Egypt, of Babylon, of China, of India; but now that
we find the hordes of Tartary possessing in the seventh
century the chief arts and institutions of an advanced
society, we shall soon have to drop the name of barbarians altogether.   The theory of M. Oppert, who

ascribes the original invention of the cuneiform letters
and a civilization anterior to that of Babylon, and Nineveh to a Turanian or Scythian race, will lose much of
its apparent improbability; for no new wave of civilization had reached these countries between the cuneiform
period of their literature and history and the time of
Hiouen-thsang's visit. In the kingdom of Okini, on
the western frontier of China, Hiouen-thsang found
an active commerce, gold, silver, and copper coinage;
monasteries, where the chief works of Buddhism were
studied, and an alphabet, derived from Sanskrit. As
he travelled on he met with mines, with agriculture,
including pears, plums, peaches, almonds, grapes,
pomegranates, rice, and wheat. The inhabitants were
dressed in silk and woolen materials. There were mu-
sicians in the chief cities who played on the flute and
the guitar. Buddhism was the prevailing religion, but
there were traces of an earlier worship, the Bactrian
fire-worship. The country was everywhere studded
with halls, monasteries, monuments, and statues.
Samarkand formed at that early time a kind of Athens,
and its manners were copied by all the tribes in the
neighborhood. Balkh, the old capital of Bactria, was
still an important place on the Oxus, well fortified, and
full of sacred buildings. And the details which our
traveller gives of the exact circumference of the cities,
the number of their inhabitants, the products of the
soil, the articles of trade, can leave no doubt in our
minds that he relates what he had seen and heard himself. A new page in the history of the world is here
opened, and new ruins pointed out, which would reward
the pickaxe of a Layard.

But we must not linger. Our traveller, as we said,

had entered India by way of Kabul. Shortly before
he arrived at Pou-lou-cha-pou-lo, i. e. the Sanskrit
Purushapura, the modern Peshawer, Hiouen-thsang
heard of an extraordinary cave where Buddha had
formerly converted a dragon, and had promised his
new pupil to leave him his shadow, in order that,
whenever the evil passions of his dragon-nature should
revive, the aspect of his master's shadowy features
might remind him of his former vow. This promise
was fulfilled, and the dragon-cave became a famous
place of pilgrimage. Our traveller was told that the
roads leading to the cave were extremely dangerous,
and infested by robbers; that for three years none
of the pilgrims had ever returned from the cave.
But he replied, "It would be difficult during a
hundred thousand Kalpas to meet one single time
with the true shadow of Buddha; how could I, having come so near, pass on without going to adore
it?" He left his companions behind, and after asking in vain for a guide, he met at last with a boy
who showed him to a farm belonging to a convent.
Here he found an old man who undertook to act as
his guide. They had hardly proceeded a few miles
when they were attacked by five robbers. The monk
took off his cap and displayed his ecclesiastical robes.
" Master," said one of the robbers, "where are you
going?" Hiouen-thsang replied, " I desire to adore
the shadow of Buddha." " Master," said the robber,
"have you not heard that these roads are full of
banditti?" " Robbers are men," Hiouen-thsang exclaimed; " and at present, when I am going to adore
the shadow of Buddha, even though the roads were
full of wild beasts, I should walk on without fear.

Surely, then, I ought not to fear you, as you are men whose heart is possessed of pity." The robbers were moved by these words, and opened their hearts to the true faith. After this little incident, Hiouen-thsang proceeded with his guide. He passed a stream rushing down between two precipitous walls of rock. In the rock itself there was a door which opened. All was dark. But Hiouen-thsang entered, advanced towards the cave, then moved fifty steps backwards, and began his devotions. He made one hundred salutations, but he saw nothing. He reproached himself bitterly with his former sins, he cried, and abandoned himself to utter despair, because the shadow of Buddha would not appear before him. At last, after many prayers and invocations, he saw on the eastern wall a dim light, of the size of a saucepan, such as the Buddhist monks carry in their hands. But it disappeared. He continued praying, full of joy and pain, and again he saw a light, which vanished like lightning. Then he vowed, full of devotion and love, that he would never leave the place till he had seen the shadow of the "Venerable of the age." After two hundred prayers, the cave was suddenly bathed in light, and the shadow of Buddha, of a brilliant white color, rose majestically on the wall, as when the clouds suddenly open and, all at once, display the marvelous image of the "Mountain of Light." A dazzling splendor lighted up the features of the divine countenance. Hiouen-thsang was lost in contemplation and wonder, and would not turn his eyes away from the sublime and incomparable object. . . . . After he awoke from his trance, he called in six men, and commanded them to light a fire in the cave, in order to burn incense ; but, as the approach of the light made the shadow of Buddha disappear, the fire was extinguished. Then five of the men saw the shadow, but the sixth saw nothing. The old man who had acted as guide was astounded when Hiouen-thsang told him the vision. " Master," he said, " without the sincerity of your faith, and the energy of your vows, you could not have seen such a miracle."

This is the account given by Hiouen-thsang's biographers. But we must say, to the credit of Hiouen-thsang himself, that in the " Si-yu-ki," which contains his own diary, the story is told in a different way. The cave is described with almost the same words. But afterwards the writer continues : " Formerly, the shadow of Buddha was seen in the cave, bright, like his natural appearance, and with all the marks of his divine beauty. One might have said, it was Buddha himself. For some centuries, however, it can no longer be seen completely. Though one does see something, it is only a feeble and doubtful resemblance. If a man prays with sincere faith, and if he has received from above a hidden impression, he sees the shadow clearly, but he cannot enjoy the sight for any length of time."

From Peshawer, the scene of this extraordinary miracle, Hiouen-thsang proceeded to Kashmir, visited the chief towns of Central India, and arrived at last in Magadha, the Holy Land of the Buddhists. Here he remained five years, devoting all his time to the study of Sanskrit and Buddhist literature, and inspecting every place hallowed by the recollections of the past. He then passed through Bengal, and proceeded to the south, with a view of visiting Ceylon, the chief seat of Buddhism. Baffled in that wish, he crossed the penin-

sala from east to west, ascended the Malabar coast,
reached the Indus, and, after numerous excursions to
the chief places of Northwestern India, returned to
Magadha, to spend there, with his old friends, some
of the happiest years of his life. The route of his
journeyings is laid down in a map drawn with exquisite
skill by M. Vivien de Saint-Martin. At last he was
obliged to return to China, and passing through the
Punjab, Kabulistan, and Bactria, he reached the Oxus,
followed its course nearly to its sources on the plateau
of Pamir, and, after staying some time in the three
chief towns of Turkistan, Khasgar, Yarkand, and
Khoten, he found himself again, after sixteen years
of travels, dangers, and studies, in his own native
country. His fame had spread far and wide, and the
poor pilgrim, who had once been hunted by imperial
spies and armed policemen, was now received with
public honors by the Emperor himself. His entry into
the capital was like a triumph. The streets were
covered with carpets, flowers were scattered, and ban-
ners flying. Soldiers were drawn up, the magistrates
went out to meet him, and all the monks of the neighborhood marched along in solemn procession. The
trophies that adorned this triumph, carried by a large
number of horses, were of a peculiar kind. First, 150
grains of the dust of Buddha; secondly a golden statue
of the great Teacher; thirdly, a similar statue of sandal-wood; fourthly, a statue of sandal-wood, representing Buddha as descending from heaven; fifthly, a
statue of silver; sixthly, a golden statue of Buddha
conquering the dragons; seventhly, a statue of sandal-
wood, representing Buddha as a preacher; lastly, a
collection of 657 works in 520 volumes. The Emperor

received the traveller in the Phœnix Palace, and, full of admiration for his talents and wisdom, invited him to accept a high office in the Government. This Hiouen-thsang declined. "The soul of the administration," he said, "is still the doctrine of Confucius;" and he would dedicate the rest of his life to the Law of Buddha. The Emperor thereupon asked him to write an account of his travels, and assigned him a monastery where he might employ his leisure in translating the works he had brought back from India. His travels were soon written and published, but the translation of the Sanskrit MSS. occupied the whole rest of his life. It is said that the number of works translated by him, with the assistance of a large staff of monks, amounted to 740, in 1,335 volumes. Frequently he might be seen meditating on a difficult passage, when suddenly it seemed as if a higher spirit had enlightened his mind. His soul was cheered, as when a man walking in darkness sees all at once the sun piercing the clouds and shining in its full brightness; and, unwilling to trust to his own understanding, he used to attribute his knowledge to a secret inspiration of Buddha and the Bodhisattvas. When he found that the hour of death approached, he had all his property divided among the poor. He invited his friends to come and see him, and to take a cheerful leave of that impure body of Hiouen-thsang. "I desire," he said, "that whatever rewards I may have merited by good works may fall upon other people. May I be born again with them in the heaven of the blessed, be admitted to the family of Mi-le, and serve the Buddha of the future, who is full of kindness and affection. When I descend again upon earth to pass through other forms of existence, I desire at every new

birth to fulfill my duties towards Buddha, and arrive at
the last at the highest and most perfect intelligence.
He died in the year 664 — about the same time that
Mohammedanism was pursuing its bloody conquests in
the East, and Christianity began to shed its pure light
over the dark forests of Germany.

It is impossible to do justice to the character of so
extraordinary a man as Hiouen-thsang in so short a
sketch as we have been able to give. If we knew only
his own account of his life and travels, — the volume
which has just been published at Paris, — we should be
ignorant of the motives which guided him and of the
sufferings which he underwent. Happily, two of his
friends and pupils had left an account of their teacher,
and M. Stanislas Julien has acted wisely in beginning
his collection of the Buddhist Pilgrims with the translation of that biography. There we learn something of
the man himself, and of that silent enthusiasm which
supported him in his arduous work. There we see him
braving the dangers of the desert, scrambling along
glaciers, crossing over torrents, and quietly submitting
to the brutal violence of Indian Thugs. There we see
him rejecting the tempting invitations of khans, kings,
and emperors, and quietly pursuing among strangers,
within the bleak wall of the cell of a Buddhist college,
the study of a foreign language, the key to the sacred
literature of his faith. There we see him rising to
eminence, acknowledged as an equal by his former
teachers, as a superior by the most distinguished
scholars of India; the champion of the orthodox faith,
an arbiter at councils, the favorite of Indian kings. In
his own work there is hardly a word about all this.
We do not wish to disguise his weaknesses, such as they

appear in the same biography. He was a credulous man, easily imposed upon by crafty priests, still more easily carried away by his own superstitions; but he deserved to have lived in better times, and we almost grudge so high and noble a character to a country not our own, and to a religion unworthy of such a man. Of selfishness we find no trace in him. His whole life belonged to the faith in which he was born, and the object of his labor was not so much to perfect himself as to benefit others. He was an honest man. And strange, and stiff, and absurd, and outlandish as his outward appearance may seem, there is something in the face of that poor Chinese monk, with his yellow skin and his small oblique eyes, that appeals to our sympathy; something in his life, and the work of his life, that places him by right among the heroes of Greece, the martyrs of Rome, the knights of the crusades, the explorers of the Arctic regions; something that makes us feel it a duty to inscribe his name on the roll of the "forgotten worthies" of the human race. There is a higher consanguinity than that of the blood which runs through our veins, — that of the blood which makes our hearts beat with the same indignation and the same joy. And there is a higher nationality than that of being governed by the same imperial dynasty, — that of our common allegiance to the Father and Ruler of all mankind.

It is but right to state that we owe the publication, at least of the second volume of M. Julien's work, to the liberality of the Court of Directors of the East India Company. We have had several opportunities of pointing out the creditable manner in which that body has patronized literary and scientific works con-

nected with the East, and we congratulate the Chair-
man, Colonel Sykes, and the President of the Board
of Control, Mr. Vernon Smith, on the excellent choice
they have made in this instance. Nothing can be
more satisfactory than that nearly the whole edition of
a work which would have remained unpublished without their liberal assistance, has been sold in little more
than a month.

April 2, 1857

XI.

THE MEANING OF NIRVÂNA.

To the Editor of "The Times."

Sir,—Mr. Francis Barham, of Bath, has protested in a letter, printed in "The Times" of the 24th of April, against my interpretations of "Nirvâna," or the *summum bonum* of the Buddhists. He maintains that the Nirvâna in which the Buddhists believe, and which they represent as the highest goal of their religion and philosophy, means union and communion with God, or absorption of the individual soul by the divine essence, and not, as I tried to show in my article on the "Buddhist Pilgrims," utter annihilation.

I must not take up much more of your space with so abstruse a subject as Buddhist metaphysics; but at the same time I cannot allow Mr. Barham's protest to pass unnoticed. The authorities which he brings forward against my account of Buddhism, and particularly against my interpretation of Nirvâna, seem formidable enough. There is Neander, the great Church historian; Creuzer, the famous scholar; and Huc, the well-known traveller and missionary,—all interpreting, as Mr. Barham says, the Nirvâna of the Buddhists in the sense of an apotheosis of the human soul, as it was taught in the Vedânta philosophy of the Brahmans, the Sufism of the Persians, and the Christian mysticism of Eckhart and Tauler, and not in the sense of absolute annihilation.

Now, with regard to Neander and Creuzer, I must observe that their works were written before the canonical books of the Buddhists composed in Sanskrit had been discovered, or at least before they had been sent to Europe, and been analyzed by European scholars. Besides, neither Neander nor Creuzer was an oriental scholar, and their knowledge of the subject could only be second-hand. It was in 1824 that Mr. Brian Houghton Hodgson, then resident at the Court of Nepal, gave the first intimation of the existence of a large religious literature written in Sanskrit, and preserved by the Buddhists of Nepal as the canonical books of their faith. It was in 1830 and 1835 that the same eminent scholar and naturalist presented the first set of these books to the Royal Asiatic Society in London. In 1837 he made a similar gift to the Société Asiatique of Paris, and some of the most important works were transmitted by him to the Bodleian Library at Oxford. It was in 1844 that the late Eugène Burnouf published, after a careful study of these documents, his classical work, "Introduction à l'Histoire du Buddhisme Indien," and it is from this book that our knowledge of Buddhism may be said to date. Several works have since been published, which have added considerably to the stock of authentic information on the doctrine of the great Indian reformer. There is Burnouf's translation of "Le Lotus de la bonne Loi," published after the death of that lamented scholar, together with numerous essays, in 1852. There are two interesting works by the Rev. Spence

Hardy, — "Eastern Monachism," London, 1850, and "A Manual of Buddhism," London, 1853; and there are the publications of M. Stanislas Julien, E. Foucaux, the Honorable George Turnour, Professor H. H. Wilson, and others, alluded to in my article on the "Buddhist Pilgrims." It is from these works alone that we can derive correct and authentic information on Buddhism, and not from Neander's "History of the Christian Church," or from Creuzer's "Symbolik."

If any one will consult these works, he will find that the discussions on the true meaning of Nirvâna are not of modern date, and that, at a very early period, different philosophical schools among the Buddhists of India, and different teachers who spread the doctrine of Buddhism abroad, propounded every conceivable opinion as to the orthodox explanation of this term. Even in one and the same school we find different parties maintaining different views on the meaning of Nirvâna. There is the school of the Svâbhâvikas, which still exists in Nepal. The Svâbhâvikas maintain that nothing exists but nature, or rather substance, and that this substance exists by itself (" svabhâvât), without a Creator or a Ruler. It exists, however, under two forms: in the state of Pravritti, as active, or in the state of Nirvritti, as passive. Human beings, who, like everything else, exist " svabhâvât," " by themselves," are supposed to be capable of arriving at Nirvritti, or passiveness, which is nearly synonymous with Nirvâna. But here the Svâbhâvikas branch off into two sects. Some believe that Nirvritti is repose, others that it is annihilation; and the former add, " were it even annihilation (' sûnyatâ '), it would still be good, man being otherwise doomed to an eternal migration through all the forms of nature; the more desirable of which are little to be wished for; and the less so, at any price to be shunned." [1]

What was the original meaning of Nirvāna may perhaps best be seen from the etymology of this technical term. Every Sanskrit scholar knows that Nirvāna means originally the blowing out, the extinction of light, and not absorption. The human soul, when it arrives at its perfection, is blown out,[2] if we use the phraseology of the Buddhists, like a lamp; it is not absorbed, as the Brahmans say, like a drop in the ocean. Neither in the system of Buddhist philosophy, nor in the philosophy from which Buddha is supposed to have borrowed, was there any place left for a Divine Being by which the human soul could be absorbed. Sânkhya philosophy, in its original form, claims the name of "an-isvara," "lordless," or "atheistic," as its distinctive title. Its final object is not absorption in God, whether personal or impersonal, but "Moksha," deliverance of the soul from all pain and illusion, and recovery by the soul of its true nature. It is doubtful whether the term "Nirvāna" was coined by Buddha. It occurs in the literature of the Brahmans as a synonyme of "Moksha," deliverance; "Nirvritti," cessation; "Apavarga," release; "Nihsreyas," summum bonum. It is used in this sense in the Mahâbhârata, and it is explained in the Amara-Kosha as having the meaning of "blowing out, applied to a fire and to a sage." [3]

[1] See Burnouf, Introduction, p. 441; Hodgson, Asiatic Researches, vol. xvi.

[2] "Calm," "without wind," as Nirvāna is sometimes explained, is expressed in Sanskrit by "Nirvāta." See Amara-Kosha, and note.

[3] Different views of the Nirvāna, as conceived by the Tîrthakas, or the

Unless, however, we succeed in tracing this term in works anterior to Buddha, we may suppose that it was invented by him in order to express that meaning of the *summum bonum* which he was the first to preach, and which some of his disciples explained in the sense of absolute annihilation.

The earliest authority to which we can go back, if we want to know the original character of Buddhism, is the Buddhist Canon, as settled after the death of Buddha at the first Council. It is called "Tripitaka," or the "Three Baskets:" the first containing the Sûtras, or the discourses of Buddha; the second, the Vinaya, or his code of morality; the third, the Abhidharma, or the system of metaphysics. The first was compiled by Ananda, the second by Upâli, the third by Kâsyapa — all of them the pupils and friends of Buddha. It may be that these collections, as we now possess them, were finally arranged, not at the first, but at the third Council. Yet, even then, we have no earlier, no more authentic documents from which we could form an opinion as to the original teaching of Buddha; and the Nirvâna, as taught in the metaphysics of Kasyapa, and particularly in the Pragnâ-pâramitâ, is annihilation, not absorption. Buddhism, therefore, if tested by its own canonical books, cannot be freed from the charge of Nihilism, whatever may have been its character in the mind of its founder, and whatever changes it may have undergone in later times, and among races less inured to metaphysical discussions than the Hindus.

The ineradicable feeling of dependence on something

else, which is the life-spring of all religion, was completely numbed in the early Buddhist metaphysicians, and it was only after several generations had passed away, and after Buddhism had become the creed of millions, that this feeling returned with increased warmth, changing, as I said in my article, the very Nothing into a paradise, and deifying the very Buddha who had denied the existence of a Deity. That this has been the case in China we know from the interesting works of the Abbé Huc, and from other sources, such as the " Catechism of the Shamans, or the Laws and Regulations of the Priesthood of Buddha in China," translated by Ch. F. Neumann, London, 1831. In India, also, Buddhism, as soon as it became a popular religion, had to speak a more human language than that of metaphysical Pyrrhonism. But, if it did so, it was because it was shamed into it. This we may see from the very nicknames which the Brahmans apply to their opponents, the Bauddhas. They call them Nâstikas — those who maintain that there is nothing ; Sûnyavâdins — those who maintain that there is a universal void.

The only ground, therefore, on which we may stand, if we wish to defend the founder of Buddhism against the charges of Nihilism and Atheism, is this, that, as some of the Buddhists admit, the " Basket of Metaphysics " was rather the work of his pupils, not of Buddha himself.[1] This distinction between the authentic words of Buddha and the canonical books in general, is men-

---

[1] See Burnouf, *Introduction*, p. 41. " Abhidharmam abhidharma-sûtram." Ib. p. 454. According to the Thibetan Buddhists, however, Buddha propounded the Abhidharma when he was fifty-one years old Asiatic Researches, vol. xx. p. 399.

tioned more than once. The priesthood of Ceylon,
when the manifest errors with which their canonical
commentaries abound were brought to their notice,
retreated from their former position, and now assert
that it is only the express words of Buddha that they
receive as undoubted truth.[1] There is a passage in a
Buddhist work which reminds us somewhat of the last
page of Dean Milman's "History of Christianity," and
where we read : —

"The words of the priesthood are good ; those of
the Rahats (saints) are better ; but those of the All-
knowing are the best of all."

This is an argument which Mr. Francis Barham
might have used with more success, and by which he
might have justified, if not the first disciples, at least
the original founder of Buddhism. Nay, there is a
saying of Buddha's which tends to show that all metaphysical discussion was regarded by him as vain and
useless. It is a saying mentioned in one of the MSS.
belonging to the Bodleian Library. As it has never
been published before, I may be allowed to quote it in
the original : "Sadasad vikâram na sahate ;" "The
ideas of being and not being do not admit of discussion ;" a tenet which, if we consider that it was
enunciated before the time of the Eleatic philosophers
of Greece, and long before Hegel's Logic, might certainly have saved us many an intricate and indigestible
argument.

A few passages from the Buddhist writings of Nepal
and Ceylon will best show that the *horror nihili* was
not felt by the metaphysicians of former ages in the
same degree as it is felt by ourselves. The famous

[1] *Eastern Monachism*, p. 171.

hymn which resounds in heaven when the luminous rays of the smile of Buddha penetrate through the clouds, is " All is transitory, all is misery, all is void, all is without substance." Again, it is said in the Pragnâ pâramitâ,[1] that Buddha began to think that he might to conduct all creatures to perfect Nirvâna. But he reflected that there are really no creatures which ought to be conducted, nor creatures that conduct; and, nevertheless, he did conduct all creatures to perfect Nirvâna. " Then," continues the text, " why is it said that there are neither creatures which arrive at complete Nirvâna, nor creatures which conduct there? Because it is illusion which makes creatures what they are. It is as if a clever juggler, or his pupil, made an immense number of people to appear on the high road, and after having made them to appear, made them to disappear again. Would there be anybody who had killed, or murdered, or annihilated, or caused them to vanish? No. And it is the same with Buddha. He conducts an immense, innumerable, infinite number of creatures to complete Nirvâna, and yet there are neither creatures which are conducted, nor creatures that conduct. If a Bodhisattva, on hearing this explanation of the Law, is not frightened, then it may be said that he has put on the great armor." [2]

Soon after, we read: " The name of ' Buddha ' is nothing but a word. The name of ' Bodhisattva ' is nothing but a word. The name of ' Perfect Wisdom ' (' Pragnâ-pâramitâ ') is nothing but a word. The name is indefinite, as if one says ' I,' for ' I' is something indefinite because it has no limits."

Burnouf gives the gist of the whole Pragnâ-pâra-

[1] Burnouf, Introduction, p. 462.   [2] Ib. p. 472.

mitâ in the following words: "The highest Wisdom, or what is to be known, has no more real existence than he who has to know, or the Bodhisattva; no more than he who does know, or the Buddha." But Burnouf remarks that nothing of this kind is to be found in the Sûtras, and that Gautama Sâkya-muni, the son of Suddhodana, would never have become the founder of a popular religion if he had started with similar absurdities. In the Sûtras the reality of the objective world is denied; the reality of form is denied; the reality of the individual, or the "I," is equally denied. But the existence of a subject, of something like the Purusha, the thinking substance of the Sânkhya philosophy, is spared. Something at least exists with respect to which everything else may be said not to exist. The germs of the ideas, developed in the Pragnâ-pâramitâ, may indeed be discovered here and there in the Sûtras.[1] But they had not yet ripened into that poisonous plant which soon became an indispensable narcotic in the schools of the later Buddhists. Buddha himself, however, though, perhaps, not a Nihilist, was certainly an Atheist. He does not deny distinctly either the existence of gods, or that of God; but he ignores the former, and he is ignorant of the latter. Therefore, if Nirvâna in his mind was not yet complete annihilation, still less could it have been absorption into a Divine essence. It was nothing but selfishness, in the metaphysical sense of the word — a relapse into that being which is nothing but itself. This is the most charitable view which we can take of the Nirvâna, even as conceived by Buddha himself, and it is the view which Burnouf derived from the canonical books of the Northern Buddhists. On the other hand, Mr. Spence Hardy, who in his works follows exclusively the authority of the Southern Buddhists, the Páli and Singhalese works of Ceylon, arrives at the same result. We read in his work: " The Rahat (Arhat), who has reached Nirvána, but is not yet a Pratyeka-buddha, or a Supreme Buddha, says: ' I await the appointed time for the cessation of existence. I have no wish to live; I have no wish to die. Desire is extinct.' "

In a very interesting dialogue between Milinda and Nágasena, communicated by Mr. Spence Hardy, Nirvána is represented as something which has no antecedent cause, no qualities, no locality. It is something of which the utmost we may assert is, that it is.

" *Nágasena.* Can a man, by his natural strength, go from the city of Ságal to the forest of Himála ?

" *Milinda.* Yes.

" *Nágasena.* But could any man, by his natural strength, bring the forest of Himála to this city of Ságal ?

" *Milinda.* No.

" *Nágasena.* In like manner, though the fruition of the paths may cause the accomplishment of Nirvána, no cause by which Nirvána is produced can be declared. The path that leads to Nirvána may be pointed out, but not any cause for its production. Why? because that which constitutes Nirvána is beyond all computation, — a mystery, not to be understood. . . . . It cannot be said that it is produced, nor that it is not produced; that it is past, or future, or present. Nor can it be said that it is the seeing of the eye, or the hearing

of the ear, or the smelling of the nose, or the tasting of
the tongue, or the feeling of the body.

"*Milinda*. Then you speak of a thing that is not;
you merely say that Nirvâna is Nirvâna;—therefore
there is no Nirvâna.

"*Nâgasena*. Great king, Nirvâna is."

Another question also, whether Nirvâna is something
different from the beings that enter into it, has been
asked by the Buddhists themselves:—

"*Milinda*. Does the being who acquires it, attain
something that has previously existed?—or is it his
own product, a formation peculiar to himself?

"*Nâgasena*. Nirvâna does not exist previously to
its reception; nor is it that which was brought into existence. Still to the being who attains it, there is Nirvâna."

In opposition, therefore, to the more advanced views
of the Nihilistic philosophers of the North, Nâgasena
maintains the existence of Nirvâna, and of the being
that has entered Nirvâna. He does not say that Buddha is a mere word. When asked by king Milinda,
whether the all-wise Buddha exists, he replies:—

"*Nâgasena*. He who is the most meritorious
(Bhagavat) does exist.

"*Milinda*. Then can you point out to me the place
in which he exists?

"*Nâgasena*. Our Bhagavat has attained Nirvâna,
where there is no repetition of birth. We cannot say
that he is here, or that he is there. When a fire is extinguished, can it be said that it is here, or that it is
there? Even so, our Buddha has attained extinction

(Nirvâna). He is like the sun that has set behind the Astagiri mountain. It cannot be said that he is here, or that he is there: but we can point him out by the discourses he delivered. In them he lives."

At the present moment, the great majority of Buddhists would probably be quite incapable of understanding the abstract speculation of their ancient masters. The view taken of Nirvâna in China, Mongolia, and Tartary may probably be as gross as that which most of the Mohammedans form of their paradise. But, in the history of religion, the historian must go back to the earliest and most original documents that are to be obtained. Thus only may he hope to understand the later developments which, whether for good or evil, every form of faith has had to undergo.

April 1857.

XII.

CHINESE TRANSLATIONS

OF

SANSKRIT TEXTS.[1]

WELL might M. Stanislas Julien put *finis* on the title-page of his last work, in which he explains his method of deciphering the Sanskrit words which occur in the Chinese translations of the Buddhist literature of India. We endeavored to explain the laborious character and the important results of his researches on this subject on a former occasion, when reviewing his translation of the "Life and Travels of the Buddhist Pilgrim Hiouen-thsang." At that time, however, M. Julien kept the key of his discoveries to himself. He gave us the results of his labors without giving us more than a general idea of the process by which those results had been obtained. He has now published his "Méthode pour déchiffrer et transcrire les noms sanscrits qui se rencontrent dans les livres chinois," and he has given to the public his Chinese-Sanskrit dictionary, the work of sixteen years of arduous labor, containing all the Chinese characters which are used for representing phonetically the technical terms and proper names of the Buddhist literature of India.

[1] *Méthode pour déchiffrer et transcrire les noms sanscrits qui se rencontrent dans les livres chinois.* Par M. Stanislas Julien, Membre de l'Institut. Paris 1861.

In order fully to appreciate the labors and discoveries of M. Julien in this remote field of oriental literature, we must bear in mind that the doctrine of Buddha arose in India about two centuries before Alexander's invasion. It became the state religion of India soon after Alexander's conquest, and it produced a vast literature, which was collected into a canon at a council held about 246 B. C. Very soon after that council, Buddhism assumed a proselytizing character. It spread in the south to Ceylon, in the north to Kashmir, the Himalayan countries, Thibet, and China. In the historical annals of China, on which, in the absence of anything like historical literature in the Sanskrit, we must mainly depend for information on the spreading of Buddhism, one Buddhist missionary is mentioned as early as 217 B. C.; and about the year 120 B. C. a Chinese general, after defeating the barbarous tribes north of the desert of Gobi, brought back as a trophy a golden statue, — the statue of Buddha. It was not, however, till the year 65 A. D. that Buddhism was officially recognized by the Chinese Emperor as a third state religion. Ever since, it has shared equal honors with the doctrines of Confucius and Lao-tse in the Celestial Empire; and it is but lately that these three established religions have had to fear the encroachments of a new rival in the creed of the Chief of the rebels.

Once established in China, and well provided with monasteries and benefices, the Buddhist priesthood seems to have been most active in its literary labors. Immense as was the Buddhist literature of India, the Chinese swelled it to still more appalling proportions. The first thing to be done was to translate the canon-

ical books.   This seems to have been the joint work of
Chinese who had acquired a knowledge of Sanskrit
during their travels in India, and of Hindus who settled in Chinese monasteries in order to assist the native
translators.   The translation of books which profess to
contain a new religious doctrine is under all circumstances a task of great difficulty.   It was so particularly
when the subtle abstractions of the Buddhist religion
had to be clothed in the solid, matter-of-fact idiom of
the Chinese.   But there was another difficulty which
it seemed almost impossible to overcome.   Many words,
not only proper names, but the technical terms also of
the Buddhist creed, had to be preserved in Chinese.
They were not to be translated, but to be transliterated.
But how was this to be effected with a language which,
like Chinese, had no phonetic alphabet ?   Every Chinese character is a word; it has both sound and meaning ; and it is unfit, therefore, for the representation of
the sound of foreign words.   In modern times, certain
characters have been set apart for the purpose of writing the proper names and titles of foreigners; but such
is the peculiar nature of the Chinese system of writing, that even with this alphabet it is only possible to
represent approximatively the pronunciation of foreign
words.   In the absence, however, of even such an alphabet, the translators of the Buddhist literature seem
to have used their own discretion — or rather indiscre-
tion — in appropriating, without any system, whatever
Chinese characters seemed to them to come nearest to
the sound of Sanskrit words.   Now the whole Chinese
language consists in reality of about four hundred
words, or significative sounds, all monosyllabic.   Each
of these monosyllabic sounds embraces a large number

of various meanings, and each of these various meanings is represented by its own sign. Thus it has happened that the Chinese dictionary contains 43,496 signs, whereas the Chinese language commands only four hundred distinct utterances. Instead of being restricted, therefore, to one character which always expresses the same sound, the Buddhist translators were at liberty to express one and the same sound in a hundred different ways. Of this freedom they availed themselves to the fullest extent. Each translator, each monastery, fixed on its own characters for representing the pronunciation of Sanskrit words. There are more than twelve hundred Chinese characters employed by various writers in order to represent the forty-two simple letters of the Sanskrit alphabet. The result has been that even the Chinese were, after a time, unable to read — i. e. to pronounce — these random transliterations. What, then, was to be expected from Chinese scholars in Europe? Fortunately, the Chinese, to save themselves from their own perplexities, had some lists drawn up, exhibiting the principles followed by the various translators in representing the proper names, the names of places, and the technical terms of philosophy and religion which they had borrowed from the Sanskrit. With the help of these lists, and after sixteen years consecrated to the study of the Chinese translations of Sanskrit works and of other original compositions of Buddhist authors, M. Julien at last caught up the thread that was to lead him through this labyrinth; and by means of his knowledge of Sanskrit, which he acquired solely for that purpose, he is now able to do what not even the most learned among the Buddhists in China could accomplish, — he is able to restore the exact form and meaning of every word transferred from Sanskrit into the Buddhist literature of China.

Without this laborious process, which would have tired out the patience and deadened the enthusiasm of most scholars, the treasures of the Buddhist literature preserved in Chinese were really useless. Abel Rémusat, who during his lifetime was considered the first Chinese scholar in Europe, attempted, indeed, a translation of the travels of Fahian, a Buddhist pilgrim, who visited India about the end of the fourth century after Christ. It was in many respects a most valuable work, but the hopelessness of reducing the uncouth Chinese terms to their Sanskrit originals made it most tantalizing to look through its pages. Who was to guess that "Ho-kia-lo" was meant for the Sanskrit "Vyâkarana," in the sense of sermons; "Po-to" for the Sanskrit "Avadâna," parables; "Kia-ye-i" for the Sanskrit "Kâsyapiyas," the followers of Kâsyapa? In some instances, Abel Rémusat, assisted by Chézy, guessed rightly; and later Sanskrit scholars, such as Burnouf, Lassen, and Wilson, succeeded in reëstablishing, with more or less certainty the original forms of a number of Sanskrit words, in spite of their Chinese disguises. Still there was no system, and therefore no certainty, in these guesses, and many erroneous conclusions were drawn from fragmentary translations of Chinese writers on Buddhism, which even now are not yet entirely eliminated from the works of oriental scholars. With M. Julien's method, mathematical certainty seems to have taken the place of learned conjectures; and whatever is to be learnt from the Chinese on the origin, the history, and the true character of Buddha's doctrine may now be had in an authentic and unambiguous form.

But even after the principal difficulties have been cleared away through the perseverance of M. Stanislas Julien, and after we have been allowed to reap the fruits of his labors in his masterly translation of the " Voyages des Pèlerins Bouddhistes," there still remains one point that requires some elucidation. How was it that the Chinese, whose ears no doubt are of the same construction as our own, should have made such sad work of the Sanskrit names which they transcribed with their own alphabet? Much may be explained by the defects of their language. Such common sounds as r, g, r, b, d, and short a, are unknown in Chinese as initials ; no compound consonants are allowed, every consonant being followed by a vowel ; and the final letters are limited to a very small number. This, no doubt, explains, to a great extent, the distorted appearance of many Sanskrit words when written in Chinese. Thus, " Buddha" could only be written " Fo-to." There was no sign for an initial b, nor was it possible to represent a double consonant, such as ddh. " Fo-to" was the nearest approach to " Buddha," of which Chinese, when written, was capable. But was it so in speaking? Was it really impossible for Fahian and Hiouen-thsang, who had spent so many years in India, and who were acquainted with all the intricacies of Sanskrit grammar, to distinguish between the sounds of " Buddha" and " Fo-to?" We cannot believe this. We are convinced that Hiouen-thsang, though he wrote, and could not but write " Fo-to" with the Chinese characters, pronounced " Buddha" just as we pronounce it, and that it was only among the unlearned that " Fo-to" became at last the recognized name of the founder of Buddhism, abbreviated even to the

monosyllabic "Fo," which is now the most current
appellation of "the Enlightened." In the same manner the Chinese pilgrims wrote "Niepan," but they
pronounced Nirvâna; they wrote "Fan-lon-mo," and
pronounced Brahma.

Nor is it necessary that we should throw all the
blame of these distortions on the Chinese. On the
contrary, it is almost certain that some of the discrepancies between the Sanskrit of their translations and
the classical Sanskrit of Pânini were due to the corruption which, at the time when Buddhism arose, and
still more at the time when Buddhism spread to China,
had crept into the spoken language of India. Sanskrit
had ceased to be the spoken language of the people
previous to the time of Asoka. The edicts which are
still preserved on the rocks of Dhauli, Girnar, and
Kapurdigiri are written in a dialect which stands to
Sanskrit in the same relation as Italian to Latin. Now
it is true, no doubt, that the canonical books of the
Buddhists are written in a tolerably correct Sanskrit,
very different from the Italianized dialect of Asoka.
But that Sanskrit was, like the Greek of Alexandria,
like the Latin of Hungary, a learned idiom, written by
the learned for the learned; it was no longer the living speech of India. Now it is curious that in many
of the canonical Buddhist works which we still possess,
the text which is written in Sanskrit prose is from
time to time interrupted by poetical portions, called
"Gâthâs" or ballads, in which the same things are
told in verse which had before been related in prose.
The dialect of these songs or ballads is full of what
grammarians would call irregularities; that is to say,
all of those changes which every language undergoes

in the mouths of the people.   In character these corruptions are the same as those which have been observed in the inscriptions of Asoka, and which afterwards appear in Pâli and the modern Prâkrit dialects
of India.   Various conjectures have been started to
explain the amalgamation of the correct prose text and
the free and easy poetical version of the same events,
as embodied in the sacred literature of the Buddhists.
Burnouf, the first who instituted a critical inquiry into
the history and literature of Buddhism, supposed that
there was, besides the canon fixed by the three convo-
cations, another digest of Buddhist doctrines composed
in the popular style, which may have developed itself,
as he says, subsequently to the preaching of Sâkya,
and which would thus be intermediate between the
regular Sanskrit and the Pâli.   He afterwards, however, inclines to another view, namely, that these
Gâthâs were written out of India by men to whom
Sanskrit was no longer familiar, and who endeavored
to write in the learned language, which they ill understood, with the freedom which is imparted by the
habitual use of a popular but imperfectly determined
dialect.   Other Sanskrit scholars have proposed other
solutions of this strange mixture of correct prose and
incorrect poetry in the Buddhist literature; but none
of them was satisfactory.   The problem seems to have
been solved at last by a native scholar, Babu Rajendralal, a curious instance of the reaction of European
antiquarian research on the native mind of India.
Babu Rajendralal reads Sanskrit, of course, with the
greatest ease.   He is a pandit by profession, but he is
at the same time a scholar and critic in our sense of
the word.   He has edited Sanskrit texts after a care-

ful collation of MSS., and in his various contributions
to the "Journal of the Asiatic Society of Bengal," he
has proved himself completely above the prejudices of
his class, freed from the erroneous views on the history
and literature of India in which every Brahman is
brought up, and thoroughly imbued with those principles of criticism which men like Colebrook, Lassen,
and Burnouf have followed in their researches into the
literary treasures of his country. His English is re-
markably clear and simple, and his arguments would
do credit to any Sanskrit scholar in England. We
quote from his remarks on Burnouf's account of the
Gâthâs, as given in that scholar's "Histoire du Buddhisme Indien:"—

"Burnouf's opinion on the origin of the Gâthâs,
we venture to think, is founded on a mistaken estimate
of Sanskrit style. The poetry of the Gâthâ has much
artistic elegance which at once indicates that it is not
the composition of men who were ignorant of the first
principles of grammar. The authors display a great
deal of learning, and discuss the subtlest questions of
logic and metaphysics with much tact and ability, and
it is difficult to conceive that men who were perfectly
familiar with the most intricate forms of Sanskrit logic,
who have expressed the most abstruse metaphysical
ideas in precise and often in beautiful language, who
composed with ease and elegance in Ârya, Totaka, and
other difficult measures, were unacquainted with the
rudiments of the language in which they wrote, and
were unable to conjugate the verb to be in all its forms.
. . . . The more reasonable conjecture appears to be
that the Gâthâ is the production of bards who were
contemporaries or immediate successors of Sâkya, who

recounted to the devout congregations of the prophet of Magadha the sayings and doings of their great teacher in popular and easy flowing verses, which in course of time came to be regarded as the most authentic source of all information connected with the founder of Buddhism. The high estimation in which the ballads and improvisations of bards are held in India, and particularly in the Buddhist writings, favors this supposition; and the circumstance that the poetical portions are generally introduced in corroboration of the narration of the prose, with the words, 'Thereof this may be said,' affords a strong presumptive evidence."

Now this, from the pen of a native scholar, is truly remarkable. The spirit of Niebuhr seems to have reached the shores of India, and this ballad theory comes out more successfully in the history of Buddha than in the history of Romulus. The absence of anything like cant in the mouth of a Brahman speaking of Buddhism, the *bête noire* of all orthodox Brahmans, is highly satisfactory; and our Sanskrit scholars in Europe will have to pull hard if, with such men as Babu Rajendralal in the field, they are not to be distanced in the race of scholarship.

We believe, then, that Babu Rajendralal is right, and we look upon the dialect of the Gâthâs as a specimen of the Sanskrit spoken by the followers of Buddha about the time of Asoka and later. And this will help us to understand some of the peculiar changes which the Sanskrit of the Chinese Buddhists must have undergone, even before it was disguised in the strange dress of the Chinese alphabet. The Chinese pilgrims did not hear the Sanskrit pronounced as it was pronounced in the Parishads, according to the

strict rules of their Sikshâ, or phonetics. They
heard it as it was spoken in Buddhist monasteries, as
it was sung in the Gâthâs of Buddhist minstrels, as it
was preached in the Vyâkaranas, or sermons of Buddhist friars. For instance. In the Gâthâs a short a
is frequently lengthened. We find "nâ" instead of
"na," no. The same occurs in the Sanskrit of the
Chinese Buddhists. (See Julien, "Méthode," pp.
18, 21.) We find there, also, "vistâra" instead
of "vistara," etc. In the dialect of the Gâthâs,
nouns ending in consonants, and therefore irregular,
are transferred to the easier declension in a. The
same process takes place in modern Greek, and in the
transition of Latin into Italian; it is, in fact, a general
tendency of all languages which are carried on by
the stream of living speech. Now this transition from
one declension to another had taken place before
the Chinese had appropriated the Sanskrit of the
Buddhist books. The Sanskrit "nabhas" becomes
"nabha" in the Gâthâs; locative "nabhe," instead
of "nabhasi." If, therefore, we find in Chinese
"lo-cho" for the Sanskrit "ragas," dust, we may
ascribe the change of r into l to the inability of the
Chinese to pronounce or to write an r. We may admit that the Chinese alphabet offered nothing nearer
to the sound of "ga" than "tcho"; but the drop-
ping of the final s has no excuse in Chinese, and finds
its real explanation in the nature of the Gâthâ dialect.
Thus the Chinese "Fan-lan-mo" does not represent
the correct Sanskrit "Brahman," but the vulgar
form "Brahma." The Chinese "so-po" for "sarva,"
all; "tho-mo" for "dharma," law, find no explanation in the dialect of the Gâthâs; but the suppression
of the r before v and m, is of frequent occurrence in

the inscriptions of Asoka. The omission of the initial *s* in words like "sthâna," place, "sthavira," an elder, is likewise founded on the rules of Pâli and Prâkrit, and need not be placed to the account of the Chinese translators. In the inscription of Girnar, "sthavira" is even reduced to "thaira." The *s* of the nominative is frequently dropped in the dialect of the Gâthâs, or changed into *o*. Hence we might venture to doubt whether it is necessary to give to the character 1780 of M. Julien's list, which generally has the value of "ta," a second value "sta." This *s* is only wanted to supply the final *s* of "kas," the interrogative pronoun, in such a sentence as "kas tadguṇaḥ?" what is the use of this? Now here we are inclined to believe that the final *s* of "kas" had long disappeared in the popular language of India, before the Chinese came to listen to the strange sounds and doctrines of the disciples of Buddha. They probably heard "ka tadguṇa," or "ka tagguṇa," and this they represented as best they could by the Chinese "kia-to-kieou-na."

With these few suggestions we leave the work of M. Stanislas Julien. It is in reality a work done once for all—one huge stone and stumbling-block effectually rolled away which for years had barred the approach to some most valuable documents of the history of the East. Now that the way is clear, let us hope that others will follow, and that we shall soon have complete and correct translations of the travels of Fahian and other Buddhist pilgrims whose works are like so many Murray's "Handbooks of India," giving us an insight into the social, political, and religious state of that country at a time when we look in vain for any other historical documents.

March 1861.

XIII.

THE WORKS OF CONFUCIUS.[1]

In reviewing the works of missionaries, we have repeatedly dwelt on the opportunities of scientific usefulness which are open to the messengers of the gospel in every part of the world. We are not afraid of the common objection that missionaries ought to devote their whole time and powers to the one purpose for which they are sent out and paid by our societies. Missionaries cannot always be engaged in teaching, preaching, converting, and baptizing the heathen. A missionary, like every other human creature, ought to have his leisure hours; and if those leisure hours are devoted to scientific pursuits, to the study of the languages or the literature of the people among whom he lives, to a careful description of the scenery and antiquities of the country, the manners, laws, and customs of its inhabitants, their legends, their national poetry, or popular stories, or again, to the cultivation of any branch of natural science, he may rest assured that he is not neglecting the sacred trust which he accepted, but is only bracing and invigorating his mind, and keeping it from that stagnation which is the inevitable result

[1] *The Chinese Classics; with a Translation, Critical and Exegetical Notes.* By James Legge, D. D., of the London Missionary Society. Hong Kong, 1861.

of a too monotonous employment. The staff of missionaries which is spread over the whole globe supplies the most perfect machinery that could be devised for the collection of all kinds of scientific knowledge. They ought to be the pioneers of science. They should not only take out, —they should also bring something home; and there is nothing more likely to increase and strengthen the support on which our missionary societies depend, nothing more sure to raise the intellectual standard of the men selected for missionary labor, than a formal recognition of this additional duty. There may be exceptional cases where missionaries are wanted for constant toil among natives ready to be instructed, and anxious to be received as members of a Christian community. But, as a general rule, the missionary abroad has more leisure than a clergyman at home, and time sits heavy on the hands of many whose congregations consist of no more than ten or twenty souls. It is hardly necessary to argue this point, when we can appeal to so many facts. The most successful missionaries have been exactly those whose names are remembered with gratitude, not only by the natives among whom they labored, but also by the savants of Europe; and the labors of the Jesuit missionaries in India and China, of the Baptist missionaries at Serampore, of Gogerly and Spence Hardy in Ceylon, of Caldwell in Tinnevelly, of Wilson in Bombay, of Moffat, Krapf, and last, but not least, of Livingstone, will live not only in the journals of our academies, but likewise in the annals of the missionary Church.

The first volume of an edition of the Chinese Classes, which we have just received from the Rev. Dr. J. Legge, of the London Missionary Society, is a now proof of what can be achieved by missionaries, if encouraged to devote part of their time and attention to scientific and literary pursuits. We do not care to inquire whether Dr. Legge has been successful as a missionary. Even if he had not converted a single Chinese, he would, after completing the work which he has just begun, have rendered most important aid to the introduction of Christianity into China. He arrived in the East towards the end of 1839, having received only a few months' instruction in Chinese from Professor Kidd in London. Being stationed at Malacca, it seemed to him then — and he adds, "that the experience of twenty-one years has given its sanction to the correctness of the judgment" — that he could not consider himself qualified for the duties of his position until he had thoroughly mastered the classical books of the Chinese, and investigated for himself the whole field of thought through which the sages of China had ranged, and in which were to be found the foundations of the moral, social, and political life of the people. He was not able to pursue his studies without interruption, and it was only after some years, when the charge of the Anglo-Chinese College had devolved upon him, that he could procure the books necessary to facilitate his progress. After sixteen years of assiduous study, Dr. Legge had explored the principal works of Chinese literature; and he then felt that he could render the course of reading through which he had passed more easy to those who were to follow after him, by publishing, on the model of our editions of the Greek and Roman Classics, a critical text of the Classics of China, together with a translation and explanatory notes. His materials were ready, but there was the difficulty of finding the funds necessary for so costly an undertaking. Scarcely, however, had Dr. Legge's wants become known among the British and other foreign merchants in China, than one of them, Mr. Joseph Jardine, sent for the Doctor, and said to him, " I know the liberality of the merchants in China, and that many of them would readily give their help to such an undertaking ; but you need not have the trouble of canvassing the community. If you are prepared to undertake the toil of the publication, I will bear the expense of it. We make our money in China, and we should be glad to assist in whatever promises to be a benefit to it." The result of this combination of disinterested devotion on the part of the author, and enlightened liberality on the part of his patron, lies now before us in a splendid volume of text, translation, and commentary, which, if the life of the editor is spared (and the sudden death of Mr. Jardine from the effects of the climate is a warning how busily death is at work among the European settlers in those regions), will be followed by at least six other volumes.

The edition is to comprise the books now recognised as of highest authority by the Chinese themselves. These are the five Kings and the four Shoos. ' King " means the warp threads of a web, and its application to literary compositions rests on the same metaphor as the Latin word *textus*, and the Sanskrit " Sûtra," meaning a yarn, and a book. " Shoo" simply means writings. The five Kings are : 1. The Yih, or the Book of Changes ; 2. The Shoo, or the Book of History ; 3. The She, or the Book of Poetry ; 4. The Le Ke, or Record of Rites ; and 5. The Chun Tsew, or Spring and Autumn ; a chronicle extending from 721 to 480 B. C. The four Shoos consist of: 1. The Lun Yu, or Digested Conversations between Confucius and his disciples ; 2. Ta Hëö, or Great Learning, commonly attributed to one of his disciples ; 3. The Chung Yung, or Doctrine of the Mean, ascribed to the grandson of Confucius; 4. Of the works of Mencius, who died 288 B. C.

The authorship of the five Kings is loosely attributed to Confucius ; but it is only the fifth, or "the Spring and Autumn," which can be claimed as the work of the philosopher. The Yih, the Shoo, and the She King were not composed, but only compiled by him, and much of the Lo Ke is clearly from later hands. Confucius, though the founder of a religion and a reformer, was thoroughly conservative in his tendencies, and devotedly attached to the past. He calls himself a transmitter, not a maker, believing in and loving the ancients (p. 59). "I am not one who was born in the possession of knowledge," he says ; "I am one who is fond of antiquity, and earnest in seeking it there " (p. 60). The most frequent themes of his discourses were the ancient songs, the history, and the rules of propriety established by ancient sages (p. 64). When one of his contemporaries wished to do away with the offering of a lamb as a meaningless formality, Confucius reproved him with the pithy sentence, " You love the sheep, I love the ceremony." There were four things, we are told, which Confucius taught, — letters, ethics, devotion of soul, and truthfulness (p. 66). When speaking of himself, he said, " At fifteen, I had my mind bent on learning. At thirty, I stood firm. At forty, I had no doubt. At fifty, I knew the decrees of Heaven. At sixty, my ear was an obedient organ

for the reception of truth.   At seventy, I could follow
what my heart desired, without transgressing what was
right " (p. 10).   Though this may sound like boast-
ing, it is remarkable how seldom Confucius himself
claims any superiority above his fellow-creatures.   He
offers his advice to those who are willing to listen, but
he never speaks dogmatically ; he never attempts to
tyrannize over the minds or hearts of his friends.   If
we read his biography, we can hardly understand how
a man whose life was devoted to such tranquil pursuits,
and whose death scarcely produced a ripple on the
smooth and silent surface of the Eastern world, could
have left the impress of his mind on millions and millions of human beings—an impress which even now,
after 2,889 years, is clearly discernible in the national
character of the largest empire of the world.   Confucius died in 478 B. C., complaining that of all the princes
of the empire there was not one who would adopt his
principles and obey his lessons.   After two generations,
however, his name had risen to be a power—the ral-
lying point of a vast movement of national and religious
regeneration.   His grandson speaks of him as the ideal
of a sage, as the sage is the ideal of humanity at large.
Though Tsz-tsz claims no divine honor for his grand-
sire, he exalts his wisdom and virtue beyond the limits
of human nature.   This is a specimen of the language
which he applies to Confucius: —

"He may be compared to heaven and earth in their
supporting and containing, their overshadowing and
curtaining all things ; he may be compared to the four
seasons in their alternating progress, and to the sun
and moon in their successive shining. . . . . Quick in
apprehension, clear in discernment, of far reaching in-

tellect and all-embracing knowledge, he was fitted to
exercise rule; magnanimous, generous, benign, and
mild, he was fitted to exercise forbearance; impulsive,
energetic, firm, and enduring, he was fitted to maintain
a firm hold; self-adjusted, grave, never swerving from
the Mean, and correct, he was fitted to command reverence; accomplished, distinctive, concentrative, and
searching, he was fitted to exercise discrimination. . . . .
All-embracing and vast, he was like heaven; deep and
active as a fountain, he was like the abyss. . . . .
Therefore his fame overspreads the Middle Kingdom
and extends to all barbarous tribes. Wherever ships
and carriages reach, wherever the strength of man
penetrates, wherever the heavens overshadow and the
earth sustains, wherever the sun and moon shine,
wherever frost and dews fall, all who have blood and
breath unfeignedly honor and love him. Hence it is
said, — He is the equal of Heaven " (p. 58).

This is certainly very magnificent phraseology, but
it will hardly convey any definite impression to the
minds of those who are not acquainted with the life
and teaching of the great Chinese sage. These may
be studied now by all who can care for the history of
human thought, in the excellent work of Dr. Legge.
The first volume, just published, contains the Confucian Analects, the Great Learning, and the Doctrine of
the Mean, or the First, Second, and Third Shoos, and
will, we hope, soon be followed by the other Chinese
Classics.[1] We must here confine ourselves to giving a
few of the sage's sayings, selected from thousands that

---

[1] Dr. Legge has since published: vol. II. containing the works of Mencius; vol. III. part 1, containing the first part of the Shoo King; vol. III.
part 2, containing the fifth part of the Shoo King.

are to be found in the Confucian Analects. Their interest is chiefly historical, as throwing light on the character of one of the most remarkable men in the history of the human race. But there is besides this a charm in the simple enunciation of simple truths; and such is the fear of truism in our modern writers that we must go to distant times and distant countries if we wish to listen to that simple Solomonic wisdom which is better than the merchandise of silver and the gain thereof than fine gold.

Confucius shows his tolerant spirit when he says, " The superior man is catholic, and no partisan. The mean man is a partisan and not catholic " (p, 14).

There is honest manliness in his saying, " To see what is right, and not to do it, is want of courage." (p. 18).

His definition of knowledge, though less profound than that of Socrates, is nevertheless full of good sense : —

" The Master said, ' Shall I teach you what knowledge is? When you know a thing, to hold that you know it; and when you do not know a thing, to allow that you do not know it, — this is knowledge ' " (p. 15).

Nor was Confucius unacquainted with the secrets of the heart : " It is only the truly virtuous man," he says in one place, " who can love or who can hate others " (p. 30). In another place he expresses his belief in the irresistible charm of virtue : " Virtue is not left to stand alone," he says ; " he who practices it will have neighbors." He bears witness to the hidden connection between intellectual and moral excellence : " It is not easy," he remarks, " to find a man who has learned

for three years without coming to be good " (p. 76)
In his ethics, the golden rule of the gospel, " Do ye
unto others as ye would that others should do to you,"
is represented as almost unattainable.   Thus we read,
" Tsze-Kung said, ' What I do not wish men to do
to me, I also wish not to do to men.'   The Master said,
' Tsze, you have not attained to that.' "   The Brahmans, too, had a distant perception of the same truth,
which is expressed, for instance, in the Hitopadesa in
the following words : " Good people show mercy unto
all beings, considering how like they are to themselves."   On subjects which transcend the limits of human understanding, Confucius is less explicit ;   but his
very reticence is remarkable, when we consider the
recklessness with which oriental philosophers launch
into the deep waters of religious metaphysics.   Thus
we read (p. 107) : —

" Ke Loo asked about serving the spirits of the dead.
The Master said, ' While you are not able to serve
men, how can you serve their spirits ? '

" Ke Loo added, ' I venture to ask about death.'   He
was answered, ' While you do not know life, how can
you know about death ? ' "

And again (p. 190) : —

" The Master said, ' I would prefer not speaking.'

" Tsze-Kung said, ' If you, Master, do not speak,
what shall we, your disciples, have to record ? '

" The Master said, ' Does Heaven speak ?   The
four seasons pursue their courses, and all things are
continually being produced ; but does Heaven say anything ? ' '

December, 1861.

XIV.

POPOL VUH.

———

A BOOK called "Popol Vuh,"[1] and pretending to be the original text of the sacred writings of the Indians of Central America, will be received by most people with a skeptical smile. The Aztec children, who were shown all over Europe as descendants of a race to whom, before the Spanish conquest, divine honors were paid by the natives of Mexico, and who turned out to be unfortunate creatures that had been tampered with by heartless speculators, are still fresh in the memory of most people; and the "Livre des Sauvages,"[2] lately published by the Abbé Domenech, under the auspices of Count Waldeck, has somewhat lowered the dignity of American studies in general. Still, those who laugh at the "Manuscrit Pictographique Américain" discovered by the French Abbé in the library of the French Arsenal, and edited by him with so much care as a precious relic of the old Red-skins of North America, ought not to forget that

———

[1] *Popol Vuh; le Livre Sacré et les Mythes de l'Antiquité Américaine, avec les Livres Héroïques et Historiques des Quichés.* Par l'Abbé Brasseur de Bourbourg. Paris: Durand. 1861.

[2] *Manuscrit Pictographique Américain, précédé d'une Notice sur l'Idéographie des Peaux-Rouges.* Par l'Abbé Em. Domenech. Ouvrage publié sous les auspices de M. le Ministre d'État et de la Maison de l'Empereur. Paris, 1860.

there would be nothing at all surprising in the existence of such MS., containing genuine pictographic writing of the Red Indians. The German critic of Abbé Domenech, M. Petzholdt,[1] assumes much too triumphant an air in announcing his discovery that the " Manuscrit Pictographique " was the work of a German boy in the backwoods of America. He ought to have acknowledged that the Abbé himself had pointed out the German scrawls on some of the pages of his MS. ; that he had read the names of Anna and Maria ; and that he never claimed any great antiquity for the book in question. Indeed, though M. Petzholdt tells us very confidently that the whole book is the work of a naughty, nasty, and profane little boy, the son of German settlers in the backwoods of America, we doubt whether anybody who takes the trouble to look through all the pages will consider this view as at all satisfactory, or even as more probable than that of the French Abbé. We know what boys are capable of in pictographic art from the occasional defacements of our walls and railings ; but we still feel a little skeptical when M. Petzholdt assures us that there is nothing extraordinary in a boy filling a whole volume with these elaborate scrawls. If M. Petzholdt had taken the trouble to look at some of the barbarous hieroglyphics that have been collected in North America, he would have understood more readily how the Abbé Domenech, who had spent many years among the Red Indians, and had himself copied several of their inscriptions, should have taken the

[1] Das Buch der Wilden im Lichte Französischer Civilisation. Mit Proben aus dem in Paris als " Manuscrit Pictographique Américain,' veröffentlichten Schmierbuche eines Deutsch-Amerikanischen Hinterwäldler Jungen. Von J. Petzholdt. Dresden, 1861.

pages preserved in the library of the Arsénal at
Paris as genuine specimens of American pictography.
There is a certain similarity between these scrawls and
the figures scratched on rocks, tombstones, and trees
by the wandering tribes of North America; and
though we should be very sorry to indorse the opinion
of the enthusiastic Abbé, or to start any conjecture of
our own as to the real authorship of the " Livre des
Sauvages," we cannot but think that M. Petzholdt
would have written less confidently, and certainly less
scornfully, if he had been more familiar than he seems
to be with the little that is known of the picture-writing of the Indian tribes. As a preliminary to the
question of the authenticity of the " Popol Vuh," a
few words on the pictorial literature of the Red
Indians of North America will not be considered out
of place. The "Popol Vuh " is not indeed a " Livre
des Sauvages," but a literary composition in the true
sense of the word. It contains the mythology and
history of the civilized races of Central America, and
comes before us with credentials that will bear the test
of critical inquiry. But we shall be better able to
appreciate the higher achievements of the South after
we have examined, however cursorily, the rude beginnings in literature among the savage races of the
North.

Colden, in his " History of the Five Nations," in-
forms us that when, in 1696, the Count de Frontenac
marched a well-appointed army into the Iroquois country, with artillery and all other means of regular
military offense, he found, on the banks of the Onon-
daga, now called Oswego River, a tree, on the trunk
of which the Indians had depicted the French army.

and deposited two bundles of cut rushes at its foot, consisting of 1,434 pieces; an act of symbolical defiance on their part, which was intended to warn their Gallic invaders that they would have to encounter this number of warriors.

This warlike message is a specimen of Indian picture-writing. It belongs to the lowest stage of graphic representation, and hardly differs from the primitive way in which the Persian ambassadors communicated with the Greeks, or the Romans with the Carthaginians. Instead of the lance and the staff of peace between which the Carthaginians were asked to choose, the Red Indians would have sent an arrow and a pipe, and the message would have been equally understood. This, though not yet *prendre la parole*, is nevertheless a first attempt at *parler aux yeux*. It is a first beginning which may lead to something more perfect in the end. We find similar attempts at pictorial communication among other savage tribes, and they seem to answer every purpose. In Freycinet and Arago's " Voyage to the Eastern Ocean," we are told of a native of the Carolina Islands, a Tamor of Sathoual, who wished to avail himself of the presence of a ship to send a trader at Botta, M. Martinez, some shells which he had promised to collect in exchange for a few axes and some other articles. He expressed to the captain, who gave him a piece of paper to make the drawing, and satisfactorily executed the commission. The figure of a man at the top denoted the ship's captain, who by his outstretched hands represented his office as a messenger between the parties. The rays or ornaments on his head denote rank or authority. The vine beneath him is a type of friendship. In the left column are depicted the number and kinds of shells sent; in the right column the things wished for in exchange, namely, seven fish-hooks, three large and four small, two axes, and two pieces of iron.

The inscriptions which are found on the Indian graveboards mark a step in advance. Every warrior has his crest, which is called his "totem," and is painted on his tombstone. A celebrated war-chief, the Adjetatig of Wabojeeg, died on Lake Superior, about 1798. He was of the clan of the Addik, or American reindeer. The fact is symbolized by the figure of the deer. The reversed position denotes death. His own personal name, which was White Fisher, is not noticed. But there are seven transverse strokes on the left, and these have a meaning, namely, that he had led seven war parties. Then there are three perpendicular lines below his crest, and these again are readily understood by every Indian. They represent the wounds received in battle. The figure of a Moose's head is said to relate to a desperate conflict with an enraged animal of this kind; and the symbols of the arrow and the pipe are drawn to indicate the chief's influence in war and peace.

There is another graveboard of the ruling chief of Sandy Lake on the Upper Mississippi. Here the reversed bird denotes his family name or clan, the Crane. Four transverse lines above it denote that he had killed four of his enemies in battle. An analogous custom is mentioned by Aristotle ("Politica," vii. 2, p. 230, ed. Güttling). Speaking of the Iberians, he states that they placed as many obelisks round the grave of a warrior as he had killed enemies in battle.

But the Indians went further; and though they

never arrived at the perfection of the Egyptian hiero-glyphics, they had a number of symbolic emblems which were perfectly understood by all their tribes. *Eating* is represented by a man's hand lifted to his mouth. *Power over man* is symbolized by a line drawn in the figure from the mouth to the heart; *power* in general by a head with two horns. A circle drawn around the body at the abdomen denotes *full means of subsistence*. A boy drawn with waved lines from each ear and lines leading to the heart represents a *pupil*. A figure with a plant as head, and two wings, denotes a *doctor* skilled in medicine, and endowed with the power of ubiquity. A tree with human legs, a *herbalist* or *professor of botany*. *Night* is represented by a finely crossed or barred sun, or a circle with human legs. *Rain* is figured by a dot or semicircle filled with water and placed on the head. The heaven with three disks of the sun is understood to mean three days' journey, and a landing after a voyage is represented by a tortoise. Short sentences, too, can be pictured in this manner. A prescription, ordering abstinence from food for two, and rest for four days, is written by draw-ing a man with two bars on the stomach and four across the legs. We are told even of war-songs and love songs composed in this primitive alphabet; but it would seem as if, in these cases, the reader required even greater poetical imagination than the writer. There is one war-song consisting of four pictures, —

1. The sun rising.

2. A figure pointing with one hand to the earth and the other extended to the sky.

3. The moon with two human legs.

4. A figure personifying the Eastern woman, i. e. the evening star.

These four symbols are said to convey to the Indian the following meaning: —

> I am rising to seek the war path;
> The earth and the sky are before me;
> I walk by day and by night;
> And the evening star is my guide.

The following is a specimen of a love song: —

1. Figure representing a god (monedo) endowed with magic power.
2. Figure beating the drum and singing; lines from his mouth.
3. Figure surrounded by a secret lodge.
4. Two bodies joined with one continuous arm.
5. A woman on an island.
6. A woman asleep; lines from his ear towards her.
7. A red heart in a circle.

This poem is intended to express these sentiments:

1. It is my form and person that make me great.
2. Hear the voice of my song, it is my voice.
3. I shield myself with secret coverings.
4. All your thoughts are known to me, blush!
5. I could draw you hence were you ever so far, —
6. Though you were on the other hemisphere.
7. I speak to your naked heart.

All we can say is, that if the Indians can read this writing, they are greater adepts in the mysteries of love than the judges of the old *Cours d'amour*. But it is much more likely that these war-songs and love-songs are known to the people beforehand, and that their writings are only meant to revive what exists in the memory of the reader. It is a kind of mnemonic writing, and it has been used by missionaries for similar purposes, and with considerable success. Thus, in a translation of the Bible in the Massachusetts language by Eliot, the verses from 25 to 32 in the thirtieth chapter of Proverbs, are expressed by " an ant, a coney, a locust, a spider, a river (symbol of motion), a lion, a greyhound, a he-goat and king, a man foolishly lifting himself to take hold of the heavens." No doubt these symbols would help the reader to remember the proper order of the verses, but they would be perfectly useless without a commentary or without a previous knowledge of the text.

We are told that the famous Testéra, brother of the chamberlain of François I., who came to America eight or nine years after the taking of Mexico, finding it impossible to learn the language of the natives, taught them the Bible history and the principal doctrines of the Christian religion, by means of pictures, and that these diagrams produced a greater effect on the minds of the people, who were accustomed to this style of representation, than all other means employed by the missionaries. But here again, unless these pictures were explained by interpreters, they could by themselves convey no meaning to the gazing crowds of the natives. The fullest information on this subject is to be found in a work by T. Baptiste, " Hiéroglyphes de la conversion, où par des estampes et des figures on apprend aux naturels à desirer le ciel."

There is no evidence to show that the Indians of the North ever advanced beyond the rude attempts which we have thus described, and of which numerous specimens may be found in the voluminous work of

Schoolcraft, published by authority of Congress, "Historical and Statistical Information respecting the History, Condition, and Prospects of the Indian Tribes of
the United States," Philadelphia, 1851–1855. There
is no trace of anything like literature among the wandering tribes of the North, and until a real "Livre
des Sauvages" turns up to fill this gap, they must continue to be classed among the illiterate races.[1]

It is very different if we turn our eyes to the people
of Central and South America, to the races who
formed the population of Mexico, Guatemala, and
Peru, when conquered by the Spaniards. The Mexican hieroglyphics published by Lord Kingsborough are
not to be placed in the same category with the totems
and the pictorial scratches of the Red-skins. They
are, first of all, of a much more artistic character,
more conventional in their structure, and hence more
definite in their meaning. They are colored, written
on paper, and in many respects quite on a level with
the hieroglyphic inscriptions and hieratic papyri of
Egypt. Even the conception of speaking to the ear
through the eye, of expressing sound by means of outlines, was familiar to the Mexicans, though they seem
to have applied their phonetic signs to the writing of
the names of places and persons only. The principal
object, indeed, of the Mexican hieroglyphic manu-
scripts was not to convey new information, but rather
to remind the reader by means of mnemonic artifices
of what he had learnt beforehand. This is acknowledged by the best authorities, by men who knew the
Indians shortly after their first intercourse with Europeans, and whom we may safely trust in what they te'l

1 Maxmardt Pictographupur, pp. 84, 89.

as of the oral literature and hieroglyphic writings of
the natives. Acosta, in his "Historia natural y moral,"
vi. 7, tells us that the Indians were still in the habit of
reciting from memory the addresses and speeches of
their ancient orators, and numerous songs composed by
their national poets. As it was impossible to acquire
these by means of hieroglyphics or written characters
such as were used by the Mexicans, care was taken that
those speeches and poems should be learnt by heart.
There were colleges and schools for that purpose,
where these and other things were taught to the young
by the aged in whose memory they seemed to be en-
graved. The young men who were brought up to be
orators themselves had to learn the ancient compositions word by word ; and when the Spaniards came
and taught them to read and write the Spanish language, the Indians soon began to write for themselves,
a fact attested by many eye-witnesses.

Las Casas, the devoted friend of the Indians, writes
as follows : —

"It ought to be known that in all the republics of
this country, in the kingdoms of New Spain and elsewhere, there was amongst other professions, that of the
chroniclers and historians. They possessed a knowledge of the earliest times, and of all things concerning
religion, the gods, and their worship. They knew the
founders of cities, and the early history of their kings
and kingdoms. They know the modes of election
and the right of succession ; they could tell the number and characters of their ancient kings, their works,
and memorable achievements whether good or bad,
and whether they had governed well or ill. They
know the men renowned for virtue and heroism in

former days, what wars they had waged, and how they had distinguished themselves; who had been the earliest settlers, what had been their ancient customs, their triumphs and defeats. They knew, in fact, whatever belonged to history; and were able to give an account of all the events of the past. . . . . These chroniclers had likewise to calculate the days, months, and years; and though they had no writing like our own, they had their symbols and characters through which they understood everything; they had their great books, which were composed with such ingenuity and art that our alphabet was really of no great assistance to them. . . . . Our priests have seen those books, and I myself have seen them likewise, though many were burnt at the instigation of the monks, who were afraid that they might impede the work of conversion. Sometimes when the Indians who had been converted had forgotten certain words, or particular points of the Christian doctrine, they began — as they were unable to read our books — to write very ingeniously with their own symbols and characters, drawing the figures which corresponded either to the ideas or to the sounds of our words. I have myself seen a large portion of the Christian doctrine written in figures and images, which they read as we read the characters of a letter; and this is a very extraordinary proof of their genius. . . . . There never was a lack of these chroniclers. It was a profession which passed from father to son, highly respected in the whole republic; each historian instructed two or three of his relatives. He made them practice constantly, and they had recourse to him whenever a doubt arose on a point of history. . . . . . But not these young historians only went to consult him;

kings, princes, and priests came to ask his advice. Whenever there was a doubt as to ceremonies, precepts of religion, religious festivals, or anything of importance in the history of the ancient kingdoms, every one went to the chroniclers to ask for information."

In spite of the religious zeal of Dominican and Franciscan friars, a few of these hieroglyphic MSS. escaped the flames, and may now be seen in some of our public libraries, as curious relics of a nearly extinct and forgotten literature. The first collection of these MSS. and other American antiquities was due to the zeal of the Milanese antiquarian, Boturini, who had been sent by the Pope in 1786 to regulate some ecclesiastical matters, and who devoted the eight years of his stay in the New World to rescuing whatever could be rescued from the scattered ruins of ancient America. Before, however, he could bring these treasures safe to Europe, he was despoiled of his valuables by the Spanish Viceroy; and when at last he made his escape with the remnants of his collection, he was taken prisoner by an English cruiser, and lost everything. The collection, which remained at Mexico, became the subject of several lawsuits, and after passing through the hands of Veytia and Gama, who both added to it considerably, it was sold at last by public auction. Humboldt, who was at that time passing through Mexico, acquired some of the MSS., which he gave to the Royal Museum at Berlin. Others found their way into private hands, and after many vicissitudes they have mostly been secured by the public libraries or private collectors of Europe. The most valuable part of that unfortunate shipwreck is now in the hands of M. Aubin, who was sent to Mexico in 1830 by the

French Government, and who devoted nearly twenty
years to the same work which Boturini had commenced
a hundred years before. He either bought the dis-
persed fragments of the collections of Boturini, Gama,
and Pichardo, or procured accurate copies; and he has
brought to Europe, what is, if not the most complete,
at least the most valuable and most judiciously arranged
collection of American antiquities. We likewise owe
to M. Aubin the first accurate knowledge of the real
nature of the ancient Mexican writing; and we look
forward with confident hope to his still achieving in his
own field as great a triumph as that of Champollion,
the decipherer of the hieroglyphics of Egypt.

One of the most important helps towards the deciphering of the hieroglyphic MSS. of the Americans is
to be found in certain books which, soon after the conquest of Mexico, were written down by natives who
had learnt the art of alphabetic writing from their conquerors, the Spaniards. Ixtlilxochitl, descended from
the royal family of Tetzcuco, and, employed as interpreter by the Spanish Government, wrote the history of
his own country from the earliest time to the arrival
of Cortez. In writing this history he followed the
hieroglyphic paintings as they had been explained to
him by the old chroniclers. Some of these very paintings, which formed the text-book of the Mexican historian, have been recovered by M. Aubin; and as they
helped the historian in writing his history, that history
now helps the scholar in deciphering their meaning.
It is with the study of works like that of Ixtlilxochitl
that American philology ought to begin. They are to
the student of American antiquities what Manetho is
to the student of Egyptian hieroglyphics, or Berosus to

the decipherer of the cuneiform inscriptions. They are written in dialects not more than three hundred years old, and still spoken by large numbers of natives, with such modifications as three centuries are certain to produce. They give us whatever was known of history, mythology, and religion among the people whom the Spaniards found in Central and South America in the possession of most of the advantages of a long established civilization. Though we must not expect to find in them what we are accustomed to call history, they are nevertheless of great historical interest, as supplying the vague outlines of a distant past, filled with migrations, wars, dynasties, and revolutions, such as were cherished in the memory of the Greeks at the time of Solon, and believed in by the Romans at the time of Cato. They teach us that the New World which was opened to Europe a few centuries ago, was in its own eyes an old world, not so different in character and feelings from ourselves as we are apt to imagine when we speak of the Red-skins of America, or when we read the accounts of the Spanish conquerors, who denied that the natives of America possessed human souls, in order to establish their own right of treating them like wild beasts.

The " Popol Vuh," or the sacred book of the people of Guatemala, of which the Abbé Brasseour de Bourbourg has just published the original text, together with a literal French translation, holds a very prominent rank among the works composed by natives in their own native dialects, and written down by them with the letters of the Roman alphabet. There are but two works that can be compared to it in their importance to the student of American antiquities and

American languages, namely, the "Codex Chimalpo-
poca" in Nahuatl, the ancient written language of
Mexico, and the "Codex Cakchiquel" in the dialect of
Guatemala. These, together with the work published
by the Abbé Brasseur de Bourbourg under the title of
"Popol Vuh," must form the starting-point of all
critical inquiries into the antiquities of the American
people.

The first point which has to be determined with regard to books of this kind is whether they are genuine
or not; whether they are what they pretend to be,
—compositions about three centuries old, founded on
the oral traditions and the pictographic documents of
the ancient inhabitants of America, and written in the
dialects as spoken at the time of Columbus, Cortez, and
Pizarro. What the Abbé Brasseur de Bourbourg has
to say on this point amounts to this,—The manuscript
was first discovered by Father Francisco Ximenes
towards the end of the seventeenth century. He was
curé of Santo-Tomas Chichicastenango, situated about
three leagues south of Santa-Cruz del Quiché, and
twenty-two leagues northeast of Guatemala. He was
well acquainted with the languages of the natives of
Guatemala, and has left a dictionary of their three
principal dialects, his "Tesoro de las Lenguas Quiché,
Cakchiquel y Tzutohil." This work, which has never
been printed, fills two volumes, the second of which
contains the copy of the MS. discovered by Ximenes.
Ximenes likewise wrote a history of the province of the
preachers of San-Vincente de Chiapas y Guatemala, in
four volumes. Of this he left two copies. But three
volumes only were still in existence when the Abbé
Brasseur de Bourbourg visited Guatemala, and they

are said to contain valuable information on the history and traditions of the country. The first volume contains the Spanish translation of the manuscript which occupies us at present. The Abbé Brasseur de Bourbourg copied that translation in 1855. About the same time a German traveller, Dr. Scherzer, happened to be at Guatemala, and had copies made of the works of Ximenes. These were published at Vienna, in 1856.[1] The French Abbé, however, was not satisfied with a mere reprint of the text and its Spanish translation by Ximenes, a translation which he characterizes as untrustworthy and frequently unintelligible. During his travels in America, he acquired a practical knowledge of several of the native dialects, particularly of the Quiché, which is still spoken in various dialects by about six hundred thousand people. As a priest he was in daily intercourse with these people; and it was while residing among them and able to consult them like living dictionaries, that, with the help of the MSS. of Ximenes, he undertook his own translation of the ancient chronicles of the Quichés. From the time of the discovery of Ximenes, therefore, to the time of the publication of the Abbé Brasseur de Bourbourg, all seems clear and satisfactory. But there is still a century to be accounted for, from the end of the sixteenth century, when the original is supposed to have been written, to the end of the seventeenth, when it was first discovered by Ximenes at Chichicastenango. These years are not bridged over. We may appeal, however, to the authority of the MS. itself, which carries the royal dynasties down to the Spanish Conquest, and ends

[1] Mr. A. Helps was the first to point out the importance of this work in his excellent *History of the Spanish Conquest in America.*

with the names of the two princes, Don Juan de Rojas and Don Juan Cortes, the sons of Tecum and Tepepul. These princes, though entirely subject to the Spaniards, were allowed to retain the insignia of royalty to the year 1558, and it is shortly after their time that the MS. is supposed to have been written. The author himself says in the beginning that he wrote "after the word of God ('chabal Dios') had been preached, in the midst of Christianity; and that he did so because people could no longer see the 'Popol Vuh,' wherein it was clearly shown that they came from the other side of the sea, the account of our living in the land of shadow, and how we saw light and life." There is no attempt at claiming for his work any extravagant age or mysterious authority. It is acknowledged to have been written when the Castilians were the rulers of the land; when bishops were preaching the word of Dios, the new God; when the ancient traditions of the people were gradually dying out. Even the title of "Popol Vuh," which the Abbé Brasseur de Bourbourg has given to this work, is not claimed for it by its author. He says that he wrote when the "Popol Vuh" was no longer to be seen. Now "Popol Vuh" means the book of the people, and referred to the traditional literature in which all that was known about the early history of the nation, their religion and ceremonies, was handed down from age to age.

It is to be regretted that the Abbé Brasseur de Bourbourg should have sanctioned the application of this name to the Quiché MS. discovered by Father Ximenes, and that he should apparently have translated it by "Livre sacré" instead of "Livre national," or "Libro del común," as proposed by Ximenes. Such small inaccuracies are sure to produce great confusion. Nothing but a desire to have a fine sounding title could have led the editor to commit this mistake, for he himself confesses that the work published by him has no right to the title of "Popol Vuh," and that "Popol Vuh" does not mean "Livre sacré." Nor is there any more reason to suppose, with the learned Abbé, that the first two books of the Quiché MS. contain an almost literal transcript of the "Popol Vuh," or that the "Popol Vuh" was the original of the "Teo-Amoxtli," or the sacred book of the Toltecs. All we know is, that the author wrote his anonymous work because the "Popol Vuh"—the national book, or the national tradition—was dying out, and that he comprehended in the first two sections the ancient traditions common to the whole race, while he devoted the last two to the historical annals of the Quichés, the ruling nation at the time of the Conquest in what is now the republic of Guatemala. If we look at the MS. in this light, there is nothing at all suspicious in its character and its contents. The author wished to save from destruction the stories which he had heard as a child of his gods and his ancestors. Though the general outline of these stories may have been preserved partly in the schools, partly in the pictographic MSS., the Spanish Conquest had thrown everything into confusion, and the writer had probably to depend chiefly on his own recollections. To extract consecutive history from these recollections, is simply impossible. All is vague, contradictory, miraculous, absurd. Consecutive history is altogether a modern idea, of which few only of the ancient nations had any conception. If we had the exact words of the "Popol Vuh," we should probably

find no more history there than we find in the Quiché
MS. as it now stands. Now and then, it is true, one
imagines one sees certain periods and landmarks, but
in the next page all is chaos again. It may be difficult
to confess that with all the traditions of the early
migrations of Cecrops and Danaus into Greece, with
the Homeric poems of the Trojan War, and the genealogies of the ancient dynasties of Greece, we know
nothing of Greek history before the Olympiads, and
very little even then. Yet the true historian does not
allow himself to indulge in any illusions on this subject, and he shuts his eyes even to the most plausible
reconstructions.

The same applies with a force increased a hundred-
fold to the ancient history of the aboriginal races of
America, and the sooner this is acknowledged, the
better for the credit of American scholars. Even the
traditions of the migrations of the Chichimecs, Col-
huas, and Nahuas, which form the staple of all American antiquarians, are no better than the Greek traditions about Pelasgians, Æolians, and Ionians; and it
would be a mere waste of time to construct out of such
elements a systematic history, only to be destroyed
again sooner or later by some Niebuhr, Grote, or
Lewis.

But if we do not find history in the stories of the
ancient races of Guatemala, we do find materials for
studying their character, for analyzing their religion
and mythology, for comparing their principles of morality, their views of virtue, beauty, and heroism, to those
of other races of mankind. This is the charm, the
real and lasting charm, of such works as that presented to us for the first time in a trustworthy trans-

lation by the Abbé Brasseur de Bourbourg.   Unfortunately there is one circumstance which may destroy even
this charm.   It is just possible that the writers of this
and other American MSS. may have felt more or less
consciously the influence of European and Christian
ideas, and if so, we have no sufficient guarantee that
the stories they tell represent to us the American mind
in its pristine and genuine form.   There are some coincidences between the Old Testament and the Quiche
MS. which are certainly startling.   Yet even if a
Christian influence has to be admitted, much remains
in these American traditions which is so different
from anything else in the national literatures of other
countries, that we may safely treat it as the genuine
growth of the intellectual soil of America.   We shall
give, in conclusion, some extracts to bear out our remarks; but we ought not to part with Abbé Brasseur
de Bourbourg without expressing to him our gratitude
for his excellent work, and without adding a hope that
he may be able to realize his plan of publishing a
"Collection of documents written in the indigenous
languages, to assist the student of the history and philology of ancient America," a collection of which the
work now published is to form the first volume.

EXTRACTS FROM THE "POPOL VUH."

The Quiché MS. begins with an account of the creation.   If we read it in the literal translation of the
Abbé Brasseur de Bourbourg, with all the uncouth
names of divine and other beings that have to act their
parts in it, it does not leave any very clear impression
on our minds.   Yet after reading it again and again,
some salient features stand out more distinctly, and

make us feel that there was a groundwork of noble conceptions which has been covered and distorted by an aftergrowth of fantastic nonsense. We shall do best for the present to leave out all proper names, which only bewilder the memory, and which convey no distinct meaning even to the scholar. It will require long-continued research before it can be determined whether the names so profusely applied to the Deity were intended as the names of so many distinct personalities, or as the names of the various manifestations of one and the same Power. At all events, they are of no importance to us till we can connect more distinct ideas than it is possible to gather from the materials now on hand, with such inharmonious sounds as Tzakol, Bitol, Alom, Qaholom, Hun-Ahpu-Vuch, Gucumatz, Qnax-Cho, etc. Their supposed meanings are in some cases very appropriate, such as the Creator, the Fashioner, the Begetter, the Vivifier, the Ruler, the Lord of the green planisphere, the Lord of the azure surface, the Heart of heaven ; in other cases we cannot fathom the original intention of such names as the feathered serpent, the white boar, *la tireur de sarbacane au corrigus*, and others ; and they therefore sound to our ears simply absurd. Well, the Quichés believed that there was a time when all that exists in heaven and earth was made. All was then in suspense, all was calm and silent ; all was immovable, all peaceful, and the vast space of the heavens was empty. There was no man, no animal, no shore, no trees ; heaven alone existed. The face of the earth was not to be seen ; there was only the still expanse of the sea and the heaven above. Divine Beings were on the waters like a growing light. Their voice was heard as they meditated and consulted, and

when the dawn arose, man appeared. Then the waters
were commanded to retire, the earth was established,
that she might bear fruit and that the light of day might
shine on heaven and earth.

" For, they said, we shall receive neither glory nor
honour from all we have created until there is a human
being — a being endowed with reason. ' Earth,' they
said, and in a moment the earth was formed. Like a
vapor it rose into being, mountains appeared from the
waters like lobsters, and the great mountains were
made. Thus was the creation of the earth, when it
was fashioned by those who are the Heart of heaven,
the Heart of the earth ; for thus were they called who
first gave fertility to them, heaven and earth being still
inert and suspended in the midst of the waters."

Then follows the creation of the brute world, and
the disappointment of the gods when they command
the animals to tell their names and to honor those who
had created them. Then the gods said to the animals :

" You will be changed, because you cannot speak.
We have changed your speech. You shall have your
food and your dens in the woods and crags; for our
glory is not perfect, and you do not invoke us. There
will be beings still that can salute us ; we shall make
them capable of obeying. Do your task ; as to your
flesh, it will be broken by the tooth."

Then follows the creation of man. His flesh was
made of earth (*terre glaise*). But man was without co-
hesion or power, inert and aqueous ; he could not turn
his head, his sight was dim, and though he had the gift
of speech, he had no intellect. He was soon consumed
again in the water.

And the gods consulted a second time how to create

beings that should adore them, and after some magic
ceremonies, men were made of wood, and they multi-
plied.   But they had no heart, no intellect, no recollection of their Creator; they did not lift up their
heads to their Maker, and they withered away and
were swallowed up by the waters.

Then follows a third creation, man being made of a
tree called "txité," woman of the marrow of a reed
called "sibac."   They, too, did neither think nor speak
before him who had made them, and they were likewise swept away by the waters and destroyed.   The
whole nature — animals, trees, and stones — turned
against men to revenge the wrongs they had suffered
at their hands, and the only remnant of that early race
is to be found in small monkeys which still live in the
forests.

Then follows a story of a very different character,
and which completely interrupts the progress of events.
It has nothing to do with the creation, though it ends
with two of its heroes being changed into sun and
moon.   It is a story very much like the fables of the
Brahmans or the German Mährchen. Some of the
principal actors in it are clearly divine beings who have
been brought down to the level of human nature, and
who perform feats and tricks so strange and incredible
that in reading them we imagine ourselves in the midst
of the Arabian Nights.   In the struggles of the two
favorite heroes against the cruel princes of Xibalba,
there may be reminiscences of historical events; but
it would be perfectly hopeless to attempt to extricate
these from the mass of fable by which they are surrounded.   The chief interest of the American tale
consists in the points of similarity which it exhibits

with the tales of the Old World. We shall mention
two only — the repeated resuscitation of the chief heroes, who, even when burnt and ground to powder and
scattered on the water, are born again as fish and
changed into men; and the introduction of animals
endowed with reason and speech. As in the German
tales, certain peculiarities in the appearance and natural
habits of animals are frequently accounted for by
events that happened " once upon a time," — for instance, the stumpy tail of the bear, by his misfortune
when he went out fishing on the ice; so we find in
the American tales, " that it was when the two principal heroes (Hun-Ahpu and Xbalanqué) had caught the
rat and were going to strangle it over the fire, that *le
rat commença à porter une queue sans poil.* Thus, because a certain serpent swallowed a frog who was sent
as a messenger, therefore *aujourd'hui encore les serpents
engloutissent les crapauds.*"

The story, which well deserves the attention of
those who are interested in the origin and spreading
of popular tales, is carried on to the end of the second
book, and it is only in the third that we hear once
more of the creation of man.

Three attempts, as we saw, had been made and
had failed. We now hear again that before the
beginning of dawn, and before the sun and moon
had risen, man had been made, and that nourishment
was provided for him which was to supply his blood,
namely, yellow and white maize. Four men are mentioned as the real ancestors of the human race, or
rather of the race of the Quichés. They were
neither begotten by the gods nor born of woman, but
their creation was a wonder wrought by the Creator.

They could reason and speak, their sight was un-
limited, and they knew all things at once. When
they had rendered thanks to their Creator for their
existence, the gods were frightened and they breathed
a cloud over the eyes of men that they might see a
certain distance only, and not be like the gods themselves. Then while the four men were asleep, the
gods gave them beautiful wives, and these became the
mothers of all tribes, great and small. These tribes,
both white and black, lived and spread in the East.
They did not yet worship the gods, but only turned
their faces up to heaven, hardly knowing what they
were meant to do here below. Their features were
sweet, so was their language, and their intellect was
strong.

We now come to a most interesting passage, which
is intended to explain the confusion of tongues. No
nation, except the Jews, has dwelt much on the problem why there should be many languages instead of
one. Grimm, in his "Essay on the Origin of Language," remarks: "It may seem surprising that
neither the ancient Greeks nor the ancient Indians
attempted to propose or to solve the question as to the
origin and the multiplicity of human speech. Holy
Writ strove to solve at least one of those riddles, that
of the multiplicity of languages, by means of the tower
of Babel. I know only one other poor Esthonian legend which might be placed by the side of this biblical solution. 'The old god,' they say, 'when men
found their first seats too narrow, resolved to spread
them over the whole earth, and to give to each nation
its own language. For this purpose he placed a
caldron of water on the fire, and commanded the

different races to approach it in order, and to select for themselves the sounds which were uttered by the singing of the water in its confinement and torture.'"

Grimm might have added another legend which is current among the Thlinkithians, and was clearly framed in order to account for the existence of different languages. The Thlinkithians are one of the four principal races inhabiting Russian America. They are called Kaljush, Koljush, or Kolosh by the Russians, and inhabit the coast from about 60° to 45° N. Lat., reaching therefore across the Russian frontier as far as the Columbia River, and they likewise hold many of the neighbouring islands. Weniaminow estimates their number, both in the Russian and English colonies, at 20,000 to 25,000. They are evidently a decreasing race, and their legends, which seem to be numerous and full of original ideas, would well deserve the careful attention of American ethnologists. Wrangel suspected a relationship between them and the Aztecs of Mexico. These Thlinkithians believe in a general flood or deluge, and that men saved themselves in a large floating building. When the waters fell, the building was wrecked on a rock, and by its own weight burst into two pieces. Hence arose the difference of languages. The Thlinkithians with their language remained on one side; on the other side were all the other races of the earth.[1]

Neither the Esthonian nor the Thlinkithian legend, however, offers any striking points of coincidence with the Mosaic accounts. The analogies, therefore, as well as the discrepancies, between the ninth chapter of

[1] Baehr, Ethnographische Skizzen über die Völker des Russischen Amerika. Halbington, 1853.

Genesis and the chapter here translated from the Quiché MS. require special attention :

"All had but one language, and they did not invoke as yet either wood or stones; they only remembered the word of the Creator, the Heart of heaven and earth.

"And they spoke while meditating on what was hidden by the spring of day; and full of the sacred word, full of love, obedience, and fear, they made their prayers, and lifting their eyes up to heaven, they asked for sons and daughters :—

"'Hail! O Creator and Fashioner, thou who seest and hearest us! do not forsake us, O God, who art in heaven and earth, Heart of the sky, Heart of the earth! Give us offspring and descendants as long as the sun and dawn shall advance. Let there be seed and light. Let us always walk on open paths, on roads where there is no ambush. Let us always be quiet and in peace with those who are ours. May our lives run on happily. Give us a life secure from reproach. Let there be seed for harvest, and let there be light.'

"They then proceeded to the town of Tulan, where they received their gods.

"And when all the tribes were there gathered together, their speech was changed, and they did not understand each other after they arrived at Tulan. It was there that they separated, and some went to the East, others came here. Even the language of the four ancestors of the human race became different. 'Alas,' they said, 'we have lost our language. How has this happened? We are ruined! How could we have been led into error? We had but one language

when we came to Tulan; our form of worship was
but one. What we have done is not good,' replied
all the tribes in the wood, and under the lianas."

The rest of the work, which consists altogether of
four books, is taken up with an account of the migrations of the tribes from the East, and their various
settlements. The four ancestors of the race seem to
have had a long life, and when at last they came to
die, they disappeared in a mysterious manner, and left
to their sons what is called the Hidden Majesty, which
was never to be opened by human hands. What it
was we do not know. There are many subjects of
interest in the chapters which follow, only we must not
look there for history, although the author evidently
accepts as truly historical what he tells us about the
successive generations of kings. But when he brings
us down at last, after sundry migrations, wars, and re-
bellions, to the arrival of the Castilians, we find that
between the first four ancestors of the human or of the
Quiché race and the last of their royal dynasties, there
intervene only fourteen generations, and the author,
whoever he was, ends with the confession : —

" This is all that remains of the existence of Quiché ;
for it is impossible to see the book in which formerly
the kings could read everything, as it has disappeared.
It is over with all those of Quiché ! It is now called
Santa Cruz !"

March, 1862.

XV.

SEMITIC MONOTHEISM.[1]

——◆——

A work such as M. Renan's "Histoire Générale
et Système Comparé des Langues Sémitiques" can only
be reviewed chapter by chapter. It contains a survey
not only, as its title would lead us to suppose, of the
Semitic languages, but of the Semitic languages and
nations; and considering that the whole history of the
civilized world has hitherto been acted by two races
only, the Semitic and the Aryan, with occasional interruptions produced by the inroads of the Turanian race,
M. Renan's work comprehends in reality half of the
history of the ancient world. We have received as
yet the first volume only of this important work, and
before the author had time to finish the second, he
was called upon to publish a second edition of the
first, which appeared in 1858, with important additions
and alterations.

In writing the history of the Semitic race it is necessary to lay down certain general characteristics common
to all the members of that race, before we can speak
of nations so widely separated from each other as the

[1] Histoire Générale et Système Comparé des Langues Sémitiques. Par
Ernest Renan, Membre de l'Institut. Seconde édition. Paris, 1858.
Nouvelles Considérations sur le Caractère Général des Peuples Sémitiques
et en particulier sur leur Tendance au Monothéisme. Par Ernest Renan.
Paris, 1859.

Jews, the Babylonians, Phenicians, Carthaginians, and Arabs, as one race or family. The most important bond which binds these scattered tribes together into one ideal whole is to be found in their language. There can be as little doubt that the dialects of all the Semitic nations are derived from one common type as there is about the derivation of French, Spanish, and Italian from Latin, or of Latin, Greek, German, Celtic, Slavonic, and Sanskrit from the primitive idiom of the ancestors of the Aryan race. The evidence of language would by itself be quite sufficient to establish the fact that the Semitic nations descended from common ancestors, and constitute what, in the science of language may be called a distinct race. But M. Renan was not satisfied with the single criterion of the relationship of the Semitic tribes, and he has endeavoured to draw, partly from his own observations, partly from the suggestions of other scholars, such as Ewald and Lassen, a more complete portrait of the Semitic man. This was no easy task. It was like drawing the portrait of a whole family, omitting all that is peculiar to each individual member, and yet preserving the features which constitute the general family likeness. The result has been what might be expected. Critics most familiar with one or the other branch of the Semitic family have each and all protested that they can see no likeness in the portrait. It seems to some to contain features which it ought not to contain, whereas others miss the very expression which appears to them most striking.

The following is a short abstract of what M. Renan considers the salient points in the Semitic character : —

" Their character," he says, " is religious rather than political, and the mainspring of their religion is the conception of the unity of God. Their religious phraseology is simple, and free from mythological elements. Their religious feelings are strong, exclusive, intolerant, and sustained by a fervor which finds its peculiar expression in prophetic visions. Compared to the Aryan nations, they are found deficient in scientific and philosophical originality. Their poetry is chiefly subjective or lyrical, and we look in vain among their poets for excellence in epic and dramatic compositions. Painting and the plastic arts have never arrived at a higher than the decorative stage. Their political life has remained patriarchal and despotic, and their inability to organize on a large scale has deprived them of the means of military success. Perhaps the most general feature of their character is a negative one, — their inability to perceive the general and the abstract, whether in thought, language, religion, poetry, or politics; and, on the other hand, a strong attraction towards the individual and personal, which makes them monotheistic in religion, lyrical in poetry, monarchical in politics, abrupt in style, and useless for speculation."

One cannot look at this bold and rapid outline of the Semitic character without perceiving how many points it contains which are open to doubt and discussion. We shall confine our remarks to one point, which, in our mind, and, as far as we can see, in M. Renan's mind likewise, is the most important of all, namely, the supposed monotheistic tendency of the Semitic race. M. Renan asserts that this tendency belongs to the race by instinct, — that it forms the rule, not the exception; and he seems to imply that without it the human race would never have arrived at the knowledge or worship of the One God.

If such a remark had been made fifty years ago, it would have roused little or no opposition. "Semitic" was then used in a more restricted sense, and hardly comprehended more than the Jews and Arabs. Of this small group of people it might well have been said, with such limitations as are tacitly implied in every general proposition on the character of individuals or nations, that the work set apart for them by a Divine providence in the history of the world was the preaching of a belief in one God. Three religions have been founded by members of that more circumscribed Semitic family,—the Jewish, the Christian, the Mohammedan; and all three proclaim, with the strongest accent, the doctrine that there is but one God.

Of late, however, not only have the limits of the Semitic family been considerably extended, so as to embrace several nations notorious for their idolatrous worship, but the history of the Jewish and Arab tribes has been explored so much more fully, that even there traces of a wide-spreading tendency to polytheism have come to light.

The Semitic family is divided by M. Renan into two great branches, differing from each other in the form of their monotheistic belief, yet both, according to their historian, imbued from the beginning with the instinctive faith in one God:—

1. The nomad branch, consisting of Arabs, Hebrews, and the neighboring tribes of Palestine, commonly called the descendants of Terah; and

2. The political branch, including the nations of Phenicia, of Syria, Mesopotamia, and Yemen.

Can it be said that all those nations, comprising the worshippers of Elohim, Jehovah, Salmoth, Moloch, Nisroch, Rimmon, Nebo, Dagon, Ashtaroth, Baal or Bel, Baal-peor, Baal-zebub, Chemosh, Milcom, Adrammelech, Annamelech, Nibhaz and Tartak, Ashima, Nergal, Succoth-benoth, the Sun, Moon, planets, and all the host of heaven, were endowed with a monotheistic instinct? M. Renan admits that monotheism has always had its principal bulwark in the nomadic branch, but he maintains that it has by no means been so unknown among the members of the political branch as is commonly supposed. But where are the criteria by which, in the same manner as their dialects, the religions of the Semitic races could be distinguished from the religions of the Aryan and Turanian races? We can recognize any Semitic dialect by the triliteral character of its roots. Is it possible to discover similar radical elements in all the forms of faith, primary or secondary, primitive or derivative, of the Semitic tribes? M. Renan thinks that it is. He imagines that he hears the key-note of a pure monotheism through all the wild shoutings of the priests of Baal and other Semitic idols, and he denies the presence of that key-note in any of the religious systems of the Aryan nations, whether Greeks or Romans, Germans or Celts, Hindus or Persians. Such an assertion could not but rouse considerable opposition, and so strong seems to have been the remonstrances addressed to M. Renan by several of his colleagues in the French Institute that without awaiting the publication of the second volume of his great work, he has thought it right to publish part of it as a separate pamphlet. In his "Nouvelles Considérations sur le Caractère Général des Peuples Sémitiques, et en particulier sur leur Tendance au Monothéisme, he endeavors to silence the objections raised against the leading idea of his history of the Semitic race. It is an essay which exhibits not only the comprehensive knowledge of the scholar, but the warmth and alacrity of the advocate. With M. Renan the monotheistic character of the descendants of Shem is not only a scientific tenet, but a moral conviction. He wishes that his whole work should stand or fall with this thesis, and it becomes, therefore, all the more the duty of the critic, to inquire whether the arguments which he brings forward in support of his favorite idea are valid or not.

It is but fair to M. Renan that, in examining his statements, we should pay particular attention to any slight modifications which he may himself have adopted in his last memoir. In his history he asserts with great confidence, and somewhat broadly, that "le monothéisme résume et explique tous les caractères de la race Sémitique." In his later pamphlet he is more cautious. As an experienced pleader he is ready to make many concessions in order to gain all the more readily our assent to his general proposition. He points out himself with great candor the weaker points of his argument, though, of course, only in order to return with unabated courage to his first position, — that of all the races of mankind the Semitic race alone was endowed with the instinct of monotheism. As it is impossible to deny the fact that the Semitic nations, in spite of this supposed monotheistic instinct, were frequently addicted to the most degraded forms of a polytheistic idolatry, and that even the Jews, the most monotheistic of all, frequently pro-

voked the anger of the Lord by burning incense to
other gods, M. Renan remarks that when he speaks of
a nation in general he only speaks of the intellectual
aristocracy of that nation. He appeals in self-defense
to the manner in which historians lay down the character of modern nations. "The French," he says,
"are repeatedly called *une nation spirituelle,*' and
yet no one would wish to assert either that every
Frenchman is *spiritual*, or that no one could be *spirit-
uel* who is not a Frenchman." Now, here we may
grant to M. Renan that if we speak of "*esprit*" we
naturally think of the intellectual minority only, and
not of the whole bulk of a nation; but if we speak
of religion, the case is different. If we say that the
French believe in one God only, or that they are
Christians, we speak not only of the intellectual aristocracy of France but of every man, woman, and child
born and bred in France. Even if we say that the
French are Roman Catholics, we do so only because
we know that there is a decided majority in France
in favor of the unreformed system of Christianity.
But if, because some of the most distinguished writers
of France have paraded their contempt for all religious
dogmas we were to say broadly that the French are
a nation without religion, we should justly be called
to order for abusing the legitimate privileges of gener-
alization. The fact that Abraham, Moses, Elijah, and
Jeremiah were firm believers in one God could not be
considered sufficient to support the general proposition
that the Jewish nation was monotheistic by instinct.
And if we remember that among the other Semitic
races we should look in vain for even four such names,
the case would seem to be desperate to any one but
M. Renan.

We cannot believe that M. Renan would be satisfied with the admission that there had been among the Jews a few leading men who believed in one God, or that the existence of but one God was an article of faith not quite unknown among the other Semitic races; yet he has hardly proved more. He has collected, with great learning and ingenuity, all traces of monotheism in the annals of the Semitic nations; but he has taken no pains to discover the traces of polytheism, whether faint or distant, which are disclosed in the same annals. In acting the part of an advocate he has for a time divested himself of the nobler character of the historian.

If M. Renan had looked with equal zeal for the scattered vestiges both of a monotheistic and of a polytheistic worship, he would have drawn, perhaps, a less striking, but we believe a more faithful portrait of the Semitic man. We may accept all the facts of M. Renan, for his facts are almost always to be trusted; but we cannot accept his conclusions, because they would be in contradiction to other facts which M. Renan places too much in the background, or ignores altogether. Besides there is something in the very conclusions to which he is driven by his too partial evidence which jars on our ears, and betrays a want of harmony in the premises on which he builds. Taking his stand on the fact that the Jewish race was the first of all the nations of the world to arrive at the knowledge of one God, M. Renan proceeds to argue that, if their monotheism had been the result of a persevering mental effort, — if it had been a discovery like the philosophical or scientific discoveries of the Greeks, it would be necessary to admit that the Jews surpassed all other nations of the world in intellect and vigor of speculation. This, he admits, is contrary to fact: —

" A part la supériorité de son culte, le peuple juif n'en a aucune autre ; c'est un des peuples les moins doués pour la science et la philosophie parmi les peuples de l'antiquité ; il n'a une grande position ni politique ni militaire. Ses institutions sont purement conservatrices ; les prophètes, qui représentent excellemment son génie, sont des hommes essentiellement réactionnaires, se reportant toujours vers un idéal antérieur. Comment expliquer, au sein d'une société aussi étroite et aussi peu développée, une révolution d'idées qu'Athènes et Alexandrie n'ont pas réussi à accomplir ? "

M. Renan then defines the monotheism of the Jews, and of the Semitic nations in general, as the result of a low, rather than of a high state of intellectual cultivation : " Il s'en faut," he writes (p. 40), " que le monothéisme soit le produit d'une race qui a des idées exaltées en fait de religion ; c'est en réalité le fruit d'une race qui a peu de besoins religieux. C'est comme minimum de religion, en fait de dogmes et en fait de pratiques extérieures, que le monothéisme est surtout accommodé aux besoins des populations nomades."

But even this minimum of religious reflection, which is required, according to M. Renan, for the perception of the unity of God, he grudges to the Semitic nations, and he is driven in the end (p. 76) to explain the Semitic Monotheism as the result of a religious instinct, analogous to the instinct which led each race to the formation of its own language.

Here we miss the clearness and precision which distinguish most of M. Renan's works. It is always dangerous to transfer expressions from one branch of knowledge to another. The word "Instinct" has its legitimate application in natural history, where it is used of the unconscious acts of unconscious beings. We say that birds build their nests by instinct, that fishes swim by instinct, that cats catch mice by instinct; and, though no natural philosopher has yet explained what instinct is, yet we accept the term as a conventional expression for an unknown power working in the animal world.

If we transfer this word to the unconscious acts of conscious beings, we must necessarily alter its definition. We may speak of an instinctive motion of the arm, but we only mean a motion which has become so habitual as to require no longer any special effort of the will.

If, however, we transfer the word to the conscious thoughts of conscious beings, we strain the word beyond its natural capacities, we use it in order to avoid other terms which would commit us to the admission either of innate ideas or inspired truths. We use a word in order to avoid a definition. It may sound more scientific to speak of a monotheistic instinct rather than of the inborn image or the revealed truth of the One living God; but is instinct less mysterious than revelation? Can there be an instinct without an instigation or an instigator? And whose hand was it that instigated the Semitic mind to the worship of one God? Could the same hand have instigated the Aryan mind to the worship of many gods? Could the monotheistic instinct of the Semitic race, if an instinct, have been so frequently obscured, or the polytheistic instinct of the Aryan race, if an instinct, so completely annihilated, as to allow the Jews to worship on all the high places round Jerusalem, and the Greeks and Romans to become believers in Christ? Fishes never fly, and cats never catch frogs. These are the difficulties into which we are led; and they arise simply and solely from our using words for their sound rather than for their meaning. We begin by playing with words, but in the end the words will play with us.

There are, in fact, various kinds of monotheism, and it becomes our duty to examine more carefully what they mean and how they arise. There is one kind of monotheism, though it would more properly be called theism, or henotheism, which forms the birthright of every human being. What distinguishes man from all other creatures, and not only raises him above the animal world, but removes him altogether from the confines of a merely natural existence, is the feeling of sonship inherent in and inseparable from human nature. That feeling may find expression in a thousand ways, but there breathes through all of them the inextinguishable conviction, " It is He that hath made us, and not we ourselves." That feeling of sonship may with some races manifest itself in fear and trembling, and it may drive whole generations into religious madness and devil worship. In other countries it may tempt the creature into a fatal familiarity with the Creator, and end in an apotheosis of man, or a headlong plunging of the human into the divine. It may take, as with the Jews, the form of a simple assertion that " Adam was the son of God," or it may be clothed in the mythological phraseology of the Hindus, that Manu, or man, was the descendant of Svayambhu, the Self-existing. But, in some form or other, the feeling of dependence on a higher Power breaks through in all the religions of the world, and explains to us the meaning of St. Paul, " that God, though in times past He suf-

fered all nations to walk in their own ways, nevertheless He left not Himself without witness, in that He
did good and gave us rain from heaven, and fruitful
seasons filling our hearts with food and gladness."

This primitive intuition of God and the ineradicable feeling of dependence on God, could only have been
the result of a primitive revelation, in the truest sense
of that word. Man, who owed his existence to God,
and whose being centred and rested in God, saw and
felt God as the only source of his own and of all other
existence. By the very act of the creation, God had
revealed Himself. There He was, manifested in His
works, in all His majesty and power, before the face
of those to whom He had given eyes to see and ears to
hear, and into whose nostrils He had breathed the
breath of life, even the Spirit of God.

This primitive intuition of God, however, was in
itself neither monotheistic nor polytheistic, though it
might become either, according to the expression which
it took in the languages of man. It was this primitive
intuition which supplied either the subject or the predicate in all the religions of the world, and without it no
religion, whether true or false, whether revealed or
natural, could have had even its first beginning. It is
too often forgotten by those who believe that a polytheistic worship was the most natural unfolding of religious life, that polytheism must everywhere have been
preceded by a more or less conscious theism. In no
language does the plural exist before the singular. No
human mind could have conceived the idea of gods
without having previously conceived the idea of a god.
It would be, however, quite as great a mistake to imagine, because the idea of a god must exist previously

to that of gods, that therefore a belief in One God preceded everywhere the belief in many gods. A belief in God as exclusively One, involves a distinct negation of more than one God, and that negation is possible only after the conception, whether real or imaginary, of many gods.

The primitive intuition of the Godhead is neither monotheistic nor polytheistic, and it finds its most natural expression in the simplest and yet the most important article of faith, — that God is God. This must have been the faith of the ancestors of mankind previously to any division of race or confusion of tongues. It might seem, indeed, as if in such a faith the oneness of God, though not expressly asserted, was implied, and that it existed, though latent, in the first revelation of God. History, however, proves that the question of oneness was yet undecided in that primitive faith, and that the intuition of God was not yet secured against the illusions of a double vision. There are, in reality, two kinds of oneness which, when we enter into metaphysical discussions, must be carefully distinguished, and which for practical purposes are well kept separate by the definite and indefinite articles. There is one kind of oneness which does not exclude the idea of plurality; there is another which does. When we say that Cromwell was a Protector of England, we do not assert that he was the only protector. But if we say that he was the Protector of England, it is understood that he was the only man who enjoyed that title. If, therefore, an expression had been given to that primitive intuition of the Deity, which is the mainspring of all later religion, it would have been, — "There is a God," but not yet "There is but 'One

God.'" The latter form of faith, the belief in One
God, is properly called monotheism, whereas the term
of henotheism would best express the faith in a single
god.

We must bear in mind that we are here speaking of
a period in the history of mankind when, together with
the awakening of ideas, the first attempts only were
being made at expressing the simplest conceptions by
means of a language most simple, most sensuous, and
most unwieldy. There was as yet no word sufficiently
reduced by the wear and tear of thought to serve as
an adequate expression for the abstract idea of an immaterial and supernatural Being. There were words
for walking and shouting, for cutting and burning, for
dog and cow, for house and wall, for sun and moon,
for day and night. Every object was called by some
quality which had struck the eye as most peculiar
and characteristic. But what quality should be pred-
icated of that Being of which man knew as yet nothing
but its existence? Language possessed as yet no auxiliary verbs. The very idea of being without the attributes of quality or action, had never entered into the
human mind. How then was that Being to be called
which had revealed its existence, and continued to make
itself felt by everything that most powerfully impressed
the awakening mind, but which as was yet known only
like a subterraneous spring by the waters which it
poured forth with inexhaustible strength? When storm
and lightning drove a father with his helpless family
to seek refuge in the forests, and the fall of mighty trees
crushed at his side those who were most dear to him,
there were, no doubt, feelings of terror and awe, of
helplessness and dependence, in the human heart which

burst forth in a shriek for pity or help from the only Being that could command the storm. But there was no name by which He could be called. There might be names for the storm-wind and the thunderbolt, but these were not the names applicable to Him that rideth upon the heaven of heavens, which were of old. Again, when after a wild and tearful night the sun dawned in the morning, smiling on man — when after a dreary and death-like winter spring came again with its sunshine and flowers, there were feelings of joy and gratitude, of love and adoration in the heart of every human being, but though there were names for the sun and the spring, for the bright sky and the brilliant dawn, there was no word by which to call the source of all this gladness, the giver of light and life.

At the time when we may suppose that the first attempts at finding a name for God were made, the divergence of the languages of mankind had commenced. We cannot dwell here on the causes which led to the multiplicity of human speech; but whether we look on the confusion of tongues as a natural or supernatural event, it was an event which the science of language has proved to have been inevitable. The ancestors of the Semitic and the Aryan nations had long become unintelligible to each other in their conversations on the most ordinary topics, when they each in their own way began to look for a proper name for God. Now one of the most striking differences between the Aryan and the Semitic forms of speech was this, — In the Semitic languages the roots expressive of the predicates which were to serve as the proper names of any subjects, remained so distinct within the body of a word, that those who used the word were

unable to forget its predicative meaning, and retained
in most cases a distinct consciousness of its appellative
power. In the Aryan languages, on the contrary,
the significative element, or the root of a word, was
apt to become so completely absorbed by the derivative elements, whether prefixes or suffixes, that most
substantives ceased almost immediately to be appellative, and were changed into mere names or proper
names. What we mean can best be illustrated by the
fact that the dictionaries of Semitic languages are
mostly arranged according to their roots. When we
wish to find the meaning of a word in Hebrew or
Arabic we first look for its root, whether triliteral or
biliteral, and then look in the dictionary for that root
and its derivatives. In the Aryan languages, on the
contrary, such an arrangement would be extremely in-
convenient. In many words it is impossible to detect
the radical element. In others after the root is discovered, we find that it has not given birth to any other
derivatives which would throw their converging rays
of light on its radical meaning. In other cases, again,
such seems to have been the boldness of the original
name-giver that we can hardly enter into the idiosyn-
crasy which assigned such a name to such an object.

This peculiarity of the Semitic and Aryan languages
must have had the greatest influence on the formation
of their religious phraseology. The Semitic man
would call on God in adjectives only, or in words which
always conveyed a predicative meaning. Every one
of his words was more or less predicative, and he was
therefore restricted in his choice to such words as expressed some one or other of the abstract qualities of
the Deity. The Aryan man was less fettered in his

choice. Let us take an instance. Being startled by
the sound of thunder, he would at first express his
impression by the single phrase, "It thunders,"
—βροντᾷ. Here the idea of God is understood rather
than expressed, very much in the same manner as the
Semitic proper names "Zabd" (present), "Abd" (servant), "Aus" (present), are habitually used for
"Abd-allah," "Zabd-allah," "Aus-allah," — the servant of God, the gift of God. It would be more in accordance with the feelings and thoughts of those who
first used these so-called impersonal verbs to translate
them by "He thunders," "He rains," "He snows."
Afterwards, instead of the simple impersonal verb "He
thunders," another expression naturally suggested itself.
The thunder came from the sky, the sky was frequently
called "Dyaus" (the bright one), in Greek Ζεύς; and
though it was not the bright sky which thundered, but
the dark, yet "Dyaus" had already ceased to be an
expressive predicate; it had become a traditional name,
and hence there was nothing to prevent an Aryan man
from saying "Dyaus," or "the sky thunders," in
Greek Ζεὺς βροντᾷ. Let us here mark the almost irresistible influence of language on the mind. The
word "Dyaus," which at first meant "bright," had
lost its radical meaning, and now meant simply "sky."
It then entered into a new stage. The idea which had
first been expressed by the pronoun or the termination
of the third person, "He thunders," was taken up into
the word "Dyaus," or "sky." "He thunders," and
"Dyaus thunders," became synonymous expressions;
and by the mere habit of speech "He" became
"Dyaus," and "Dyaus" became "He." Henceforth
"Dyaus" remained as an appellative of that unseen

though ever present Power, which had revealed its existence to man from the beginning, but which remained without a name long after every beast of the
field and every fowl of the air had been named by
Adam.

Now, what happened in this instance with the name
of " Dyaus," happened again and again with other
names. When men felt the presence of God in the
great and strong wind, in the earthquake, or the fire,
they said at first, " He storms," " He shakes," " He
burns." But they likewise said, the storm (" Marut ")
blows, the fire (" Agni ") burns, the subterraneous
fire (" Vulcanus ") upheaves the earth. And after a
time the result was the same as before, and the words
meaning originally wind or fire were used, under
certain restrictions, as names of the unknown God.
As long as all these names were remembered as mere
names or attributes of one and the same Divine Power,
there was as yet no polytheism, though, no doubt, every
new name threatened to obscure more and more the
primitive intuition of God. At first, the names of God,
like fetishes or statues, were honest attempts at expressing or representing an idea which could never
find an adequate expression or representation. But
the *eidolon*, or likeness, became an *idol*; the *nomen*, or
name, lapsed into a *numen*, or demon, as soon as they
were drawn away from their original intention. If the
Greeks had remembered that Zeus was but a name or
symbol of the Deity, there would have been no more
harm in calling God by that name than by any other.
If they had remembered that Kronos, and Uranos, and
Apollon were all but so many attempts at naming the
various sides, or manifestations, or aspects, or persons

of the Deity, they might have used these names in the hours of their various needs, just as the Jews called on Jehovah, Elohim, and Sabaoth, or as Roman Catholics implore the help of Nunziata, Dolores, and Notre-Dame-de-Grace.

What, then, is the difference between the Aryan and Semitic nomenclature for the Deity? Why are we told that the pious invocations of the Aryan world turned into a blasphemous mocking of the Deity, whereas the Semitic nations are supposed to have found from the first the true name of God? Before we look anywhere else for an answer to the question, we must look to language itself, and here we see that the Semitic dialects could never, by any possibility, have produced such names as the Sanskrit "Dyaus" (Zeus), "Varuna" (Uranos), "Marut" (Storm, Mars), or "Ushas" (Eos). They had no doubt names for the bright sky, for the tent of heaven, and for the dawn. But these names were so distinctly felt as appellatives, that they could never be thought of as proper names, whether as names of the Deity, or as names of deities. This peculiarity has been illustrated with great skill by M. Renan. We differ from him when he tries to explain the difference between the mythological phraseology of the Aryan and the theological phraseology of the Semitic races, by assigning to each a peculiar theological instinct. We cannot, in fact, see how the admission of such an instinct, i. e. of an unknown and incomprehensible power, helps us in any way whatsoever to comprehend this curious mental process. His problem, however, is exactly the same as ours, and it would be impossible to state that problem in a more telling manner than he has done.

"The rain," he says (p. 79), "is represented, in all
the primitive mythologies of the Aryan race, as the
fruit of the embraces of Heaven and Earth."   "The
bright sky," says Æschylus, in a passage which one
might suppose was taken from the Vedas, "loves to
penetrate the earth; the earth on her part aspires to
the heavenly marriage.   Rain falling from the loving
sky impregnates the earth, and she produces for mortals pastures of the flocks and the gifts of Ceres."
In the Book of Job,[1] on the contrary, it is God who
tears open the waterskins of heaven (xxxviii. 37) who
opens the courses for the floods (Ib. 25), who engen-
ders the drops of dew (Ib. 28) : —

> "He draws towards Him the mists from the waters,
> Which pour down as rain, and form their vapors.
> Afterwards the clouds spread them out,
> They fall as drops on the crowds of men."   (Job
>   xxxvi. 27, 28.)

> "He charges the night with damp vapors,
> He drives before Him the thunder-bearing cloud.
> It is driven to one side or the other by His com-
>   mand,
> To execute all that He ordains
> On the face of the universe,
> Whether it be to punish His creatures
> Or to make thereof a proof of his mercy."   (Job
>   xxxvii. 11-13.)

Or, again, Proverbs xxx. 4 : —

"Who hath gathered the wind in His fists?   Who

---

[1] We give the extracts according to M. Renan's translation of the Book
of Job (Paris, 1860, Michel Lévy).

hath bound the waters in a garment? Who hath
established all the ends of the earth? What is His
name, and what is His Son's name, if thou canst
tell?"

It has been shown by ample evidence from the Rig-
veda how many myths were suggested to the Aryan
world by various names of the dawn, the day-spring of
life. The language of the ancient Aryans of India
had thrown out many names for that heavenly appari-
tion, and every name, as it ceased to be understood, became, like a decaying seed, the germ of an abundant
growth of myth and legend. Why should not the
same have happened to the Semitic names for the
dawn? Simply and solely because the Semitic words
had no tendency to phonetic corruption; simply and
solely because they continued to be felt as appellatives,
and would inevitably have defeated every attempt at
mythological phraseology such as we find in India and
Greece. When the dawn is mentioned in the book of
Job (ix. 7), it is God "who commandeth the sun and
it riseth not, and sealeth up the stars." It is His
power which causeth the day-spring to know its place,
that it might take hold of the ends of the earth, that
the wicked might be shaken out of it (Job xxxviii.
12, 13; Renan, "Livre de Job," pref. 71). "Shahar,"
the dawn, never becomes an independent agent; she is
never spoken of as Eos rising from the bed of her husband Tithonos (the setting sun), solely and simply
because the word retained its power as an appellative,
and thus could not enter into any mythological meta-
morphosis.
Even in Greece there are certain words which have

remained so pellucid as to prove unfit for mythological refraction. "Selene" in Greek is so clearly the moon that her name would pierce through the darkest clouds of myth and fable. Call her "Hecate," and she will bear any disguise, however fanciful. It is the same with the Latin "Luna." She is too clearly the moon to be mistaken for anything else; but call her "Lucina," and she will readily enter into various mythological phases. If, then, the names of sun and moon, of thunder and lightning, of light and day, of night and dawn, could not yield to the Semitic races fit appellatives for the Deity, where were they to be found? If the names of Heaven or Earth jarred on their ears as names unfit for the Creator, where could they find more appropriate terms? They would not have objected to real names such as "Jupiter Optimus Maximus," or Ζεὺς ὕπατος μήστωρ, if such words could have been framed in their dialects, and the names of Jupiter and Zeus could have been so ground down as to become synonymous with the general term for "God." Not even the Jews could have given a more exalted definition of the Deity than that of *Optimus Maximus* — the Best and the Greatest; and their very name of God, "Jehovah," is generally supposed to mean no more than what the Peleiades of Dodona said of Zeus, Ζεὺς ἦν, Ζεὺς ἐστίν, Ζεὺς ἔσσεται· ὦ μεγάλε Ζεῦ, "He was, He is, He will be, O great Zeus!" Not being able to form such substantives as Dyaus or Varuna or Indra, the descendants of Shem fixed on the predicates which in the Aryan prayers follow the name of the Deity, and called Him the Best and the Greatest, the Lord and King. If we examine the numerous names of the Deity in the Semitic dialects we find that

they are all adjectives, expressive of moral qualities.
There is " El," strong; " Bel " or " Baal," Lord;
" Beel-samin," Lord of Heaven; " Adonis " (in Phœnicia), Lord; " Marnas " (at Gaza), our Lord; " Shet,"
Master, afterwards a demon; " Moloch," " Milcom,"
" Malika," King; " Elion," the Highest (the God of
Melchisedek); " Ram " and " Rimmon," the Exalted;
and many more names, all originally adjectives and expressive of certain general qualities of the Deity, but
all raised by one or the other of the Semitic tribes to
be the names of God or of that idea which the first
breath of life, the first sight of this world, the first consciousness of existence, had forever impressed and im-
planted in the human mind.

But do these names prove that the people who invented them had a clear and settled idea of the unity
of the Deity? Do we not find among the Aryan nations that the same superlatives, the same names of
Lord and King, of Master and Father, are used when
the human mind is brought face to face with the Divine,
and the human heart pours out in prayer and thanksgiving the feelings inspired by the presence of God?
" Brahman," in Sanskrit, meant originally Power, the
same as El. It resisted for a long time the mythological contagion, but at last it yielded like all other names
of God, and became the name of one God. By the first
man who formed or fixed these names, " Brahman,"
like El, and like every name of God, was meant, no
doubt, as the best expression that could be found for
the image reflected from the Creator upon the mind of
the creature. But in none of these words can we see
any decided proof that those who framed them had arrived at the clear perception of One God, and were

thus secured against the danger of polytheism. Like
Dyaus, like Indra, like Brahman, Baal and El and Moloch were names of God, but not yet of the One God.

And we have only to follow the history of these
Semitic names in order to see that, in spite of their
superlative meaning, they proved no stronger bulwarks
against polytheism than the Latin *Optimus Maximus.*
The very names which we saw explained before as
meaning the Highest, the Lord, the Master, are represented in the Phenician mythology as standing to each
other in the relation of Father and Son. (Renan, p.
60.) There is hardly one single Semitic tribe which
did not at times forget the original meaning of the
names by which they called on God. If the Jews had
remembered the meaning of El, the Omnipotent, they
could not have worshipped Baal, the Lord, as different
from El. But as the Aryan tribes bartered the names
of their gods, and were glad to add the worship of
Zeus to that of Uranos, the worship of Apollon to that
of Zeus, the worship of Hermes to that of Apollon, the
Semitic nations likewise were ready to try the gods of
their neighbours. If there had been in the Semitic race
a truly monotheistic instinct, the history of those nations
would become perfectly unintelligible. Nothing is
more difficult to overcome than an instinct : "naturam
expellas furcâ, tamen usque recurret." But the history
even of the Jews, is made up of an almost uninterrupted series of relapses into polytheism. Let us admit, on the contrary, that God had in the beginning
revealed Himself as the same to the ancestors of the
whole human race. Let us then observe the natural
divergence of the languages of man, and consider the
peculiar difficulties that had to be overcome in framing

names for God, and the peculiar manner in which they were overcome in the Semitic and Aryan languages, and everything that follows will be intelligible. If we consider the abundance of synonymes into which all ancient languages burst out at their first starting, — if we remember that there were hundreds of names for the earth and the sky, the sun and the moon, we shall not be surprised at meeting with more than one name for God both among the Semitic and the Aryan nations. If we consider how easily the radical or significative elements of words were absorbed and obscured in the Aryan, and how they stood out in bold relief in the Semitic languages, we shall appreciate the difficulty which the Shemites experienced in framing any name that should not seem to take too one-sided a view of the Deity by predicating but one quality, whether strength, dominion, or majesty; and we shall equally perceive the snare which their very language laid for the Aryan nations, by supplying them with a number of words which, though they seemed harmless as meaning nothing except what by tradition or definition they were made to mean, yet were full of mischief owing to the recollections which, at any time, they might revive. "Dyaus" in itself was as good a name as any for God, and in some respects more appropriate than its derivative "deva," the Latin *deus*, which the Romance nations still use without meaning any harm. But "Dyaus" had meant "sky" for too long a time to become entirely divested of all the old myths or sayings which were true of Dyaus, the sky, but could only be retained as fables, if transferred to Dyaus, God. Dyaus, the Bright, might be called the husband of the earth; but when the same myth was repeated of Zeus,

the god, then Zeus became the husband of Demeter,
Demeter became a goddess, a daughter sprang from
their union, and all the sluices of mythological madness
were opened.   There were a few men, no doubt, at all
times, who saw through this mythological phraseology,
who called on God, though they called him " Zeus," or
" Dyaus," or Jupiter."   Xenophanes, one of the earliest Greek heretics, boldly maintained that there was
but " one God, and that he was not like unto men,
either in body or mind." [1]   A poet in the Veda asserts
distinctly, " They call him ' Indra,' ' Mitra,' ' Varuna,' ' Agni ; ' then he is ' the well-winged heavenly
Garutmat ; ' that which is One the wise call it many
ways, — they call it ' Agni,' ' Yama,' ' Mâtariçvan.' " [2]

But, on the whole, the charm of mythology prevailed
among the Aryan nations, and a return to the primitive
intuition of God and a total negation of all gods, were
rendered more difficult to the Aryan than to the
Semitic man.   The Semitic man had hardly ever to
resist the allurements of mythology.   The names with
which he invoked the Deity did not trick him by
their equivocal character.   Nevertheless, these Semitic names, too, though predicative in the beginning,
became subjective, and from being the various names
of One Being, lapsed into names of various beings.
Hence arose a danger which threatened wellnigh to
bar to the Semitic race the approach to the conception
and worship of the One God.

Nowhere can we see this danger more clearly than

[1] Xenophanes, about contemporary with Cyrus, as quoted by Clemens
Alex., Strom. v. p. 601, — εἷς θεὸς ἔν τε θεοῖσι καὶ ἀνθρώποισι μέγιστος, οὔτι
δέμας θνητοῖσιν ὁμοίιος οὐδὲ νόημα.

[2] History of Ancient Sanskrit Literature, by M. M., p. 567.

in the history of the Jews. The Jews had, no doubt, preserved from the beginning the idea of God, and their names of God contained nothing but what might by right be ascribed to Him. They worshipped a single God, and, whenever they fell into idolatry, they felt that they had fallen away from God. But that God, under whatever name they invoked Him, was especially their God, their own national God, and His existence did not exclude the existence of other gods or demons. Of the ancestors of Abraham and Nachor, even of their father Terah, we know that in old time, when they dwelt on the other side of the flood, they served other gods (Joshua xxiv. 2). At the time of Joshua these gods were not yet forgotten, and instead of denying their existence altogether, Joshua only exhorts the people to put away the gods which their fathers served on the other side of the flood and in Egypt, and to serve the Lord: "Choose ye this day," he says, "whom you will serve; whether the gods which your fathers served that were on the other side of the flood, or the gods of the Amorites, in whose land ye dwell: but as for me and my house, we will serve the Lord."

Such a speech, exhorting the people to make their choice between various gods, would have been unmeaning if addressed to a nation which had once conceived the unity of the Godhead. Even images of the gods were not unknown to the family of Abraham, for, though we know nothing of the exact form of the teraphim, or images which Rachel stole from her father, certain it is that Laban calls them his gods (Genesis xxxi. 19. 30). But what is much more significant than those traces of polytheism and idolatry is the hesitat-

ing tone in which some of the early patriarchs speak
of their God. When Jacob flees before Esau into
Padan-Aram and awakes from his vision at Bethel,
he does not profess his faith in the One God, but he
bargains, and says, "If God will be with me, and will
keep me in this way that I go, and will give me bread
to eat, and raiment to put on, so that I come again to
my father's house in peace, then shall the Lord be my
God: and this stone, which I have set for a pillar, shall
be God's house: and of all that thou shalt give me, I
will surely give the tenth unto thee" (Genesis xxviii.
20–22). Language of this kind evinces not only a
temporary want of faith in God, but it shows that the
conception of God had not yet acquired that complete
universality which alone deserves to be called monotheism, or belief in the One God. To him who has seen
God face to face there is no longer any escape or doubt
as to who is to be his god; God is his god, whatever
befall. But this Jacob learnt not until he had strug-
gled and wrestled with God, and committed himself to
His care at the very time when no one else could have
saved him. In that struggle Jacob asked for the true
name of God, and he learnt from God that His name
was secret (Genesis xxxii. 29). After that, his God
was no longer one of many gods. His faith was not
like the faith of Jethro (Exodus xxvii. 11), the priest
of Midian, the father-in-law of Moses, who when he
heard of all that God had done for Moses acknowledged that God (Jehovah) was greater than all gods
(Elohim). This is not yet faith in the One God. It
is a faith hardly above the faith of the people who were
halting between Jehovah and Baal, and who only when
they saw what the Lord did for Elijah, fell on their
faces and said, "The Lord He is the God."

And yet this limited faith in Jehovah as the God of the Jews, as a God more powerful than the gods of the heathen, as a God above all gods, betrays itself again and again in the history of the Jews. The idea of many gods is there, and wherever that idea exists, wherever the plural of god is used in earnest, there is polytheism. It is not so much the names of Zeus, Hermes, etc., which constitute the polytheism of the Greeks; it is the plural of gods, which contains the fatal spell. We do not know what M. Renan means when he says that Jehovah with the Jews "n'est pas le plus grand entre plusieurs dieux; c'est le Dieu unique." It was so with Abraham, it was so after Jacob had been changed into Israel, it was so with Moses, Elijah, and Jeremiah. But what is the meaning of the very first commandment, "Thou shalt have no other gods before me?" Could this command have been addressed to a nation to whom the plural of God was a nonentity? It might be answered that the plural of God was to the Jews as revolting as it is to us; that it was revolting to their faith, if not to their reason. But how was it that their language tolerated the plural of a word which excludes plurality as much as the word for the centre of a sphere? No man who had clearly perceived the unity of God, could say with the Psalmist (lxxxvi. 8), "Among the gods there is none like unto Thee, O Lord, neither are there any works like unto Thy works." Though the same poet says, "Thou art God alone," he could not have compared God with other gods, if his idea of God had really reached that all-embracing character which it had with Abraham, Moses, Elijah and Jeremiah. Nor would God have been praised as the "great king above all

gods " by a poet in whose eyes the gods of tho heathen
had been recognized as what they were — mighty shadows, thrown by the mighty works of God, and inter-
cepting for a time the pure light of the Godhead.

We thus arrive at a different conviction from that
which M. Renan has made the basis of the history of
the Semitic race. We can see nothing that would jus-
tify the admission of a monotheistic instinct, granted to
the Semitic, and withheld from the Aryan race. They
both share in the primitive intuition of God, they are
both exposed to dangers in framing names for God,
and they both fall into polytheism. What is peculiar
to the Aryan race is their mythological phraseology,
superadded to their polytheism; what is peculiar to the
Semitic race is their belief in a national god — in a god
chosen by his people as his people had been chosen by
him.

No doubt M. Renan might say that we ignored his
problem, and that we have not removed the difficulties
which drove him to the admission of a monotheistic instinct. How is the fact to be explained, he might ask,
that the three great religions of the world in which the
unity of the Deity forms the key-note, are of Semitic
origin, and that the Aryan nations, wherever they have
been brought to a worship of the One God, invoke
Him with names borrowed from the Semitic languages?

But let us look more closely at the facts before we
venture on theories. Mohammedanism, no doubt, is
a Semitic religion, and its very core is monotheism.
But did Mohammed invent monotheism? Did he invent even a new name of God? (Renan, p. 28.) Not
at all. His object was to destroy the idolatry of the
Semitic tribes of Arabia, to dethrone the angels, the

sin, the sons and daughters who had been assigned to
Allah, and to restore the faith of Abraham in one God.
(Renan, p. 87.)

And how is it with Christianity? Did Christ come
to preach a faith in a new God? Did He or His disciples invent a new name of God? No, Christ came
not to destroy, but to fulfill; and the God whom He
preached was the God of Abraham.

And who is the God of Jeremiah, of Elijah, and of
Moses? We answer again, the God of Abraham.

Thus the faith in the One living God, which seemed
to require the admission of a monotheistic instinct,
grafted in every member of the Semitic family, is
traced back to one man, to him "in whom all families of the earth shall be blessed" (Genesis xii. 3;
Acts iii. 25; Galatians iii. 8). If from our earliest
childhood we have looked upon Abraham, the friend of
God, with love and veneration; if our first impressions
of a truly god-fearing life were taken from him, who
left the land of his fathers to live a stranger in the
land whither God had called him, who always listened
to the voice of God, whether it conveyed to him the
promise of a son in his old age, or the command to sacrifice that son, his only son Isaac, his venerable figure
will assume still more majestic proportions when we
see in him the life-spring of that faith which was to
unite all the nations of the earth, and the author of that
blessing which was to come on the Gentiles through
Jesus Christ.

And if we are asked how this one Abraham possessed not only the primitive intuition of God as He
had revealed Himself to all mankind, but passed
through the denial of all other gods to the knowl-

edge of the one God, we are content to answer that
it was by a special Divine Revelation. We do not
indulge in theological phraseology, but we mean every
word to its fullest extent. The Father of Truth
chooses His own prophets, and He speaks to them in
a voice stronger than the voice of thunder. It is the
same inner voice through which God speaks to all of
us. That voice may dwindle away, and become hardly
audible; it may lose its Divine accent, and sink into
the language of worldly prudence; but it may also,
from time to time, assume its real nature with the
chosen of God, and sound into their ears as a voice
from Heaven. A "divine instinct" may sound more
scientific, and less theological; but in truth it would
neither be an appropriate name for what is a gift or
grace accorded to but few, nor would it be a more
scientific, i. e. a more intelligible word than "special
revelation."

The important point, however, is not whether the
faith of Abraham should be called a divine instinct or
a revelation; what we wish here to insist on is that
that instinct, or that revelation, was special, granted to
one man, and handed down from him to Jews, Christians, and Mohammedans, — to all who believe in the
God of Abraham. Nor was it granted to Abraham
entirely as a free gift. Abraham was tried and tempted
before he was trusted by God. He had to break with
the faith of his fathers; he had to deny the gods who
were worshipped by his friends and neighbors. Like
all the friends of God, he had to hear himself called
an infidel and atheist, and in our own days he would
have been looked upon as a madman for attempting to
slay his son. It was through special faith that Abra-

ham received his special revelation, not through instinct, not through abstract meditation, not through
ecstatic visions. We want to know more of that man
than we do; but, even with the little we know of him,
he stands before us as a figure second only to one in
the whole history of the world. We see his zeal for
God, but we never see him contentious. Though
Melchizedek worshipped God under a different name,
invoking Him as Elion, the Most High, Abraham at
once acknowledged in Melchizedek a worshipper and
priest of the true God, or Elohim, and paid him tithes.
In the very name of Elohim we seem to trace the con-
ciliatory spirit of Abraham. Elohim is a plural, though
it is followed by the verb in the singular. It is generally said that the genius of the Semitic languages
countenances the use of plurals for abstract conceptions, and that when Jehovah is called Elohim, the
plural should be translated by "the Deity." We do
not deny the fact, but we wish for an explanation,
and an explanation is suggested by the various phases
through which, as we saw, the conception of God
passed in the ancient history of the Semitic mind.
Eloah was at first the name for God, and as it is
found in all the dialects of the Semitic family except
the Phenician (Renan, p. 61), it may probably be
considered as the most ancient name of the Deity,
sanctioned at a time when the original Semitic speech
had not yet branched off into national dialects. When
this name was first used in the plural, it could only
have signified, like every plural, many Eloahs; and
such a plural could only have been formed after the
various names of God had become the names of independent deities, i. e. during a polytheistic stage.

The transition from this into the monotheistic stage could be effected in two ways: either by denying altogether the existence of the Elohim, and changing them into devils, as the Zoroastrians did with the Devas of their Brahmanic ancestors; or by taking a higher view, and looking upon the Elohim as so many names invented with the honest purpose of expressing the various aspects of the Deity, though in time diverted from their original purpose. This is the view taken by St. Paul of the religion of the Greeks when he came to declare unto them "Him whom they *ignorantly worshipped*," and the same view was taken by Abraham. Whatever the names of the Elohim, worshipped by the numerous clans of his race, Abraham saw that all the Elohim, were meant for God, and thus Elohim, comprehending by one name everything that ever had been or could be called divine, became the name with which the monotheistic age was rightly inaugurated, —a plural, conceived and constructed as a singular. Jehovah was all the Elohim, and therefore there could be no other God. From this point of view the Semitic name of the Deity, Elohim, which seemed at first not only ungrammatical but irrational, becomes perfectly clear and intelligible, and it proves better than anything else that the true monotheism could not have risen except on the ruins of a polytheistic faith. It is easy to scoff at the gods of the heathen, but a cold-hearted philosophical negation of the gods of the ancient world is more likely to lead to Deism or Atheism than to a belief in the One living God, the Father of all mankind, "who hath made of one blood all nations of men, for to dwell on all the face of the earth; and hath determined the times before appointed, and the bounds of their habitation; that they should seek the Lord, if haply they might feel after him, and find Him, though He be not far from every one of us; for in Him we live, and move, and have our being; as certain also of your own poets have said, For we are also His offspring."

Taking this view of the historical growth of the idea of God, many of the difficulties which M. Renan has to overcome by most elaborate, and sometimes hair-splitting arguments, disappear at once. M. Renan, for instance, dwells much on Semitic proper names in which the names of the Deity occur; and he thinks that, like the Greek names "Theodorus" or "Theodotus," instead of "Zenodotus," they prove the exist-ence of a faith in one God. We should say they may or may not. As "Devadatta," in Sanskrit, may mean either "given by God," or "given by the gods," so every proper name which M. Renan quotes, whether of Jews, or Edomites, Ishmaelites, Ammonites, Moab-ites, and Themanites, whether from the Bible, or from Arab historians, from Greek authors, Greek inscrip-tions, the Egyptian papyri, the Himyaritic and Sinaitic inscriptions and ancient coins, are all open to two in-terpretations. "The servant of Baal" may mean the servant of the Lord, but it may also mean the servant of Baal, as one of many lords, or even the servant of the Baalim or the Lords. The same applies to all other names. "The gift of El" may mean "the gift of the only strong God;" but it may likewise mean "the gift of the El," as one of many gods, or even "the gift of the El's," in the sense of the strong gods. Nor do we see why M. Renan should take such pains to prove that the name of "Orotal" or "Orotalat,"

mentioned by Herodotos (III. 8), may be interpreted
as the name of a supreme deity; and that "Alilat,"
mentioned by the same traveller, should be taken, not
as the name of a goddess, but as a feminine noun expressive of the abstract sense of the deity. Herodotos
says distinctly that Orotal was a deity like Bacchus;
and Alilat, as he translates her name by Οὐρανίη, must
have appeared to him as a goddess, and not as the
Supreme Deity. One verse of the Koran is sufficient
to show that the Semitic inhabitants of Arabia worshipped not only gods, but goddesses also. "What
think ye of Allat, al Uzza, and Manah, that other
third goddess?"

If our view of the development of the idea of God
be correct, we can perfectly understand how, in spite
of this polytheistic phraseology, the primitive intuition
of God should make itself felt from time to time, long
before Muhammed restored the belief of Abraham in
one God. The old Arabic prayer mentioned by Abul-
faraj may be perfectly genuine: "I dedicate myself to
thy service, O God! Thou hast no companion, except
thy companion, of whom thou art absolute master, and
of whatever is his." The verse pointed out to M.
Renan by M. Caussin de Perceval from the Moallaka
of Zoheyr, was certainly anterior to Mohammed:
"Try not to hide your secret feelings from the sight of
Allah; Allah knows all that is hidden." But these
quotations serve no more to establish the universality
of the monotheistic instinct in the Semitic race than similar quotations from the Veda would prove the existence
of a conscious monotheism among the ancestors of the
Aryan race. There too we read, "Agni knows what
is secret among mortals" (Rig-veda VIII. 80, 6)

and again: "He, the upholder of order, Varuna, sits down among his people; he, the wise, sits there to govern. From thence perceiving all wondrous things, he sees what has been and what will be done."[1] But in these very hymns, better than anywhere else, we learn that the idea of supremacy and omnipotence ascribed to one god did by no means exclude the admission of other gods, or names of God. All the other gods disappear from the vision of the poet while he addresses his own God, and he only who is to fulfill his desires stands in full light before the eyes of the worshipper as the supreme and only God.

The Science of Religion is only just beginning, and we must take care how we impede its progress by preconceived notions or too hasty generalizations. During the last fifty years the authentic documents of the most important religions of the world have been recovered in a most unexpected and almost miraculous manner. We have now before us the canonical books of Buddhism; the Zend-Avesta of Zoroaster is no longer a sealed book; and the hymns of the Rig-veda have revealed a state of religion anterior to the first beginnings of that mythology which in Homer and Hesiod stands before us as a mouldering ruin. The soil of Mesopotamia has given back the very images once worshipped by the most powerful of the Semitic tribes, and the cuneiform inscriptions of Babylon and Nineveh have disclosed the very prayers addressed to Baal or Nisroch. With the discovery of these documents a new era begins in the study of religion. We begin to see more clearly every day what St. Paul meant in his sermon at Athens. But as the excavator

[1] *History of Ancient Sanskrit Literature*, by M. M., p. 534.

at Babylon or Nineveh, before he ventures to reconstruct the palaces of these ancient kingdoms, sinks his shafts into the ground slowly and circumspectly lest he should injure the walls of the ancient palaces which he is disinterring; as he watches every corner-stone lest he mistake their dark passages and galleries, and as he removes with awe and trembling the dust and clay from the brittle monuments lest he destroy their outlines, and obliterate their inscriptions, so it behooves the student of the history of religion to set to work carefully, lest he should miss the track, and lose himself in an inextricable maze. The relics which he handles are more precious than the ruins of Babylon; the problems he has to solve are more important than the questions of ancient chronology; and the substructions which he hopes one day to lay bare are the world-wide foundations of the eternal kingdom of God.

We look forward with the highest expectations to the completion of M. Renan's work, and though English readers will differ from many of the author's views, and feel offended now and then at his blunt and unguarded language, we doubt not that they will find his volumes both instructive and suggestive. They are written in that clear and brilliant style which has secured to M. Renan the rank of one of the best writers of French, and which throws its charm even over the dry and abstruse inquiries into the grammatical forms and radical elements of the Semitic languages.

April, 1860.